GANGSTER ON THE RUN

Praise for *Gangster on the Run*

'In this immersive journey into the heart of India's gangland, Puja captures the varied textures of the criminal world with her storytelling genius. A thrilling, unputdownable read from a prolific journalist!'

> – Rakesh Maria, former chief, Maharashtra Anti-Terrorism Squad, and former Commissioner of Police, Mumbai

'Through its honest and riveting rendition, this remarkable book shows how the underworld builds gangsters, and how some, unexpectedly, break free from the blood and gore to build an inspiring life. A must-read for true-crime lovers!'

> – Ravi Subramanian, bestselling author

'In this thoroughly enthralling read, Puja provides an insider's view of the underworld in a kaleidoscopic testimony of crime and punishment, survival and redemption.'

> – Siddharth Roy Kapur, film producer

'One of our finest crime reporters returns with her latest offering – a pacy, gritty read, about the life of an underworld criminal who changed his life around to become an ultra-marathoner. Brilliantly detailed and researched, written with a sharp reporter's eye and empathy, this is a book that you just cannot put down.'

> – Kiran Manral, bestselling author

'Only Bombay can script such a life where a Goodfella turns Forrest Gump! Puja packs this incredible life in a stunning, powerful narrative. This is for sure a series in the making.'

> – Vasan Bala, film director

'An astounding storyteller with a strong, distinctive voice, Puja has an eye for nuance and an ear for detail. A dazzling story told in the most affecting manner; a triumph of humanity over forces of violence.'

> – Fatima Sana Shaikh, actor

GANGSTER ON THE RUN

THE TRUE STORY OF A REFORMED CRIMINAL

PUJA CHANGOIWALA

Dear Sara,
I'm just so glad to have met you. You're so evolved, so adorable & such a beautiful writer.. Much more than you give yourself credit for. Until we meet again.. & we will!
Love,
Puja
March 22, 2022.

HarperCollins *Publishers* India

First published in India in 2020 by
HarperCollins *Publishers*
A-75, Sector 57, Noida, Uttar Pradesh 201301, India
www.harpercollins.co.in

2 4 6 8 10 9 7 5 3 1

P-ISBN: 978-93-5357-731-5
E-ISBN: 978-93-5357-732-2

Typeset in 11.5/15.2 Adobe Garamond Pro at
Manipal Technologies Limited, Manipal

Printed and bound at
Thomson Press (India) Ltd

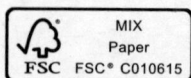

MIX
Paper
FSC FSC® C010615

This book is produced from independently certified FSC® paper to ensure
responsible forest management.

Author's Note

This is a work of non-fiction. I have used pseudonyms to protect the identities of some of the individuals involved.

For Dadoo,
my talisman

Contents

1

In Search of the Horizon

———◆———

Where the sky meets the sea, where the sun just always is,
You'll see her silhouette against that horizon, that's where she is.

As ten-year-old Rahul shut his eyes before he blew the candles on his fresh, home-baked birthday cake, he saw his best friend's smiling face, how her eyes lit up when she jumped into a puddle of muck. The boy smiled too, and made his birthday wish – he wished to see her again. His birthday song echoed in the room as he quickly sliced the chocolate cake into uneven pieces. Soon, with no heed to his favourite samosas or mango drink, he walked out of his home, looking for the horizon.

While he was growing up, Rahul had heard countless stories about a creek near his home in Dombivli, a city on the outskirts of Mumbai. Flamingos would visit the rivulet, delicious tamarind and gooseberries abundant along its shore, and local trains would disappear into its majestic mountains. Although the air tasted salty from the heaps of garbage dumped into the backwater, the sky here was the purest blue – blue as the southern sea.

'Take me there, maa,' the child would tell his mother.

Each time, his request was shunned with, 'There's a demon in that creek, who feeds off young boys. As soon as he spots a kid, the waters swallow him up. Don't you dare go anywhere close.'

Rahul's parents were reasonable in designing the phantasms. The creek was a secluded, marshy wasteland, where local addicts indulged in gambling, hooch and homegrown marijuana. To the young boy, the forbiddance made the illusive inlet more attractive. Unaware of the creek's location, he would walk by the gutter under his building, following its course, hoping it would eventually merge with the bay and take him with it. On one such expedition, eight months before his tenth birthday, he met Dina Lohar, his first best friend.

Dina was six years older than Rahul, but she was unlike any of the elders the boy had known – while his parents and siblings admonished him when he jumped into the gutter, Dina jumped in with him. While they had barred his visit to the creek, Dina took him to it. Every afternoon, after he returned from school, Rahul would cross the road outside his building, and disappear into a tiny forest, where Dina lived. She would wait for him by a well near her hut. As soon as he arrived, the two would walk one and a half kilometres to get to the stream. Rahul particularly loved their journey through a bamboo forest – dense and isolated, with rustling leaves playing a soothing symphony in their welcome. He would feel at peace in that jungle, as if he were finally home.

The children would bathe in the still, dirty waters of the rivulet, and build muck castles ashore. They would catch 'long-tailed fish', which were in fact tadpoles, and Rahul would put them in a small tank at home. Over a few weeks, the 'fish' would turn into frogs, and the boy would be ecstatic. 'Magic!' he'd exclaim each time he witnessed the metamorphosis. *The world is a wizard, or maybe it's my best friend, Dina.*

While at the creek, if the two grew hungry, they would walk to a tiny temple nearby, and feast on the coconut offerings left for the deity. The shrine lay isolated on most days. When the priest was around – an old man with a kind face – he would give them milk cakes. The two would savour the treat and return home, content.

As days melted into months, Rahul realized Dina had never been to school. She was skinny because she did not have enough to eat. She would wear the same pair of salwar kameez every day because she did not have other clothes. Belonging to a tribal family, her migrant parents worked as labourers, who could not afford the luxury of education or regular meals for their three children. She, too, was forbidden from visiting the creek, he learnt – and their association soon became a cherished secret affair.

On his tenth birthday, Rahul's father returned from work with the boy's favourite Indian sweet, gulab jamun. Friends and neighbours had gathered at his home to celebrate his special day, but Rahul packed four of the treats in a plastic bag and told his mother he would return soon. He crossed the road, and rushed towards Dina's hut. She was by the well as usual, looking deep into its bottomless waters. He'd always wondered what she'd stare at inside that well. He had even asked her a few times, but being Dina, she had always brushed the query aside with a story about a new bird she'd spotted or a colourful insect that had entered her hut.

'It's my birthday, Didi,' Rahul spoke to her back, beaming. 'Here, look what I got for you. They're my favourite.'

Dina turned around and hugged him. Her brown, sunken cheeks wet with tears, she was trembling. She wasn't shivering, no. She was trembling, as if it were freezing, as if she couldn't breathe. Within seconds, she broke the embrace, climbed onto the well's side-rail, and jumped.

Splash. Rahul heard her hit the water. Splash and silence. Silence so dark, so dark.

As locals rushed over in reaction to the sound, the boy, without turning around, began to retreat. He ran towards the temple near the creek. At a distance, he could hear the quiet turn into wailing. Too shocked for tears, he kept running as fast as he could, away from that conundrum, towards his friend. The boy had heard that when people die, they go to the gods. His mother had told him that. Dina, he was certain, was at the temple.

'Is she here?' the boy asked the priest. 'Is Dina here?'

'Come here, child,' the priest, dressed in a white dhoti, said and asked Rahul to sit on his lap. 'Tell me what happened.'

'She jumped into the well. She died. She must come here now. Any minute, any minute.'

'She won't come here, boy,' the priest explained. 'Here, have some water, catch your breath.'

'I don't want water. Do you know where I can find her?'

'You cannot find her, child. When people die, they go to the horizon – where the sky meets the sea, where the sun never sets. She's there, too far.'

Tears now welling up in his eyes, Rahul jumped off the priest's lap, and started running home. As his parents admonished him for making guests wait, he walked to the sponge cake and sliced it. He then turned to his school bag, took out the twenty rupees his father had given him that morning, and left.

Dressed in a t-shirt and trousers, Rahul walked until he reached the Kalyan–Shilphata Road, three kilometres from his home. When he spotted the first hillock off the highway, he decided to scale it. As the sun began to set over the city, the boy made his way through the weeds and stones on the hillock's shoulder. Within an hour, he was at the top. The world looked dangerously non-negotiable from that spot – much too large, much too complex – thriving under the gradually greying skies, but without the company of a sea. Desperate and disappointed, he began to weep.

As his silent cries turned into sobs atop the peak, Rahul remembered his family trips to south Bombay's Girgaum Chowpatty – the splendid sand beach by the Arabian Sea. He would find Dina there, he told himself, and immediately started the fifty kilometre walk to Mumbai. Too taken aback by her sudden death, he would walk for a couple of metres, and then break into frantic runs. He'd be deadpan for a few metres; during others, he'd burst into unrestrained howls. He would call out Dina's name, and wait for the lonely night to respond to his anguished prayers. But, silence, as peaceful as a grave.

After asking directions from a host of strangers, mostly drunks and the homeless, Rahul reached the beach at five the following morning. He had covered the distance on foot; the soles of his rubber slippers had given way and his head throbbed with hunger. The lethargic winter sun was yet to rise, and although the boy could see the waters under the charcoal sky, he could not spot the horizon. He'd have to wait till morning, he told himself. Exhausted, he made a pillow of the golden sand, and drifted into sleep.

Back home, Rahul's family, neighbours and friends were wide awake, scouring railway stations, hospitals, police stations, and streets all over Dombivli. Astrologers were telephoned, impromptu pujas were performed, and birds were fed seeds and nuts in the middle of the night. There was still no trace of the boy. His parents, who started imagining the worst, worried that their son had been kidnapped.

When Rahul woke up after a few hours, he narrowed his eyes at the meeting of the sky and the sea. The horizon was breathtaking. The earth's star had left it with a blush of scarlet, the warmth of tangerine. The tides, too, were competing to get to it. To get to Dina.

Elated, he jumped up, and ran into the waters. The sea, too proud to let him pass, pushed the tiny boy out. With saltwater in his eyes and mouth, he tried to battle the mighty waves again. Yet, the sea, with no regard for his endeavour, forced him ashore. On his third attempt, a man rushed into the waters behind Rahul, caught him by the arm, and pulled him to the shore.

'Are you out of your mind, you stupid boy? Where are your parents?' the stranger demanded.

'My father is around, uncle. He's getting me breakfast.'

'What's with the crying then? And who's Dina?' the man asked, escorting Rahul to a corner of the beach and seating him on a rock. 'Stay here.'

As soon as the stranger turned to look for Rahul's father, the boy got up and started running away from the beach. He knew he could never see Dina again. The horizon was too far. She had gone too far.

———————

A boy, who lost his innocence to the Mumbai mafia; a painter, who lost his art to the 9 mm pistol; a dreamer, who lost his ambition to cheap whisky; a romantic, who lost his love to dimly lit bars and brothels; and a son, who lost his ideals to hard cash – this is the story of Rahul Ramakant Jadhav – a gangster, a gunrunner, a sharpshooter, an alcoholic, a de-addiction crusader and an ultra marathoner. A saga of grime and grit, it starts in one of the darkest phases of post-Independence India, when democracy was hijacked, left reeling under Prime Minister Indira Gandhi's Emergency.

Rahul was born on 11 February 1976, during the twenty-one-month state of Emergency. The historic chaos, however, hardly affected life in his sleepy, unimportant town of Dombivli, sixty kilometres northeast of Bombay. No enemies of Mrs Gandhi were being jailed here – the first prison in the district was only under construction at the time. There were no newspaper presses to have their electricity lines disconnected. No one came looking for antigovernment propagandists or to impose 'graveyard discipline', and no one bothered with strikes, marches or riots. It was as if the world was oblivious to this city, until Rahul dragged its name to the news headlines.

Rahul's seventy-two-year-old mother, Shalini, vouches for the accord in her city during the Emergency, when she was to deliver her third child. 'No, they did not come after us to neuter my husband. Yes, we had easy access to public transport. No, we were not arbitrarily detained. In fact, it was a peaceful time. Buses had never been as punctual.'

Dombivli, now the biggest middle-class township in the Mumbai Metropolitan Region, derives its name from its first inhabitants – the 'Dombs', who conduct cremation rites at funeral pyres. Although the city is now a dormitory town, which works hard to keep the country's financial capital breathing, it was not the same in the 1970s. The wooded commune had a population of 51,108 then, as opposed to its current 1.2 million. The land was rough and rocky, water was scarce, and wolves and foxes roamed the wilderness within the metropolis.

'As I said, peaceful,' the arthritic septuagenarian asserts, lying with her eyes shut on the only cot in her 150-square-foot home, the same one where the underworld hitman was born.

A garlanded poster of a multi-faced Hindu god adorns one of the walls, the lone item that qualifies for the apartment's humble decor. The paint has long lost its lustre, and the only other furniture the home boasts of is a plastic chair and a wooden stool. With a single cupboard to accommodate the family's belongings, various parts of the living room lie strewn with heaps of human possessions – photo albums, books, clothes, toilet cleaners, cold creams and ageing iron trunks – placed artfully one above the other. A small television sits atop one of the piles, playing old Hindi songs, as if in tribute to the monochromatic life outside. '*Ajeeb dastaan hai yeh…*'

'We've never owned many things,' says Rahul. 'It's the first emotion I ever remember feeling – longing, pining for the littlest of things.'

When Rahul was growing up, his father, Ramakant, was employed as a quality inspector with a razorblade-manufacturing company. His monthly salary of Rs 6000 was enough to cover the family's rent, meals and the three children's school fees. It could not accommodate the luxuries of refrigerators, television sets or comfortable holidays. There was never enough money for new schoolbooks, and Rahul would study from hand-me-downs from his two older siblings – his sister Mangala and brother Mangesh. His clothes, too, had first belonged to Mangesh.

The children would go to a neighbour's home to watch television. The night before they would leave for their annual hometown holiday, the brothers would carry pillows and covers to sleep on a footpath outside the bus station. They had to queue up for tickets at the break of dawn – before they were sold out. The government bus, although overcrowded and rickety, was the cheapest way to travel to their village in Ratnagiri.

Rahul was deeply disgruntled with the family's limited means, but he noticed that his mother never complained. All she cared about was the public faucet near their building, where, armed with two buckets, she would make multiple trips every day to ensure the household never ran out of water. Shalini never asked her husband for anything extravagant, and Ramakant never denied the few wishes she expressed. When she asked for something, he'd take some time, but he'd make sure he had the desire fulfilled. Like the time she asked him for a water filter – first came a clay pot, then a steel tank, and a couple of years later, the coveted purifier.

'Everything is borrowed in this house, Baba – everything second-hand, even my school bag and crayons,' the boy once confronted his father. 'This shoe rack, that suitcase, and now this teapoy. Why do you keep accepting charity from others? You work so hard, Baba. Why can't we buy things on our own?'

The boy's father, a tiny, soft-spoken man, who never once lost his temper with his kids, stayed quiet. He probably understood his son's fury. He had possessed it once, too – before he realized it was a price he'd have to pay for his honest ways. The boy, however, would misunderstand his father's silence for weakness. He did not share his humble aspirations. He questioned their finite existence, dreamed, and decided at a very young age that if he desired something, he would make sure he got it.

'As a boy, he would love cycling,' recollects his eighty-year-old father. 'Because we couldn't afford a bicycle, he would stand by our apartment window, watching other kids cycle. A few months later, he figured a way out. He offered to run errands for the boys, like buying milk and bread for their homes, or getting cereals milled at the flour mill. In exchange, they would let him ride their bicycles for an hour. He'd also save up on his daily pocket money of ten paise to rent bicycles for two rupees every few days.'

Rahul also maintained a dairy, where most of his daily musings were about the elusive two-wheeler:

> *I wish I had a bike; it'd be a lot easier to find the creek…*
> *I rode my friend's bike today, and fell in that dirty gutter near our building. So much fun…*
> *Why can't Baba get me a bike? All the other boys have one. I'm going to talk to Ma…*
> *Ma refused…*
> *If I had my own bike, I would pedal away, I'd never come back…*

Rahul's parents had known how much he wanted a bycicle. A few years later, his father surprised him with a chocolate-coloured BSA Mach 1 bike, bringing his yearning to temporary rest.

'And it wasn't just any bicycle. It was a high-end racer bike, on which you'd have to crouch your torso,' says Rahul. The innocent glee looks almost inappropriate on his hard face, as if trying to prove that the former gangster once had childlike ingenuity.

'It's one of the only two precious things my father ever bought me,' he adds. The other one was a second chance at life.

———⊪———

The youngest of the three children, Rahul was nicknamed 'Chotu'. When he was growing up, his tiny, papery frame came to embody the sobriquet. The boy would always be coughing and sneezing, and fighting a fever every few days. When his body temperature crossed 102° Fahrenheit, he would drift into a state of hypnagogic hallucinations.

While asleep, he would see ashes rain from the sky, and hear screams rend the hazy air. He'd see darkness with a hint of luminous white, and hear thumping sounds of gigantic feet. With every passing moment, he would sense the strides get quicker, the monster inch closer. He'd press a pillow against his head to drown out the sounds, to make the demon go away. The behemoth would remain persistent. Defenceless, the child would launch into frantic apologies.

'I'm sorry, Thatrak. Please don't hurt me, Thatrak. I'm sorry. I'm sorry. I swear,' he would mumble in his sleep, desperate to fend off the imaginary monster, puzzled at the origins of his name.

After he saw Dina jump to her death, Thatrak's visits grew frequent, coaxing Rahul to let go of Dina's memory. She was a friend who had abandoned him; a story with an anticlimax. The boy started taking to more and more habits, which kept him from friends, and the heartbreak of their sudden desertions. Always a sincere student, he immersed himself in his academics. His textbooks served a dual purpose – they got his mind off Dina, and made him believe that if he studied well, he wouldn't have to live on the breadline like his father. Rahul was studying in a Marathi-medium school, Swami Vivekananda Vidya Mandir, Dombivli, at the time. For the next few years, he put everything he had into his schooling.

Rahul particularly enjoyed history – stories of Shivaji Maharaj and Adolf Hitler, and other warrior kings and world leaders. He relished their journeys, the way they had built empires from the ground up, and the battles they fought to protect their legacies. The boy did not bother if the men were noble or ignoble, if they'd left their mark on the world or scars. All he cared about was their magnificence and their power, their conquests and their triumphs. He, too, would do what it takes – the boy decided at an unreasonably young age – and his story, too, would outlive him.

When he wasn't studying, Rahul would write his diary, and he'd draw pictures of animals, landscapes, gods and distinguished personalities. One of the portraits, which he had preserved for the longest time, was that of Mikhail Gorbachev, including the port wine stain on the Russian politician's forehead. Rahul was in awe of the USSR leader, who was constantly in the news following the 1986 Chernobyl nuclear disaster. A peasant boy with a difficult childhood, Gorbachev joined the Communist Party as an activist, and rose to become its chief. The Soviet leader's tale left the young boy inspired. It convinced him that he, too, could flourish. 'With everything second-, third- or fourth-hand, I also have Mr Gorbachev's tragic childhood!'

Despite his efforts, Rahul was always an 'average' student. He once complained to his dairy, 'My neighbour's son, he is the same age as me, he plays as much as me, but he still gets 85 per cent. That's despite studying in an English school, while I'm stuck with this stupid 70. After every report card day, I go to his house to compare our mark sheets, and every time, I return disappointed.'

Tinier than most in his classroom, Rahul would also fall prey to school bullies, who'd beat him up and snatch his kites. The boy was already disgruntled – his parents would buy him the small, five-paise kite, and not the big 'kauwa', which cost five times more. The bullies would rob him of that, too. After every such instance, he would rush to his mother, crying. One day, his mother slapped him.

'Why do you run to me for rescue each time?' she yelled, 'Am I going to come save you all your life? Go, confront them. Tell them you won't have any more of this nonsense.'

As the boy didn't have the nerve for a face-off, he stopped flying kites altogether, and retired to his creek – the one where he'd spend his afternoons with Dina, where he'd later test-fire his 7.65 mm pistol as he set out to terrorize his city.

2
Money Can Buy Happiness

———◦‖◦———

4 December, 1988. Ashok Joshi, a powerful ganglord in east Bombay, was driving towards Pune with four associates. At 5 a.m. on a deserted road near Panvel, five vehicles overtook his car, and its occupants jumped out. Armed with AK-47 assault rifles and handguns, they fired 180 rounds into Joshi's vehicle. The gangster and his henchmen succumbed on the spot – their bodies riddled with the volley of bullets, their blood splattered all over the hatchback. The hit squad – don Dawood Ibrahim's men led by his then top lieutenant, Chhota Rajan, sped away, cheering.

Bombay in the 1980s, when Rahul was growing up, resembled Chicago of the 1930s. It was run by the sultans of the Bombay underworld, who controlled an enormous underground economy, ran extra-judicial governments, and lived above the law. A decade before, when Bombay's mafia was dominated by a few dons – Haji Mastan, Karim Lala, Yusuf Patel and Varadarajan Mudaliar – there had been morality to organized crime and dictates of conscience among criminals.

Territories were carefully carved out. Family's blood was considered sacrosanct. But the brash brand of gangsters who took over reins from the old dons conformed to no such etiquette. New alliances, new chieftains, emerged in the 1980s. They raged a battle of might against each other to usurp land, power and a giant share of Bombay. The police stood watching on the sidelines, helpless.

Newspapers screamed of the bloodbath unleashed by the transitioning narrative of the Bombay mafia, the power struggle, the doom. 'This year Bombay has witnessed a dramatic upsurge in gangland warfare,' wrote journalist S.N. Vasuki in December 1988. 'The old underworld order has given way to a new ruthlessness. Audacity has marked action: weapons have become sophisticated. And gangsters have discarded the cloak of darkness, brazenly carrying out shoot-outs in broad daylight. The city is passing through one of its bloodiest phases of underworld violence.'

Every gangland corpse would make page-one headlines in Bombay, and the horror would inevitably spill over to newspaper pages in its satellite towns. Joshi's murder was the thirteenth such killing that year. The shoot-out was widely reported in Dombivli as the spot where the bloody face-off took place was only thirty kilometres from here. Everyone in the city – on roads, in buses, in trains, and in Rahul's home – seemed to be talking about the slain ganglord.

'I know more blood will follow. Joshi's men are not going to take this in silence,' Rahul's paternal aunt told his father during a visit after the killing. She stayed in Kanjurmarg, east Bombay, where the assassinated don once ran his flourishing syndicate. 'I worry for my daughters.'

In the years preceding Joshi's murder, Rahul, on countless occasions, had heard his aunt's alarming stories about the gang, how knife attacks and gunshots were commonplace under their reign. No one was safe, not even her twelve-year-old daughter, who would be harassed with sexual remarks from the 'godless hooligans' every time she passed by a crossroad. Now, with their boss murdered, the gang was to get brash as brass.

Rahul was in class seven when Joshi was murdered. It was the first time his family discussed the Bombay mafia in detail, when the horror arrived home. The killing was an act of revenge, the boy learned from the grapevine. A D-company lieutenant, Sunil Sawant, alias Sautya, was infuriated since Joshi had insulted him in a Bombay prison, wounding his pride. Sautya, relatively small-boned in the world of organized crime, vowed retribution. When an opportune moment arrived, his assault rifles served his revenge. Young Rahul began to like Sautya. He saw him as the torchbearer of hope – the commoner who killed the king, the David to Bombay's Goliath.

With no television at home, Rahul followed the thrilling trail to Joshi's killers in Marathi newspapers. The black, bold headlines, the cliffhanging reports and the graphic images stirred a voyeur in the little boy. He particularly enjoyed news pieces that called out the law enforcement agency's inability to control the warring gangs. The reports accused the Bombay Police commissioner of doing nothing but 'attending to VIPs' as the city rattled with echoes of Berettas and machine guns.

'These were men who'd killed a high-flying don in an action sequence straight out of a Bollywood potboiler. They'd also made the glorious Bombay Police look impotent. How could I not be impressed? How could *anyone* not be impressed? Even newspapers were venerating them! Sautya, Rajan and Dawood were the Al Capones of India,' says Rahul, an ardent admirer of the American gangster.

With the hullabaloo around Joshi's death, Rahul was introduced to a new genre of achievers: gangsters. He started admiring the outlaws, and realized there wasn't just one road to ambition. He needn't be a great student, painter, orator or runner – gigs he'd given up on – to stand out. There were plenty other, more glamorous, ways. All he had to do was choose between extremities, and excel at his choice – be the light or night, philanthropist or mercenary, Mahatma Gandhi or Dawood Ibrahim.

Convinced that academics would never get him too far, Rahul was glad to have discovered a new avenue to realize his wild fancies, to ensure he did not die like a commoner from a small town: a death unnoticed, and a life forgotten. He no longer had to be the saint his father was. No, sir. Demons were in vogue.

———•❦•———

It was the exhilaration of being greater than social statutes that attracted the teenager most towards the world of organized crime – that, and having one's name published in newspapers. Rahul was especially irked with his father around this time, and the fury lent further energy to the budding rebel in him. The family's ancestral property was being split. His uncles got the good lands – close to the highway, where real-estate rates were soaring. Ramakant was given a piece in the forest, which wasn't good to inhabit or cultivate. Yet, he did not protest.

Ramakant wasn't up for sour blood in the family, but to his youngest son, the composure proposed that he 'probably enjoyed being treated like a doormat.' Rahul was convinced that his father, who had been a polite, helpful man all his life, only had hardship to show for it. Too naive, the boy started thinking of his old man, 'border-line stupid'.

'And it isn't that we can afford his niceties,' Rahul complained to his mother after the property split. 'We are a lower-middle-class family despite all that integrity of his. I'm thinking honesty is over-rated, Ma. Had it paid, Baba would have been the richest man in the world.'

Rahul did not want to inherit the burden of his father's virtues. After Sautya, he learnt he didn't have to. It wasn't that his paternal grudges or the sharpshooter's story could turn him into a criminal overnight. Of course, they couldn't. They did, however, open gates to a netherworld, where men favoured anarchy over order, pleasure over paradigms. The boy started looking for these parallels in his classroom, and found them on its backbenches. The notorious kids were happier than the accomplished scorers – even when asked to kneel outside the classroom, or chased after with wooden rulers. Rules were antidotes to fun, the teenager soon realized: adolescent rebellion was wisdom.

Rahul soon found himself on the farthest bench in the classroom, throwing paper planes during classes, and eating out of his lunch box when teachers faced the blackboard. During break time, the boys – a group of eight to ten – would go to a grocery store near their school, distract the old shopkeeper, and steal toffees and candies off his counter. On other days, after bunking classes, they would watch B-grade films at a local cinema hall. Since the nudity-heavy movies allowed only adult audiences, the group would wear multiple layers, including oversized shirts and caps, to look eighteen. During evenings, they would catch the action live, loitering about couples in public gardens.

It was the first time after Dina that Rahul was enjoying the company of his friends. His classmates would laugh at his antics, and he'd like the attention, especially from the opposite sex. He had never had the nerve to talk to any of the girls in his class. No one had told him he was good-looking, so the fair, tall, athletic boy assumed he wasn't. He wouldn't bother with his hair or his recently arrived, uneven moustache, and would always be dressed in a pair of shorts and t-shirt. Once, when he told his friends he was infatuated with a girl, they insisted he approach her. He dressed up, mustered all his courage, and walked up to her one evening. Within moments, he was seen running, too nervous to utter the lines he had memorized.

Although his friends laughed at him for days, Rahul was happy. It wasn't just their company. Through the little acts that challenged norms, the boy was experimenting with identity. He had realized that he preferred being the predator to prey. He was relieved that he couldn't be strong-armed anymore, and that he was the one snatching kites now, making the frailer kids cry.

Through his gang, Rahul was introduced to another group of boys in school – rich kids, who belonged to families of businesspersons, politicians, landowners and local ganglords. While other students walked to school, they would arrive in cars, even bullock carts for amusement. They'd harass girls and get away with it. They wouldn't write a word in their examination papers and still graduate to the next grade. They'd be caught for underage driving, but they'd beat up cops and drive away.

It was his proximity with these boys that convinced Rahul that money could buy happiness. Even if it couldn't, misery in a mansion seemed far more congenial than misery in a hutment. A hefty bank balance, he realized, changes the game. The rules, which govern laymen, are different for the rich. In fact, there are no rules for the rich.

When these boys would call out to Rahul from under his building, Shalini would warn him against mingling with them.

'They can afford to be brats. They have their fathers' golden thrones to inherit. Your pop is leaving you no such legacy. Pay attention to your studies,' his mother would say.

'You don't understand, Ma,' the teenager would argue, 'So many of their fathers are school dropouts. Still, they're rich. Do you think Chhatrapati Shivaji went to college? You don't need to study to become great. You don't need to work as hard as Baba does. There are other ways, much easier ways.'

'Really? And what are these ways?' Shalini would laugh off her son's banter.

'I don't know yet. But when I find out, I'll get you everything that Baba couldn't.'

Rahul had wanted to get far from his father's old-world benevolence. With his adolescent non-compliance, he believed the journey had commenced. The change wasn't a rebellion against his family, an authority, or any of his handicaps. It wasn't self-pity. It was adventure. It was a young boy's acceptance of himself, of the wild possibilities he held within.

———•||•———

Rahul scraped through class eight, with a marked difference in his academic performance. He was no more the studious kid his parents boasted about. He was no more an introvert. He took centre stage wherever he went, commanding attention, unconcerned whether negative or positive. So what if he didn't score the first rank? So what if he couldn't excel at any of the listed extracurriculars? If he couldn't fit in, he would stand out. For that, the boy decided, he would first have to be completely free – from every norm, every restriction that tried to govern his adolescence. Free to draft his own rules. Free to design his own restrictions. Free to fail. Free to fly.

'When Shivaji Maharaj was planning to annexe neighbouring kingdoms, do you think his mother forcibly put him to bed at ten every night?' he once asked his mother.

It was sheer dissent that also brought Rahul back to Bombay, and close to the first time he thought of hurting a man. He had been walking for two days, shivering because he hadn't eaten, and his clothes – a white t-shirt and trousers – had turned brown with dust and sweat. Hoping to rob an old man at knifepoint, the fourteen-year-old followed the senior citizen into a dark alley in south Bombay.

The grocer, who had just shut his shop, was counting his earnings from the day when Rahul pulled out his pocket knife. Moments before accosting him, he decided to call his plan off. Rahul was tall, but thin and weak. The grocer could easily rough him up. He led with a request instead, 'May I borrow ten rupees, sir? I want to go home.'

Rahul had left home two days earlier – as abruptly as he had after Dina leapt into the well. Only this time, he was looking for himself. He knew school wasn't the answer to his big future. He wanted to know what was. He left home on a Friday evening, and walked all night until he reached Bombay. Once at Girgaum Chowpatty, he ran into the waters, happy to embrace his first best friend again. The reunion felt good. After Dina's suicide, Rahul did not have the heart to visit or condole with her family. When he did, two years later, they had moved. The well stood, unapologetic.

The teenager returned home only on Sunday night – after two days of communal toilets, public faucets, vada pavs and footpath-beds. Upon seeing him, his mother hugged him and cried.

'Many friends and neighbours gathered to see the boy, who, once again, had miraculously come back alive,' says Sachin Shivale, Rahul's childhood friend. 'But no one hounded him with questions. It was clear that he did not want to be bothered. After he returned, he didn't talk to anyone. He just asked his mother for food, ate too many chapattis and bhaji, covered his face with a bedsheet and slept. Of course, we were still in the room.'

The boy was at peace, smiling under the white sheet. He still hadn't found his answers, but he knew his solo escapade had limited the questions from his kin.

Another time Rahul threw his family into a crazed frenzy was a few months later, when he got inebriated on bhang. It was Holi eve, and the boys decided to celebrate with some forbidden cannabis. The group of six walked to a local dairy, and each gulped two glasses of milk, mixed with a paste of marijuana buds and leaves. To ensure the drug kicked in, they also picked up some round, peppery bhang tablets.

'It still hasn't hit me,' Rahul complained to his friends after popping the goli. 'That motherfucking doodhwala is the biggest con on this planet.'

'Sweets, boss,' one of the boys suggested. 'We need sweets.'

'Yes, yes. They'll kick the bhang right in,' agreed another. 'Boom Shankar.'

The boys returned to the dairy, and bought caramel-coloured pedas. They also confronted the milkman, who offered a money-back guarantee if 'this maal doesn't fire up your loins'. The cannabis, however, still failed them. About half an hour later, the teenagers returned to their respective homes.

Still hopeful about the loin's fire, Rahul sat with a sugar jar in the living room, gobbling spoon after spoon. A few minutes later, he lay flat on the cot, gripping its sides, trying hard not to fly away. He laughed and squealed in excitement, as if he was on a roller-coaster ride. Soon, he broke into tearful howling.

Rahul's sister, Mangala, was the only one at home. She pulled her brother up, shook him and pinched him. She told him that his friends were about to light the Holi pyre. She hoped he would sober up since he had worked hard to gather wood for it. Rahul responded, but rushed to the window to jump off their first-floor apartment. Mangala could not stop weeping. Her little brother was hallucinating, and she could barely keep him off the window. Eventually, her wails brought in neighbours, who tied Rahul down, poured some mustard oil in his ears, and waited for him to pass out.

Mangala was seven years older than Rahul – almost as much as Dina. Fiercely protective of her youngest sibling, she would defend him against their parents, and shield him against bullies. She would walk him to school and carry his bag. Despite a warm relationship, Rahul was strongly opposed to holding his sister's hand on their way to school. After Dina, he gave up on the grumble. He'd gladly hold

Mangala's hand, but still couldn't tell her about his lost friend. He did not have the heart to. He still doesn't.

'Chotu was always aloof,' says Mangala, 'But he was a good kid. Once, on Raksha Bandhan, he picked up a kilogram of chikoos that father had bought for us, and got onto a local train alone. Over the next few stations, he sold the fruits for ten paise each and gifted me a pen.'

Although he was close to his sister, Rahul would often be at war with his older brother, Mangesh. The quarrels, like most rivalry between young siblings, were short-lived, but one left a permanent scar on Rahul's forehead. In the days preceding Diwali one year, Ramakant had bought firecrackers, and distributed them equally among his three children. Each had ten crackers for the ten-day holiday. Too fond of 'ear-numbing dhamakas', a love that later translated into the clamour of gunshots, Rahul burst his share within the first few days.

With Diwali at its peak, the fifteen-year-old hankered for more thunder bombs, bottle rockets and sparklers. He started looking for Mangesh's crackers, and found them hidden under the cot. He picked a bomb, went down and lit it up. The pyrotechnics left him elated, and over the next few minutes, he had blown up half of his brother's stock. When Mangesh found out, he was furious. He confronted Rahul, but the boy was unapologetic.

'I found them, I burst them,' he said matter-of-factly. 'Next time, use that brain before you hide your crackers.'

Incensed, Mangesh grabbed his brother by his neck, and banged his head against a wall. Hearing Rahul scream, Shalini rushed out of the kitchen and slapped her older son.

'He's the one at fault here,' eighteen-year-old Mangesh retorted between his tears, 'You never recognize his mistakes. Can't you see? He's turning into a monster.'

3

A Good Gamble

Kaan: Rupees 100
Aadha kaan: Rupees 50
Chidiya: Pager
Jhadu: Sten gun
Guitar: AK47
Apple: Bomb

The underworld has its own language, more of an anti-language. A mercurial beast that keeps evolving, the anti-language may not be a poetic representation of the criminal world; but it does the job – befuddles lawkeepers. When Rahul started with the basics of the language at age fifteen, he wasn't looking to befuddle. The secret argots just made him feel closer to one of his favourite heroes, the luminous anti-knight with a 'guitar' – Dawood Ibrahim.

By the 1990s, Dawood had emerged as the one constant factor in the shifting landscape of the Bombay mafia. Many men had killed, and died, to protect their claim over Bombay. The underworld crown had changed several heads. The man, who had rapidly emerged tall from the bloodshed, was Dawood.

Like Gorbachev, Hitler and Sautya, Dawood's humble origins impressed Rahul the most. A police constable's son, the mobster grew to be one of India's most wanted men – a Dubai-based crime lord, running a Rs 150 crore bullion-smuggling empire. Dawood ruled Bombay in absentia through a battalion of lieutenants, far from the clutches of the likes of his father. Rahul adored the don. He, too, had travelled far from his old man's footsteps.

Dombivli, at the time, was home to many youths like Rahul, who idolized infamous gangsters like Dawood, say officers with Mumbai's anti-extortion cell. The city was a recruitment ground for low-budget mafia gangs in Bombay, who scoured the developing metropolis for gangsters, hitmen and any thug who could extract bundles of cash at knifepoint. Street corners and crossroads would be crowded with underworld aspirants in Dombivli, discussing crime, plotting more. One such crossroad introduced Rahul to the anti-language, and later got him inducted into the anti-society.

Rahul met the gang through a game of cricket. An ace spinner, according to his childhood friends, the boy had 'the reflexes of a starving cat'. His deceptive throws quickly translated into popularity in his neighbourhood, and he started receiving invitations for matches outside his residential area. During one such game, he famously took six wickets in an over and won the tournament for his team, beating seventeen others. His teammates carried him around the cricket field as the crowd ringed in thunderous applause for the 'Badshah of Underarm'.

The boy slept well that night. The following morning, he woke up smiling. It was new, that feeling. A taste of recognition, which had evolved into a sense of achievement by dawn, was something he had never experienced before.

'Most of those six wickets were clean bolds, Ma,' he boasted at breakfast. 'They're the most difficult and the most offensive.'

As days passed, Rahul started spending more time with his new team, playing with them, winning accolades for them. The adulation remained consistent, and as most flattery does, it brought him closer to sycophants. The equation would have been harmless, had the boys not been delinquents.

Rahul's new friends were five to six years older than him, all school dropouts, and most with criminal records. Some had been locked up for extortion threats, some for theft, some for street fights, and yet others had been roughed up for behaving inappropriately with women. Most boys had the same story – sent to prison for petty offences, they had befriended local dons inside and returned with opportunities for graver crimes.

Rahul and his new group spent their days at a street corner outside Dombivli railway station – sipping tea, smoking cigarettes, discussing crime and girls. The underworld hopefuls, who hardly bothered with hygiene, would stand unwashed and dishevelled. Despite their insanitary appearances, they'd look at women passersby with sincere aspirations, hoping one of them would agree to be theirs. Rahul, too, had one such pedestrian love-interest.

'I remember him for a wise fool,' says one of his friends from the street corner, 'This girl he had a crush on – the moment she'd walk out of the railway station, he'd run half a kilometre towards her home only to start walking back. This way, he could look at her as she walked past him. We'd ask him why he'd go through all that trouble, and the moron would go all women's empowerment on us. He'd say he'd kill any boy who'd dare to trail his sister.'

The busy crossroad was home to grocery stores, bars, restaurants, men's salons and vegetable and fruit vendors. Outlaws from many local gangs would visit the taverns. Gradually, having spent two years with the boys, Rahul could identify every important criminal in Dombivli. He knew who had killed whom, and who could be bumped off soon.

It was with his new friends that Rahul also witnessed his first instance of violence. One evening, he was at the street corner when he saw some of his friends rushing towards his group.

'He's in the next train, bhai,' one said.

'Who?'

'The maderchod who assaulted Yusuf yesterday. The train was overcrowded when our friend was trying to get in. This man lost his mind, pushed Yusuf out and beat him up.'

'Let's go.'

The group of eight boys, including Rahul, waited as the train approached the railway platform. As its pace lowered, Yusuf pointed at his assaulter in one of the bogies. The group grabbed the man by his shirt and pulled him out. Once he fell to the floor, they held a chopper to his throat. The weapon was only to scare him. None of them were murderers yet. Their kicks and blows, however, spared no part of his body. Commuters begged the boys to stop, but they did not – not until the man had shed a few litres of blood. The passersby didn't dare to intervene. Dombivli, at the time, was known for its unruly boys and their ugly street fights.

This was the first time Rahul saw wilful bloodshed in his sixteen years. The bruised man, who lay unconscious on the floor, should have left him moved, if not disturbed. Blood expects that reaction. The oozing injuries evoked no such emotion. To the ideal underworld aspirant, blood meant nothing more than raw material.

'No, of course I wasn't scared. Nor did I feel sorry for the man.' Rahul laughed, mocking the possibility of compassion when one of his friends confronted him. 'I was improvising on the action sequence in my head. You should have kicked him in the nuts instead of his belly, punched him with your knuckles instead of bare hands, called out his whore of a mother instead of throwing those random curses.'

Although unmoved, the violence did not tempt Rahul. He did not feel the compulsive urge to assault – a need that would eventually take over his life. That evening, he only realized he was dispassionate, and that if he ever became a gangster, he'd be better than most.

———||———

At Dombivli's South Indian Association Junior College, where Rahul was enrolled as a commerce student, he did not enjoy popularity from his street corner. At the naaka, checkpoint, he was a star bowler, more admired than the rest. Unlike the group of brash underworld hopefuls, he was well read, and did not allow impulse to dictate action. He would take his time to absorb circumstances, and when he spoke, he'd offer fail-safe solutions. Like the time his gang was about to assault a grocer who had refused to pay hafta.

'Broken bones are temporary. They heal in weeks. They also invite cops,' Rahul countered his friends, leaning on a light pole, blowing out circles of cigarette smoke for drama. 'Find out where he sources his groceries from. Ask the source to stop giving him goods on credit. Then threaten him, say if he doesn't pay up, he'll have to kiss his dhanda goodbye. If he has the slightest sign of a brain, he'll bring you the cash.'

Rahul's logic was simple – the grocer would rather have three fourths of a pumpkin than a full pea. Convinced, the group took his suggestion and the relucatant grocer soon turned into an eager payee. Like the grocer, the group targeted dozens of shopkeepers in the vicinity. The threat worked on most occasions. Once the boys had made enough money, they offered Rahul a portion of their earnings, even an expensive stealth knife. He refused. For then, a loaded mind was as good as a weapon.

The intellect, however, wouldn't accompany Rahul to college. Having studied in a Marathi-medium school up to class ten, he wasn't fluent in English. He would struggle to weave sentences when teachers, before a full classroom, asked him to introduce himself. His body would melt in embarrassment. When they taught, he would note down most words, and look them up in a dictionary upon returning home. *Meddy-turr-onion. Vole-kay-no.*

The teenager was already irked. He wanted to study science, but was compelled to take up commerce. He had passed his class ten examinations with 64.75 per cent, but on his second attempt. The first time, he had blacked out on his answer sheet, down with a severe bout of typhoid. When he finally cleared school, the principal of the next institution refused to consider his illness.

'Fresh students have first preference,' the headmistress told Rahul.

'But I was forced to drop a year, madam. I wasn't well,' he tried to explain. 'Students, who have scored lesser than me this year, have secured science admissions.'

'I do not make the rules.'

With his stream of interest denied to him and his embarrassing English-language skills, Rahul lost the little inclination he had for academics. The boy had always suspected that his books could never take him too far. Now, the thought was rapidly growing to become a belief. Within weeks of joining college, Rahul started finding more time for the naaka, his cigarettes, the occasional drink and regular criminal banter. His new lifestyle required money – the root of most felony.

———⊦———

At eighteen, when Rahul committed his first extortion bid for the Mumbai mafia, he did not know that a recruiter from a prominent underworld gang was gauging his potential. The handler, also a regular feature at the naaka, was closely watching Rahul's naturally terrorizing moves. He noted his ease as he grabbed his first victim by the collar, and held a chopper to his throat. Rahul had looked perfectly murderous in that moment – his eyes bloodshot, his tall, thin frame trembling with anger – as if he was genuinely furious, as if he'd really kill. A good actor, the handler noted – 'There's no stopping this boy in the underworld.'

The recruiter, Aarif Pardesi, spotted Rahul when he was setting up his don Daya Mahajan's empire in Dombivli. Mahajan, a top lieutenant of Chhota Rajan, started his illegal business by stealing iron scrap from railway workshops in Bombay. A start extortionist, he shot to fame after he gunned down MLA Vitthal Chavan in a sensational killing at the latter's residence in 1991. Thereafter, he joined forces with Rajan and fled the country to join his new boss in Dubai.

Rajan, at the time, was a close associate of Dawood Ibrahim. He, too, had had a stellar rise – from a petty bootlegger to Dawood's Man Friday in the late 1980s. Following the 1993 Bombay blasts, Rajan parted ways with D-Company. Dawood was accused of perpetrating the coordinated attacks, which killed 257. Rajan walked out, announcing he was a nationalistic Hindu don, who did not support 'traitors'. Rajan then established a new syndicate, operating from different South East Asian countries with close associates, including Mahajan and fugitive gangster Jaidev Reddy.

To announce the onset of the new gang in Dombivli, Pardesi had to ready a battalion of foot soldiers. He targeted three types of youths: First, those like Rahul – college boys from lower middle-class families with expensive lifestyles, who would take to crime to sustain vices like alcohol, drugs and prostitutes. Second, unemployed youths from financially weak households, who are desperate for money and, third, immigrants with criminal records, who are experienced and make for cheaper labour.

To identify potential recruits, all Pardesi had to do was lurk around street corners, where such boys spent their days. Like all underworld handlers, he preferred boys, who had exhibited some sort of dare devilry, or had past cases of crimes against them. Rahul had neither of those qualifications, but he 'did seem to have balls.'

There were other idiosyncrasies, too. Unlike other boys at the street ghetto, Rahul was well mannered. He would dress decently and was tech-savvy – he spoke about using pagers and cell phones. He was well informed as he monitored underworld developments through newspapers and his own network of khabris. He would talk about bringing order to ill-organized companies and system to reckless crime; and he'd talk with passion. Most of all, he had a smouldering desire to prove his mettle.

The handler gauged Rahul would do anything – not as much to soar in the universe of organized crime, or for the money, but for his personal sense of achievement. He was power-hungry the way authoritarians are. He was a dreamer the way cutthroats are. Crime adores virtue-free ambition, and the day he met Rahul, Pardesi knew that the boy would either grow into an invincible don or end up dead. Either way, he was a good gamble.

A few days after his class twelve examinations, on a summer morning in April 1994, Rahul reached a Dombivli-based under-construction site with Pardesi and two other youths. A housing complex was being built at the site – six buildings, seven storeys each. The job for the day, which was part of Rahul's underworld entrance examination, was to threaten the project's real-estate developer. The businessman had to pay protection money for the elaborate society he was building in Mahajan's ilaka.

The quartet walked past the iron entrance gate, and entered a fifty-square-foot makeshift cabin on the left. Upon inquiry, the receptionist informed that the builder wasn't in office, but the project manager was available at the site. As the men walked towards the plot, they noticed heaps of sand bags and heavy machinery strewn around the open space. Work had barely begun, and only a few foundation pillars stood footed. Seven labourers – four men, three women – plied materials and supplies in their galvanized iron pans. The manager stood at a distance, supervising the transfers.

'Aye, who's in charge here?' Rahul's two friends, also potential recruits, started rather meekly. 'Stop. Stop the work now.'

The manager and labourers failed to notice them. Determined, the boys repeated their call. No response.

Rahul chuckled. *This isn't doing squat.*

Pardesi stood behind the trio, observing them. This could be their initiation ceremony. Bravery, strong presence of mind or an innovative curse would add to their ratings, while nervousness, poor impact, or inability to accomplish the task would earn negative markings.

A few minutes later, the boys still hadn't managed to draw the staff's attention. Aghast, Rahul picked up a red brick and hurled it at the manager with a loud, unmistakeable 'maderchod'. *This'll do it.*

Rahul was over six feet tall, with a frail frame but a deep, penetrating gaze. His curse, coupled with his baritone, quickly reached the manager. The man ducked to dodge the brick. Having established his presence, Rahul then turned to the labourers: '*Chalo, ghar chalo*. Holiday today, unless you want to stay here and watch this bald fuck die.'

Rahul glanced at the manager through a corner of his eye, and knew the middle-aged, bespectacled man was alarmed. To magnify the moment, he whipped out a chopper and charged towards him. Labourers abandoned their iron pans and rushed out of the main gate, while Rahul stood with his arm around his victim's neck, the chopper lightly touching his Adam's apple. As the manager struggled to escape the young boy's hold, Rahul turned him around and held him by the collar.

'Gandu, get your shit straight.' He looked deep into the manager's eyes – the man was almost as old as his father. Putting a piece of paper in the manager's breast pocket, he added, 'This is Bhai's number. Daya Mahajan. You must have heard of him. Tell the developer to call him and pay up. Or next time, uncle, this chopper won't return clean.'

While the manager stood shaking, Pardesi was impressed with Rahul's 'glib threats and charming delivery'. The boy was a natural sociopath, one who did not bow to pressure. He had acted when his peers failed, when they stood foolishly, pondering over their next steps. Had Rahul not stepped in, the bid would have been a failure.

As he walked out of the construction site, Rahul noticed the manager's scooter near the entrance. He kicked the two-wheeler to the floor. Smiling, the vandal turned around, and waved goodbye to his victim.

4
The Tempting Defeat

———◆I◆———

Dear Aarti,
A very happy birthday to you. They say there's little difference between a wise man and a fool when they fall in love. Just wanted to say I'm happy to be your fool. Thank you for being mine. I love you.
Yours,
Rahul

Rahul fell for Aarti Diwan the moment he saw her. She wasn't the most beautiful girl in college. Her splendour lay in her minimalism. Dressed in a black cotton kurta and blue jeans, she held her head high, and wore no make-up nor excessive jewellery. Her long, ebony-black hair was neatly tied in a braid, and her fair face glowed with simplicity. She was larger than the two-dimensional catwalk models on magazine covers. Five feet seven, she was slightly robust, but real. And her talkative eyes, they offered a peek into her soul, the colour of cheer.

'I want to be your friend,' Rahul walked up to her in college one morning, and offered a friendship band. The abrupt, unorthodox move did not make him falter. The eighteen-year-old was brimming with self-confidence at the time. His first job for the Mumbai mafia had been a success. The developer had paid up following his threat, strongly validating his work, and bringing him Rs 10,000 in cash – as much as his father's monthly salary.

Two months after his first crime for the underworld, having scored 51 per cent in his class twelve examinations, Rahul entered his first year of commerce at Thane's Sheth NKTT College, where he met Aarti. Probably impressed with his audacity, she accepted the embroidered bracelet.

'Yes!' the teenager threw a punch in the air, as she walked away laughing. The laughter was of a child's – loud, carefree, all the teeth showing.

Although he was infatuated with Aarti, Rahul did not attempt to talk to her after that first interaction. A rapidly progressing egotist, his pride demanded her to make the next move. As he waited, he went about his college life, showing his money off. He would wear branded clothes – Crocodile t-shirts and Buffalo jeans – a first in his family. While other kids lived off limewater and vada pavs in the college canteen, he'd splurge on soft drinks and cheese toast sandwiches 'with extra cheese'. The cash convinced him he was above his impoverished college-mates, even his teachers.

Once, when he walked in half an hour late for a class, his Accounts professor lost his temper. The long-haired, bandana-donning Rahul was casual in his stride, far from assuming the courtesy of an apology.

'You!' the professor, a small-statured, healthy man, said, furious. 'Is this your private estate? How dare you enter the class without asking for my permission?'

'*Yeda hai kya*, boss?' Rahul laughed, looking around the classroom, expecting agreement.

'Get out. Get out at once.'

In response, Rahul charged towards the blackboard and grabbed the professor's wrist.

'Don't you dare tell me what I should do, old man. I'll leave if I want to; I'll stay if I want to.' He stared into the professor's eyes. 'Some balls you have, talking to me like that. Come on, do it again. I dare you. Do. It. Again.'

As a stunned silence gripped the classroom, the professor mulled over his next move. He knew Dombivli was flooded with defiant and 'daring' kids like Rahul – armed boys, mesmerized by the glamour of guns and ganglords, waiting to arrive in the underworld with a sensational killing. He decided against being the first blood for this likely aspirant.

'Please, tell him this is not how one speaks to their teacher,' the lecturer requested the class.

Rahul laughed at the man's submission, and released his chalk powder-covered wrist.

Soon, as tales of his bravado travelled across classrooms, everyone learnt of the seemingly rich kid, who had frightened a professor. Pleased with the attention, Rahul's antics grew graver – he'd draw caricatures of lecturers on classroom boards, and would write 'refer to textbook' for questions in his exam sheets. Every time, he would manage to get away with a warning. Teachers did not want to confront him about his pranks, poor attendance or poorer academic performance. His tales had reached them, too.

Brazen and disrespectful, Rahul's demeanour softened only when he got close to Aarti. It did not start well. Without speaking to her, he had told his college-mates that she was a 'special friend'. When word reached Aarti, she was miffed.

'But you took the band. Doesn't that make us friends?' he asked her, as they stood in the classroom corridor.

'You are my friend, but you're not special. People think we are dating. I don't want you spreading such rumours. Please stay away from me.' She walked off.

An irate Rahul swore distance. A few days later, she apologized. He asked her if she would be his girlfriend, but she declined. She said she was her parents' only child. A secret affair would mean betrayal.

During the Diwali vacation that year, Rahul met Aarti by a lake, went down on his knees, and pleaded with her to say yes. His desperation ruptured his ego a little, but he gave in. From all the romantic sagas he had watched, read and heard, the teenager knew that to win in love, one has to lose their pride. He was happy to surrender. She had made the defeat tempting.

Despite his pleas, Aarti wasn't moved. Rahul did not hear from her for days. When lectures resumed after holidays, he noticed she wasn't attending college. He enquired from her friends and learnt she had consumed sleeping pills. He wanted to barge into her house, admonish her and hold her in his arms as she wept. Before he could, she visited college. As soon as she spotted Rahul, she hugged him.

'I will be with you, yes,' she cried on his chest. 'My mother always suspected me of having affairs, but I never did. I never hid anything from her. I also told her that I like you. Things went out of hand and I had to take the pills.'

To Rahul, Aarti's suicide attempt was disconcerting. However, love is nothing if not dramatic, he told himself – if it doesn't push one to the edge of their seat. With Dina's suicide still squatting in a corner of his mind, Rahul decided to take extra care of his new girlfriend. Thereafter, the couple would spend their days in college together. Outside the institution, Aarti would refuse to go out with Rahul alone, finding it 'inappropriate'. If he insisted on meeting, he would have to accompany her for errands like buying groceries and paying bills. Within months, the excuses started disappearing, and the girl, too, raised a white flag to her feelings.

'It was magical, that time,' says Rahul. 'Albeit short.'

———I|I———

The year he started dating Aarti, Rahul met another person, who would alter the course of his life. One evening, after his workout at a nearby gym, the delinquent arrived at his regular street corner. Unlike most days, his friends were missing. The loud discussions around the underworld had been replaced by an unusual, almost unsettling quiet. Rahul looked for cigarette butts on the floor. Their absence told him that no one had visited the naaka that day. The shut tea stall and locked bar explained that something was gravely amiss.

A few seconds later, as Rahul stood looking for familiar faces, a teenager popped up from behind a parked car, and waved at him. He was holding his forefinger to his lip, instructing Rahul to walk the few metres between them in silence.

'Get out of here, quick,' the boy, one of Rahul's friends from the street corner, said in a whisper.

'Why?' Rahul ducked behind the vehicle.

'Don't you know? The Mumbai Crime Branch was here. They have stationed men all around here. Officers in plain clothes, looking for each one of us.'

'Why us?' asked Rahul, confident that none of his crimes had attracted police complaints. After his first offence, the recruiter had kept him busy with regular extortion jobs. Each time, he had ensured his victims were petrified enough to deliver cash and keep mum.

'They came here for Bhaijaan. They want us, too. They think he's our friend.'

'Who the fuck is Bhaijaan?'

'Arre, don't you remember? He'd stand at the naaka with us. We'd borrow his cigarettes. He's about forty-two, average height, beer belly, oiled hair. His name is Joshi, but everyone calls him Bhaijaan.'

'Damn, I didn't know he was a gangster. I assumed he'd return from office every day – in those formal shirts and trousers, and that leather briefcase.'

'Yeah, he'd have guns in that briefcase. They picked him up today. He killed two of Dawood's top gangsters in Mumbai. He's a famous sharpshooter. When they searched his home, they found two pistols and a carbine. A fucking carbine. Now, get out of here. They're out to get everyone, everyone who has anything to do with the naaka.'

As Rahul turned to leave, he saw a woman approaching. He didn't know her, but she recognized him from the street corner and burst into tears.

'They were beating him when they put him in the van, they were beating him,' she said weeping.

Seeing Rahul puzzled, she added, 'I'm Inayat, Joshi's wife. Can you find me a lawyer?'

Rahul promised to help and offered to visit Bhoiwada Court in Mumbai, where Bhaijaan was to be produced before a magistrate the following morning. As decided, he met Inayat at the court's entrance. The thirty-eight-year-old woman was relieved to see the boy, who had sincerely dressed up in formal clothes for the hearing – full-sleeved white shirt, trousers, leather shoes and a backpack. Even Bhaijaan was glad to see Rahul. No one, not even his closest friends or fellow gunrunners, had bothered to show up.

The sharpshooter called for a generous serving of chicken biryani and lassi for Rahul during lunchtime. Towards the day's end, when he was being taken to the police van to be escorted back to prison, he slipped a chit into Rahul's hand.

'Go to an ISD booth, call this number. Tell Mahajan Bhai I'm at Arthur Road Jail,' Bhaijaan quietly instructed.

The underworld hierarchy is such that young boys like Rahul, who largely work with local handlers, never land the coveted opportunity of being in direct touch with the Bhai or CEO of the company. The chief always remains a glamorous, elusive figure, accessible only in news literature and the grapevine of glories. Boys commit their lives to their Bhais without as much as a conversation. It was only obvious that Rahul would remain one of these ordinary recruits. Only if fate didn't have a mind of its own.

Outside the Mumbai court that evening, Bhaijaan had handed Mahajan's personal number to Rahul. The ganglord, one of the most notorious dons of the country, was a lead co-runner of the Rajan syndicate, the only considerable competition to the illustrious D-Company.

'Hello, Bhai,' said Rahul, slightly nervous, mostly ecstatic.

'Who's calling?'

'Bhai, Rahul. You may not know me. I'm one of the new recruits, and this is about Joshi.'

'What about him?'

'The Mumbai Crime Branch have arrested him. He's at Arthur Road Jail.'

'Okay, I'll take care of it.'

'Bhai, I've done a couple of jobs for you recently,' Rahul broke in, sensing the don was about to disconnect the line.

'Like?'

'I'm the new boy, who threatened the Dombivli site manager in April, got him to pay up. Pardesi Bhai said you were happy with my work.'

'Yes, of course. That's why I've been sending you more gigs. We need boys like you. And now, you're helping us get Joshi out. There's no nobler deed than helping a trapped man, beta – especially one trapped with the ruthless Mumbai Police. Do some good work and I'll have you moved to Kuala Lumpur or Bangkok.'

The budding gangster was awed. The don was authoritative yet gracious in his diction. Unlike his naaka friends, who would utter one curse per word, Mahajan's idiolect commanded reverence. It was a classic underworld trick, Rahul learnt much later: Since recruits are usually underachievers, with low self-esteem, they find emotional boosts in the kind words of high-flying dons. Ganglords are known to buy loyalty with flattering phrases. Dawood's top man Chhota Shakeel, for example, would often say to his recruits: 'Beta, what do you think I am going to do with all this money? It's for all of us.'

Rahul didn't respond to the don's proposition, but gleamed. He had finally found a man – and no ordinary man – who recognized his aptitude.

'Tell me, child,' Mahajan continued. 'Is everything good at home? Do you need money?'

'No, Bhai, not at all.'

'Very well then,' replied the CEO, 'Tell Joshi not to worry. I have him covered.'

Before Rahul could hang up, the don added, 'and beta, welcome to the family.'

On the exterior, the underworld seems like a heartless dystopia. However, men close to the ground know that on the inside, syndicates thrive on relationships between the boss and his employees – much closer relationships than in any other profession. It takes emotions to kill another man, not a lack of them. And recruits do it for their bhais, their ideals, their words.

If a don likes a recruit, he often uses emotional weaponry to buy loyalty for his syndicate – praise, so the new footsoldier takes pride in his work, and affection so he feels loved and develops a sense of belonging towards the gang. The third weapon is money, so he gets used to expensive wine and women, and continues to commit crimes to afford his vices. When Rahul spoke to Mahajan for the first time, the don had been generous with his praise and affection. To ensure the boy had enough money, he started employing him for more extortion jobs.

As thousands of rupees poured in every month, Rahul's education became a hurdle in his up-and-coming professional life. He had already failed three times in his graduation years, and soon dropped out of college. He would visit the institution only to see Aarti, who was still unsuspecting of his crimes.

Once, she spotted him walk out of Thane Central Prison, three buildings away from their college. Rahul was visiting a gangster, who, like Bhaijaan, was picked up on murder charges. When Aarti questioned, he said he was friends with a prison official. She believed him. It was love and its renowned blindfold.

A few weeks after he spoke to Mahajan, Rahul saw Bhaijaan walk towards him at the street corner one evening. The sharpshooter, with the don's help, had managed bail. He invited Rahul home for dinner, and the boy gladly accepted. On their way, they visited a local butcher to buy chicken and a wine shop for scotch.

'Are they that afraid of you?' a perplexed Rahul enquired when vendors refused money from the gangster.

'No. Of course, not,' Bhaijaan stated. 'They know I was arrested. They must think I'm low on cash.'

'So? Why do they care?'

'Because on many an occasion before, I've paid them way more than their dues. God helps those who help others.' Bhaijaan smiled.

'Do you believe in God?' Rahul saw the irony. The man was a murderer, ineligible to preach godliness.

'I believe in the devil, and I believe in balance. The devil exists, so there must be his antidote, too.'

The sharpshooter was at least two decades older than Rahul. Dark-skinned and bespectacled with a medium built, he did not dress like a gangster. He would wear formal clothes, and his shoulders drooped like that of an ordinary, hard-working man. Rahul immediately fell for his conventional attire and counterintuitive ways. Unlike stereotypical gangsters, he wasn't an oppressor. Fear wasn't his only weapon. He was polite, even kind, just like Mahajan had been over the phone.

'Until your arrest, I assumed you were some nice uncle who came to the naaka only to smoke cigarettes,' Rahul told him on their way home.

'Yes, of course.' Bhaijaan laughed. 'That street corner is a big hit with law-abiding, principled uncles.'

Rahul did not mind the mockery. He could tell the sharpshooter liked him. That dinner invitation was a privilege not afforded to many.

'My dear boy, the game of organised crime is much bigger than its pawns; men like you and I,' the underworld veteran continued. 'To be powerful, you needn't flaunt your Benz or AK to the world. You need not take to the roof, proclaim you're a Bhai. It's the most commonly travelled road to mediocrity, this mindless display of power. Look poor. It guarantees no one will remember you.'

'Meaning?'

'Show your power when you're looking into your victim's eyes, when you're about to shoot his brain out, only in that moment. The remaining time, try to make up for that moment with some genuine compassion.'

'Why compassion? Do you think what you're doing is wrong?'

'No. It's a business, just a dirty one. And like all dirty businesses, it needs to have a strong social responsibility wing. Why do you think dons do so much charity? They build temples, fund festivals and feed the needy by the thousands. It helps them sleep better at night.'

As the duo reached Bhaijaan's residence, Rahul realized they were entering a dark, isolated under-construction site. They walked hundreds of metres to the farthest end, and reached the lone building on the plot. Still unpainted, only one of the apartments appeared lit in the four-storey structure.

'A developer offered me the place for a few days,' Bhaijaan turned to Rahul to douse his queries, 'Until the cops cool down.'

'Of course.'

When Rahul reached the 450-square-foot apartment on the third floor, he noticed it had nothing more than a few basic eassentials – a mattress, a gas stove, a few utensils and vegetables, a bucket, empty whisky bottles, a table fan and a few books. Two yellow bulbs were the only sources of light, and one of them illuminated something striking – an old newspaper in a corner of the room strewn with seven firearms and dozens of bullets with varied diameters.

'Yes, go for them,' Bhaijaan read Rahul's mind. 'First gunmetal feels better than your first pussy.'

Rahul reached for one of the pistols and ran his fingers on its grip. His adrenaline shot up, and he pointed the gun at a tree outside the window.

'Fire away,' Bhaijaan encouraged. 'No one can hear you here.'

'I don't know how to.'

'Bring it to me.'

When Rahul walked up to the sharpshooter with one of the revolvers, Bhaijaan was pleased. 'You've picked the most precious one,' he said.

'They look the same to me.'

'The one you've picked is a 0.45 mm revolver. This one's called the "real man-stopper".' Bhaijaan smiled. 'Beautiful range, gorgeous precision. We source these from the Indian military. Even their bullets, which are much fatter and leave larger wound cavities, have to be procured from the army.'

'These must be expensive, no?'

'Yes, of course. Regular underworld shooters use 9 mms, available for 60,000 to 75,000 rupees. 0.45s cost double the amount. Carbines are even more expensive, more than 1.5 lakh a gun.'

Rahul could tell that the sharpshooter was passionate about his weapons. He spoke of their calibre, penetration and capacities like a doting father would praise his children. As the two sat discussing the features of various firearms, Bhaijaan's wife Inayat entered the living room. Rahul noticed how pretty she was when stress didn't crease her forehead. She was dressed in a peach salwar kameez, and her skin was a perfect bronze. Willowy and graceful, her big, brown eyes lit up every time she looked at Bhaijaan, matching the tiny diamond stud on her perfect nose.

'Don't you dare teach him how to use those killing machines,' Inayat admonished her husband. 'He's a decent boy.'

'And how do shooting skills make one indecent, my love?' Bhaijaan smiled.

'Shut up,' she said. 'Throw your twisted one-liners at that illiterate wife of yours. I'm done with your word play. What good is it if it can't get you out of prison?'

'This lovely lady here is my second wife.' Bhaijaan looked at Rahul to clarify. 'The first wife's back in the village, with my parents.'

'Yes, yes,' Inayat teased, mischief in her grin. 'First one doesn't know he's a murderer, or that he's a maderchod. That's only for me.'

'Enough now.' Bhaijaan laughed, pulling her close. 'Come, let's drink.'

5
Mumbai ka King Kaun?

—•|•—

> 'Mumbai *ka king kaun?*'
> 'Rahul Ramakant Jadhav.'

Standing atop a Mumbai cliff, when iconic ganglord Bhiku Mhatre, in the 1998 film *Satya*, shouted, 'Who's the king of Mumbai?,' Rahul yelled back his own name in response. It was almost laughable, that proclamation in a full, dark cinema hall. But the twenty-two-year-old did not care if his declaration made him cut a foolish figure. In that instance, he was consumed with the testosterone running through his veins, feeling as powerful, as alive as the mighty Bhiku himself.

After that first time, whenever Rahul watched the film – eighteen times over the next year – he'd watch it academically, learning more from Bhiku's character than his crimes. The gangster opera, with its dark undertones and noir lighting, covers the ruthlessness and brutality of the Mumbai underworld around the turn of the twenty-first century – when Rahul made his foray into the world of organized crime.

'He was so influenced that he also took on Bhiku as his gangland pseudonym,' says David Machmach, one of Rahul's friends and co-accused, 'Initially, he'd ask us to call him that. But as days passed, as he started living up to the character behind the sobriquet, the name caught on. Everyone in the underworld, even the cops, would refer to him as Bhiku – with all the respect that name deserves.'

When Rahul entered the underworld, it was partly Bhiku's audacity, which extended him the courage to dream big. Although a newbie, he told himself he was a conqueror, one who would create the largest mafia empire of contemporary India, become one of history's most successful gang commanders. He was a fantasist, distant from reason. To bridge the gap, he had the underworld veteran Bhaijaan, his newfound mentor, his guru.

'You have a clean record, don't get into this shit,' Bhaijaan would tell Rahul when the latter asked him for tips and training. The sharpshooter probably felt protective about the underworld hopeful, like an older brother. He would reiterate, 'It's all glamour and guns on the outside, beta – and guilt and grime on the inside.'

'I don't think I've ever felt guilty, Bhaijaan,' Rahul once replied. 'I've made men older than my father cry. Even after threatening so many of them, I can't tell what remorse feels like.'

'I know, gandu,' Bhaijaan lightly slapped his cheek. 'That's exactly why I try to keep you away from this shit.'

New recruits in the underworld usually work far from sharpshooters and gang heroes like Bhaijaan. Rahul had managed the unparalleled opportunity. All he had done was show up when Bhaijaan needed help. It was instinct that took Rahul to the court that day, a moment that froze to become his criminal life.

Rahul would spend every day at Bhaijaan's home following the sharpshooter's bail, fiddling with pistols and carbines, loading and unloading them, learning their complicated mechanisms. Late at nights, he would fire the guns, irking sleeping birds and Bhaijaan's wife. When Mahajan called, an exuberant Rahul would note down particulars of the assignments for the hitman – names, numbers and addresses of extortion and murder victims, details of arms dealers and money deliverers.

'Did you really kill two of Dawood's men?' Rahul asked Bhaijaan one evening, venturing into the murders that led to his arrest.

'Of course, I did,' the sharpshooter replied. 'It's part of the game. The Bhais and their companies are battling for the underworld throne, for Mumbai. Casualties, like in any war, are lieutenants on the frontier, men like me and the ones I killed.'

'If you know it's a game, why do you take part?'

'Because it isn't just a turf war anymore. It's a battle of ideologies. A gangster is nothing if not loyal, Rahul – and loyalty demands a price. I love my don. I believe in his beliefs. The 1993 Bombay blasts should not have happened. Those 257 innocents should have been alive. Dawood doesn't deserve Mumbai; all his men deserve to die,' Bhaijaan declared with the conviction of a revolutionary. The hitman was genuinely enraged – his nostrils flared, jaw clenched and teeth gnashed.

'When Dawood's name emerged in the 1993 blasts, I was shocked, even disappointed,' Rahul offered. 'They were burning his effigies, chanting "deshdrohi Dawood Ibrahim". He was my hero. I couldn't understand why he'd done that. He's a gangster, not a terrorist.'

'Your hero's dragged the underworld's name through the mud,' Bhaijaan spat, his face now turning red. 'Gangsters are men of ethics. We don't steal, rob, rape or bother the poor. We target the rich, who are anyway sitting on empires built on deprived men's sweat and blood. We have principles. We don't kill in temples, hospitals or in front of one's family. We take care of the area we live in. No one can mess with our women, elderly or our kids. We're respectable men, and he's made us look like terrorists.'

'That's also probably why everybody – from politicians to the police and the legislature – is so pissed with the underworld.'

'Yes, of course,' said Bhaijaan, 'The Mumbai Police is running wild for our capture. The bastards have chased and gunned down 600 of us in seven years. The state is enacting the mindlessly stringent Maharashtra Control of Organised Crime Act. Now, there will be special courts to prosecute gangsters, and the khaki-clad "Dirty Harrys" will have even more liberty to shove their sticks up our asses.'

'Wow,' mused Rahul. 'It's a really bad time to enter the underworld.'

––|––

It was through Bhaijaan that Rahul, over months, learnt the intricacies of organized crime – the hierarchy of criminal companies, the various departments, and their many showrunners. To the underworld aspirant, the information was gold. He would repeat the details to himself after he left Bhaijaan's home and, still an avid sketcher, he'd draw flowcharts in his diary:

THE COMPANY

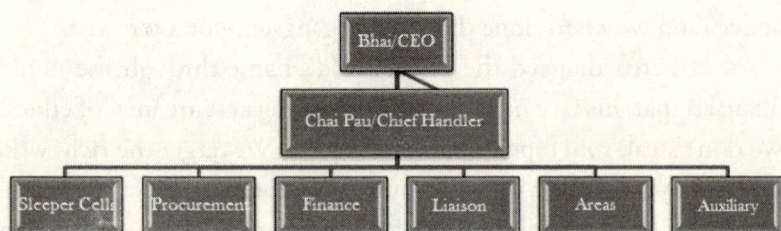

Bhai/CEO
Chai Pau/Chief Handler
Sleeper Cells | Procurement | Finance | Liaison | Areas | Auxiliary

Chai Pau: The CEO's right hand man, one who is close enough to the Bhai to drink tea and break bread with him. He oversees every company operation and supervises heads of all departments:

- Sleeper Cell Head: Manages recruitment and maintenance of special contract killers and sharpshooters like Bhaijaan, spread across sleeper cells all over the country. These are activated only for important hit jobs.
- Procurement Head: Manages recruitment of boys for smaller jobs, also handles arrangement of stolen motorbikes, weapons, and other paraphernalia required in execution of crimes.
- Finance Head: Manages bag boys – money launderers, collectors and distributors. He is in touch with illegal finance networks across borders as well as investors within the country.
- Liasion Head: More educated and polished than other department heads, he handles lawyers, politicians, law enforcement agencies and other stakeholders, who can protect the company against the law.
- Areas Head: Manages supervisors of the various geographies under the don's command.
- Auxiliary Head: Manages hideouts and shelters for gangsters once they have executed their tasks. Also identifies trusted locals in various cities, who can act as weapons repository, and offer their premises to hoard arms and hold meetings.

Department Heads	→	Multiple Handlers	→	Boys like Me

Rahul's charts brusquely told him that he was at the lowest rung of the underworld hierarchy. He consoled himself, saying he does interact with the head of the company, but soon realized it was mostly as Bhaijaan's Chai Pau. He did not have an individual relationship with the CEO. He had done nothing to deserve his camaraderie, yet.

'I must win him over,' Rahul found himself thinking, 'I must do something that stays with him for long, establishes my potential. I could threaten a big realtor and arrange for a huge extortion amount. Oh wait, I could bump off a D-Company gangster.'

As Rahul sat plotting his boisterous arrival in the world of organized crime, fate once again intervened to do the job for him. The Mumbai Crime Branch learnt of Bhaijaan's involvement in a third murder, and he was soon re-arrested, putting Rahul in close touch with the CEO.

—————

Rahul landed his first hawala job in 1998 by mere chance. Hawala, the illegal process of transferring funds by skirting traditional banking channels, ensures gangsters have enough money to grease the crime machinery. Since Bhaijaan needed cash to pay his lawyer, the CEO asked Rahul to pick up the amount, awarding him his first job as an underworld bag boy.

'It's nothing complicated, beta,' Mahajan explained. 'All you have to do is go near the McDonalds outlet outside Andheri railway station, and exchange codes with the delivery person. Once he hands you the cash, deliver it at the addresses I share with you.'

'Understood.'

As instructed, Rahul arrived near the McDonalds outlet the following morning, looking for the delivery person dressed in black jeans and grey shirt, carrying a blue duffle bag. The man spotted Rahul and stood next to him.

'Jai?' the deliverer asked Rahul in whispers.

'Yes, Veeru,' Rahul completed the code based on lead protagonists of the classic Bollywood film *Sholay*.

In response, the man handed him the bag.

On his way in an autorickshaw to the first Mumbai address, Rahul partly unzipped the bag and discovered several bundles of 500-rupee notes. He estimated the cash must amount to at least five lakh rupees. Three destinations later, including Bhaijaan's lawyer's, he returned to Dombivli.

'The job is done, Bhai,' Rahul called Mahajan from an ISD booth. 'I have one stack left. It's Rs 25,000. Whom do I give this to?'

'That one's for you, beta,' the CEO replied.

The money, which meant little to the don, instantly bought Rahul's loyalty. To the 23-year-old, the amount was substantial. 'More than double of Baba's salary,' he again compared himself to his father – 'twice as much, for a four-hour job.'

Standing inside the telephone booth, the receiver still in his hand, Rahul started dreaming of the overpriced restaurants he would take Aarti to. He could even bring her to the Gateway of India or the Taj Mahal Hotel of Mumbai, and buy her a private boat-ride across the Arabian Sea. *And then, as the sun sets, we'll have our first kiss.*

Ecstatic with the easy money, Rahul decided to dive deeper into the illegal banking channel, and realized how massive the business was. The practice originated in India, he learnt, and the country had lost trillions of dollars in tax avoidance since Independence, around half of which could be accounted to hawala transactions. By the mid 1990s, such dealings stood at US $112 million.

The underground remittance system transfers money without actually moving it, Rahul deciphered – and the cash is dispensed through hawaladars or hawala dealers.

'Say, a South Africa-based don wants to perpetrate bombings in Mumbai,' a Crime Branch officer explains. 'He'll call a hawala operator in South Africa, who, in turn, will get in touch with his Mumbai counterpart. After the Mumbai operator confirms the cash is ready, the African hawaladar will call the don with the time, venue, code and description of clothing of the delivery boy. The don's crony will meet the delivery boy in Mumbai, exchange codes and pick up the cash.'

An extremely quick remittance system, which ensures cash delivery in less than 24 hours, hawala pays more than official currency exchange rates, and ensures two things that gangsters hold dear – anonymity and conversion of unaccounted black money.

'The most important part of hawala is the trust factor. In fact, one of the meanings attached to the word hawala is "trust",' Bhaijaan once told Rahul. 'Hawala operators go to any length to protect their clients, which works well for the dons. Your hero, Mr Ibrahim, financed his 1993 blasts through hawala. Funds for the bombings, especially to buy explosives and pay the bombers, came through operators in the United Kingdom, Dubai and India.'

Thereafter, Rahul participated in dozens of such transactions. He'd pick up five to twenty-five lakh rupees at a time, sorting cash in autorickshaws and public toilets, delivering it at various addresses all over Mumbai. The job appeared uncomplicated, but it had its perils, even temptations.

If he were travelling in trains, Rahul would constantly be paranoid about being robbed. If he saw cops on the road, he would turn around and walk in the opposite direction. If rickshaw or taxi drivers stared through their rear view mirrors, he would duck to the floor to count the cash. At times, he would also think of pilfering a bundle or two, but he couldn't risk the don's faith. *A gangster is nothing if not loyal.*

From picking up and distributing cash in Mumbai, Rahul quickly graduated to travelling to other Indian cities, where he would buy arms in exchange for the hawala money arranged for him there. His margins, like his first hawala job, were phenomenal. He began to grow fond of the trade.

Apart from hawala, Rahul would also pick up extortion money from Mahajan's many rich victims. He enjoyed the fear on the men's faces when they delivered cash in those expensive automobiles. Their petrified eyes and dry mouths would make him grin, lend him power.

'I'm meeting really important men – from arms agents and contract killers to cops and lawyers,' a thrilled Rahul told Bhaijaan outside a Mumbai courtroom one afternoon. The veteran was still in prison, brought to court for proceedings. 'Plus, it's introducing me to hawaladars all over the world.'

'And it's teaching you about money, the underworld's raw material as well as end product,' said Bhaijaan. 'The don must really trust you.'

'I think he does, yes. But my girlfriend and family are getting suspicious. Ma used to be happy with the cash I gave her. Lately, she has been raising questions. And Aarti, I took her to Mumbai's Oberoi Trident the other day. She kept asking how a college dropout like me could afford a meal at the five-star restaurant. Saala, I wanted to have dinner, but left after having tea and some complimentary cookies.'

'Too much money is always a crisis.' Bhaijaan smiled. 'Why don't you tell them you're doing a job?'

'I did! I said I'm into marketing, but they don't believe me. In fact, Aarti definitely knows I'm up to something. She's said it. She said if I don't mend my ways, I'll end up as a gangster.'

'But you're already a gangster! Extortion and hawala, you're building up your criminal CV quite impressively. Plus, I hear you're also taking up a lot of ambassadorial gigs.'

'Meaning?'

'Diplomatic poaching,' Bhaijaan explained. 'Didn't you get that sharpshooter to quit Dawood's gang and join ours?'

'Oh, that! Yes, of course. Even months after his arrest, Dawood's men hadn't shown up for his rescue. Through my sources in prison, I learnt he was pissed with the D-company. So I approached a lawyer and paid for his bail. Grateful, he was happy to switch loyalties.'

'The don was quite impressed with that switch. Your acquisition is a good shooter – trained, experienced and doesn't return without game.'

'I've been getting our own gang members out, too, Bhaijaan,' Rahul boasted to his mentor. 'There was one, who was arrested for six extortion cases. The don wanted him out at any cost. I found a lawyer, got bail for our boy, and gifted a Nokia cell phone worth Rs 17,000 to that lawyer.'

'Good, looks like you're developing your own sources.'

'Yes, yes. Just that I need to hide this better from the women in my life.'

The budding gangster grew no better at dodging suspicion. He had now become a close aide of the CEO. He could be trusted with money – an asset in any profession. Countless hawala jobs had also established his control over the pulse of organized crime. He was now well versed with the confederation of small and big gangs who worked for his Bhai, the lawyers who helped with incarcerated gangsters from the company, and money launderers who'd be ready with cash whenever the ganglord called.

The money, the 'unparalleled honour' of being in direct touch with the head of the syndicate, the mounting admiration for his work, and his rocketing sense of self-worth – all of these were making Rahul fall in love with the underworld. Just that this steamy affair had also put him on the cop radar. He was being watched, his phone tapped.

6

The Golden Fucking Eggs

— ◆ —

> 'Your son, Jadhav saheb – he has the gaze of a sharpshooter.'
> – A Thane Crime Branch official to
> Ramakant Jadhav, December 1998

As the police SUV raced along the deserted Shilphata Road towards the Crime Branch headquarters, Rahul sat amused on a bench in its cargo space with two policemen, his hands cuffed to metal loops on the ceiling. The cold December breeze rushed into the speeding vehicle as the cop on the middle seat opened its door, and tried to push Rahul's presumed accomplice out. The man, a sand supplier, was one of Rahul's extortion victims, and was picked up with the gangster from Dombivli railway station. The supplier wailed and begged for mercy, oblivious that his right hand, which was cuffed to a handrail above the door, wouldn't permit the fall.

'Don't encounter me, sahib. Please don't encounter me. I have a wife, two children. I'm a husband, a father,' he made his case.

The cops were resolute.

'You're Chhota Rajan's man, aren't you, gandu?' the officer next to the supplier lowered the man's head towards the SUV's rapidly rotating rear wheel. His cuffed arm stretched, making him bellow in agony.

'I don't know any chhota-mota Rajan, sahib,' he shouted back, the wind distorting his words. 'I'm no Bhai-vhai. I'm a husband, a father.'

'Yes, yes.' The police officer pulled him in. 'Sing another song.'

'Aye, let him go,' the cop on the front seat intervened. 'This Bhiku is the maderchod who needs to be pushed out.'

At the Crime Branch office, Rahul and his victim were ordered to a bench in a corner of the room, where they waited for senior officers to arrive. They were told that they had been picked up under Section 151 of the Code of Criminal Procedure, which allows the police to arrest any person likely to commit a cognizable offence. The supplier tried to explain that his detention was a mistake, but was told that senior officers would take a call on his fate. When Rahul tried to argue, demanding an arrest warrant or a magistrate's order, they said that law did not require them to furnish either.

'You're fucked, son,' a cop informed the gangster.

A few hours later, two police officers – one tall, one short – entered the room. They walked past Rahul, and the tall one reached out for the supplier's collar. The duo, like the cops in the SUV, was probably fooled by Rahul's civilized attire. The clean-shaven gangster looked younger than his twenty-four years. His white formal shirt was tucked in neatly on his tall, muscular frame, and his formal trousers and backpack indicated purpose.

The tall cop threw the supplier to the floor, and the short one kicked him. One of their colleagues intervened within seconds, and pointed out that Rahul was the one who deserved the kicking.

'*Yeh chikna?*' the short one asked, surprised. The supplier quietly stood up, and walked to a distant spot in the room, where he could cower in peace.

'I was going to Mumbai for a job interview, sahib. You may check my bag,' Rahul stated.

The short cop with a red, round face laughed. 'Thank you for the permission, sahib,' he said, 'Come, I'll take your job interview. Tell me, why are you in touch with Daya Mahajan? And where is he now?'

Rahul remained silent. The tall cop pushed him to the floor and searched him – there were two mobile phones and negligible cash.

'Ahh, these are the phones you use to call your Bhai, haan?' the short one kicked the gangster, and pulled out a revolver, '*Bolta hai ki karu* encounter?'

With his experience with incarcerated gangsters, Rahul knew he could not protest – the law legitimized the interrogation, even the threat. That moment was beyond his control. A slight fear crept into his nerves, but he knew this wasn't the day he was going to die: Since there were no formal complaints against him, if the cops shot him dead, they'd have nothing to show for his corpse. They had picked him up on suspicion, not evidence. There's only so much assault that suspicion grants. Besides, he knew important men who could get him out within minutes – if only he could make one phone call.

A few kicks and blows later, before the assault could break the gangster, his wish was granted. Rahul's father walked into the Crime Branch office, accompanied by his friends from the naaka, and two representatives of a prominent local politician. A word with the cops, and Rahul was bailed from the situation. Amidst steely-eyed death glares from police officers, he walked out of the Crime Branch office.

'Remember my words,' said the short, round one, approaching Rahul's father. 'Your son is out to terrorize this city. Stop him, or the state will do it for you.'

When Rahul returned home that evening, he was met with a full living room – his mother, brother, sister and her husband. The gangster was embarrassed upon spotting his brother-in-law, Kishor. His sister had got married only a few months ago. As he smiled apologetically at her, he remembered her wedding day, how she had hugged him before leaving with her new family. It had felt strange, that first embrace between siblings, her tears on his chest. It had left him moved, almost shaken.

'Namastey, Bhauji,' Rahul touched Kishor's feet.

He then turned to his sister, 'You have put on weight, Mangala. Marriage agrees with you.'

The gangster looked dishevelled – torn shirt, muddy pants, and oozing wounds all over his body. Blood had frozen below his nostrils, and he was walking with a limp.

'What's the matter? Why this assembly?' he enquired, 'I'm not a criminal, Ma.'

'Let's get this straight,' said Kishor, 'Your past – anything you've done until this morning – doesn't matter to me. I'm here to discuss your future.'

As Rahul stared at the floor, Kishor continued, 'Do you want one, Chotu? A future?'

Had it been his parents or siblings, the gangster would have argued or snubbed their arguments with disrespect or a walk-off. He could not have done that with his brother-in-law. The relationship demanded his respect.

'Of course, Bhauji.'

'Good,' replied Kishor, 'There are many opportunities in technology after the internet came to us five years ago. It's only going to get bigger. You've already dropped out of college, and I'm assuming you don't want to return. Join a computer course. With that training, you can land a well-paying job in web designing, graphic designing, animation technology, any specialization you choose.'

'You're doing the course,' declared Rahul's mother before he could protest. 'I'm not having any more of this nonsense.'

The gangster gave in. With the crime branch's eyes fixed on him, he could use the course for an alibi. If the cops picked him up, he could say he's changed, that he's now studying computers to ensure a bloodless future. The classes would also settle the arguments he was having with his girlfriend.

Aarti did not know of the detention, but she had been pestering Rahul to complete his graduation so she could tell her parents about him, and the two could get married. The couple had spent three beautiful years together, and she was certain she wanted to marry Rahul. When her parents brought portfolios of eligible grooms, Aarti would consume a few sleeping pills to shut them up. She would survive the suicide attempts, and return to Rahul with the same request.

'I know you keep lying to me about your job,' she would tell him. 'If you do not get serious, we'll have to break up. I know you don't want that either. So please, become a little responsible. Life isn't just naaka and cigarettes and daru. It's us. Don't walk out on us.'

When Rahul joined the coaching class to learn graphic designing in early 1999, Mumbai was reeling with gunshots, and the underworld was down on its knees. The police's encounter squad had killed gangsters by the hundreds. Towards the end of the century, even the Bhais were weary of all the blood. The dons, most of whom were now settled overseas, were worried. With so many of their foot soldiers wiped off, they feared being reduced to far-flung kings without armies.

It was a common realization in the underworld that the gang wars, the brazen murders, the kidnappings and contract killings had to give way to more sophisticated means of organized crime. What emerged as a solution was a reign of extortion. The crime did not require investment nor covert arrangements that could attract attention of law-enforcement agencies. All that the gangsters had to do was make a call and sit back. Even the smallest businessperson would pay 'protection money' of lakhs of rupees. Mumbai was full of such entrepreneurs then, and as many gangsters – small and big – extorting money from them. Every call was suspect, every contract a cause for worry.

'During the late 1990s, Mumbai would witness at least thirty-five extortion attempts a day. Everybody who was anybody was threatened, asked to dole out lakhs or crores of rupees. You could not drive a Mercedes in this city without getting calls from the underworld. You couldn't get your children married,' says an encounter specialist with the Mumbai Police, who rose to fame in the 1990s after he purportedly gunned down eighty gangsters.

Estimates suggest that by the year 2000, the extortion business was officially pegged at Rs 150 million a year in Mumbai, while unofficial figures put the stakes at Rs 10 billion annually. Gangs targeted real-estate developers, hoteliers, financiers, industrialists, traders and Bollywood bigwigs. The crime soon started demanding blood, and the final years of twentieth century saw a spate of extortion-related shootouts in Mumbai. Music baron Gulshan Kumar, for instance, was gunned down at point-blank range in suburban Mumbai on 12 August 1997. The forty-one-year-old singer's bullet-riddled body lay on the road as a warning from the underworld: those unwilling to meet a don's demands would face death for destiny.

With every new murder, Rahul got desperate to get a piece of the extortion pie. He was impatient to establish his name in Dombivli and then move on to bigwigs in Mumbai. Following his detention, as he diligently plotted the road to his rise, the computer course incidentally, helped him with directions.

—◦—

To evade police suspicion after his detention, Mahajan stopped being in direct touch with Rahul, and introduced him to his associate, Jaidev Reddy. Rahul did not mind the transition. He knew Reddy would have important lessons for him. A famed extortionist, the gangster was known to have murdered high-flying developers in the early 1990s.

Born in a small village in Karanataka, Reddy had moved to Bombay with his family in the 1980s. He worked in a suburban tea stall in the city. He met gangsters who would frequent the stall, and soon killed a local criminal. The underworld henchmen, impressed with his audacity, got him recruited with Rajan. After a spate of important killings, he grew to be a close confidant of the don's. In the early 1990s, he shifted base to Dubai, where, with Rajan, he worked for Dawood. When Rajan walked away from D-Company, Reddy, like Mahajan, walked with him.

After the introduction, Rahul was in regular touch with Reddy, but he decided to lie low. His hawala, money collection and delivery, threats to local developers, diplomatic poaching and weapon purchasing had come to a temporary halt. Since scouting for extortion targets wouldn't immediately attract cops, he continued with the job. He would travel through Dombivli, looking for under-construction real-estate projects. After identifying their developers, he would pass on their contacts to Reddy. The remaining time, he would drink and explore computers.

One evening in April 1999, about five months after the Crime Branch picked him up, Reddy asked Rahul to find the contact number of a business tycoon he wished to extort money from. Although Rahul wanted to impress 'Anna', a term for older brother in south India, he was feeling lazy – finding personal numbers of well-heeled victims was tedious. At the time, underworld gangs had collectively employed over 5,000 youths only to collect intelligence and contact data of potential extortion victims. It would be weeks before Rahul could wade through a complex web of khabris, and find the final link, which was in close proximity to the target.

Rahul decided to procrastinate, and went to his computer class at midnight. Apart from the one-hour coaching sessions in the afternoon, the gangster would spend six hours in the class every midnight to 6 a.m. Busy coders, website developers and animators, who owned the class, would accompany him. The men were happy to accommodate the unusual hours for Rahul – an enthusiastic learner, he'd quietly occupy one of the fifteen computers in the 300-square-foot room, revising his lessons from the day – Photoshop, Corel Draw, GIF animator, Flash and Illustrator. He had started with the basics, learning what CPUs and monitors were, and was quickly mastering some of the most complicated software.

The class introduced Rahul to the internet. Like most first-time explorers, he was hooked. He realized that the web, like the underworld, was a parallel universe. In fact this was a far better world than the real one – here, he had anonymity. No one knew what websites he was browsing, or the information he was looking up. He had no footprints to trail. *The anonymity can be put to better use*, Rahul found himself thinking. Soon, he knew how. He looked up the internet for the businessman Anna had mentioned, and found his number within minutes.

'How did you manage the number in a day?' Reddy was stunned.

'Not a day, Anna,' the gangster was ecstatic. 'Twenty minutes.'

'How?'

'The internet! BSNL, Thane's telecommunications service provider, has a website with all numbers listed. I cracked it; I figured out the keywords. Now, I can find you any number you want within minutes, not just in Dombivli, even other cities in the Thane district.'

'Well done, beta. This is going to save us months, no, years!'

Spurred with Anna's enthusiasm, Rahul decided to scour the internet for more resources. He wanted to graduate from his Rampuris and the petty threats to local shopkeepers and builders. He wanted to foray into real extortion, target the biggest fishes. Now, he had found an effortless way in.

Like other gangsters, Rahul would not have to tap informers for weeks, or physically recce construction sites, or get developers' office numbers off hoardings. He need not follow the cumbersome process. He devised an easier one on his own, which could get him the direct line to his victim. It involved five key steps:

1. Look up newspaper advertisements of real-estate projects and note the phone number listed for enquiry on the property.
2. Insert this number on the search bar on BSNL's website.
3. The BSNL site, in its search results, would come up with the official name of the developer.
4. Insert this official name in BSNL's search bar, and the site would share every phone number registered under that name.
5. Call each of the listed numbers – reception, accounts, marketing, and offices in various cities – until you've reached the developer's direct line.

Rahul would make at least fifteen to eighteen calls to zero in on the developer's direct number. It was still easier than the months that other gangsters took for the job. Convinced with his method, he started exploring the MTNL website, the telecom service provider for Mumbai. Over the next year, he had gathered details of hundreds of the most prominent realtors in Mumbai and its neighbouring cities, neatly stacked in a pile of A4s. He also extended his search to other flourishing businessmen, and was quickly in possession of their contact details.

Rahul would pass on the numbers to Reddy. He cannot tell how many of these men were threatened, but he knew his research had many victims, and that Anna was a generous man. His pockets had never been heavier.

———⊪———

During one of his web searches, Rahul stumbled upon another important website, Film Guild India, a Mumbai-based producers' body. The site had listed a database of some of the most eminent Bollywood producers in the country – their names, addresses and telephone numbers. The gangster knew he had struck it rich.

The underworld was known for financing films through black money. At times, the storyline was also dictated by the Bhais, who liked to promote their favourite heroes and heroines. The film industry, in turn, lent glamour and pomp to scores of underworld parties. Towards the end of the twentieth century, the equation started changing. The cash-strapped underworld began to spot gullible, wealthy victims in Bollywood.

Journalists Ajith Pilai and Saira Menezes, in 1997, noted, 'In the last two years, the dons haven't been magnanimous enough in writing off losses on failed films. For one, money from real-estate investments is drying up because of the market slump. Then, of their traditional sources of income – narcotics, gold smuggling, illicit liquor trade and prostitution – only the first remains lucrative. Naturally, the underworld has turned to the film industry with renewed interest.'

Extortion found innumerable Bollywood casualties in the late 1990s. Gulshan Kumar was killed. Directors Mahesh Bhatt and Rakesh Roshan were attacked. Threats were issued to director Subhash Ghai, and producer Mukesh Duggal was gunned down. The industry was left in a state of panic. The strikes meant the dons had upped their ante, and cash-rich segments had no option other than to pay the Bhais. Police protection was extended to the likes of Amitabh Bachchan and Lata Mangeshkar, while many others reached out to private security agencies.

Actor Anupam Kher, during a press interview in 1998, stated, 'The time has come when we all have to be together. Each man cannot stand up for himself. We have to do something collectively and we have to involve the police and the government for the well-being of the industry. You can't possibly do creative work when there is this level of fear.'

In all the blood and mayhem, in every new attack, Rahul only saw opportunity. With the Film Guild India website, he was certain he had a breakthrough, and dialled his boss immediately.

'We should call them, Anna. We should call and threaten each of these motherfuckers,' he rushed. 'I have numbers of all the important producers in the country. You just name them.'

Reddy was silent, probably in disbelief. Rahul could not have those numbers. It was years of work.

Rahul continued: 'The industry employs one million people, and the bastards have an annual turnover of Rs 1,250 crore. A large chunk of the financial transactions are through black money. They'll be happy to pay up a few crores in exchange for their lives. Even if we don't get cash out of them, scared Bollywoodwallahs will call the cops, and we'll have your name on news headlines. That means more publicity for you. Plus, inducing fear into Bollywood will also boost the gang's morale. Our boys, like everyone in the country, are overawed by the film industry. They'd be mighty proud if we made the celebs kneel.'

'Get me the numbers and we'll see,' said the don, still hesitant.

After the call, the gangster went to a public telephone booth and started dialling the numbers he had noted from the Film Guild India website. He realized the numbers belonged to office receptions, and not the producers' desks. To get personal numbers of prospective Bollywood victims, Rahul came up with another five-step process:

1. Get the producer's number from Film Guild India.
2. Insert this number on the MTNL website's search bar.
3. The MTNL site, in its search results, would come up with the official name of the production house.
4. Insert this official name in MTNL's search bar, and the site would share every phone number registered under that name.
5. Call each of the listed numbers – reception, accounts, marketing, et al. – until you've reached the producer's direct line.

Rahul realized there was another important benefit of his unique approach – other gangs would remain in the dark about his company's extortion targets. At the time, when a gang deputed lieutenants to identify a target's contact details, rival gangs would quickly learn about the attempt through the web of khabris. Gangs would then compete to threaten the potential target, or the cops would step in to help the prospect with protection. Rahul's method had no such hindrances.

When Rahul knew he had a producer on the line, he would speak instead of abruptly disconnecting the call. Throwing a fake name, he would say, 'Write down my boss's number.'

'What is this about?'

'A business deal,' Rahul would then dictate an international phone number and disconnect the line.

A couple of hours later, Reddy would follow up on Rahul's threat, calling the producer on his direct line. 'Maderchod,' he would start, 'Didn't my boy ask you to call me? Don't you know how many of your industry have been gunned down like dogs? I'll send a boy to collect Rs 75 lakh tomorrow. Keep it ready.'

Gradually, Rahul also started speaking to developers, and passed their numbers to Reddy after his initial conversation. An average of six of ten would pay up, and Rahul made dozens of such calls every month. The extortion amounts for producers were fixed – 50 lakh rupees to a crore, depending on their stature. For developers, rates varied in accordance with geography – ten lakh rupees for a housing complex in Dombivli or elsewhere in Thane, 25 to 50 lakh rupees for a society on immediate outskirts of Mumbai, and a minimum of one crore for properties in Mumbai.

'The internet is our dino-fucking-saur, Anna – one that lays golden-fucking-eggs,' a thrilled Rahul told his don. 'I can't believe my family bought it for me!'

7

The Carnival of Longing

—◦⟡◦—

15 February 2001. 3.15 a.m. Standing outside Aarti's apartment, Rahul pulled out his 9 mm pistol. He ejected the magazine, and started loading it with ammunition that he had thrown carelessly in his jeans pocket. One bullet, two, three, four – 'That should be enough. I'll shoot the motherfucker at point blank range, one shot in the middle of his fat forehead, another in his heart. Of course, the first bullet will rip his brain apart, but he deserves two.' Smiling at the image of the old man's bloodied corpse, Rahul inserted the magazine into the pistol's handgrip and briskly pushed it inside. Click, the handgun announced it was ready to fire.

Rahul pressed his right ear against the apartment's wooden door. He tried to listen in for movement. All he could hear was black noise – the colour of silence, intermittently interrupted by the dark shades of his shrieking thoughts. His dilemma was grave, and the bottle of whisky, which he had downed only a few hours ago, was only adding to the conundrum. He was almost certain that he wanted to kill Aarti's father. After all, he was the one who got her married to another man, declared that the 'college dropout, worthless' gangster wasn't good enough for his daughter.

'He deserves to die,' Rahul spoke out aloud. As the anger rushed through his veins, he pulled the pistol's slide to its farthest position, and released it to chamber a round. He affirmed his position in front of the door, his arms stretched, pistol staring down the peephole. He reached out to the trigger with his right index finger, while the left moved towards the doorbell.

'She'll hate you more if you kill him,' a voice in Rahul's head countered his body. 'She'll never forgive you.'

Confused, he threw himself to the floor, and sat with his back resting on the apartment door. The alcohol flooded his bloodstream, slowing his judgement, and accelerating his heartbeat. He thought of the day he last saw Aarti. It was three months ago. She was dressed in a light green salwar kameez; her kohl-black tresses free, her chattering eyes silent. Rahul had felt like grabbing her by her waist, drowning the tense second with a passionate kiss. He remembered the sugary, strawberry taste of her lips, and the way she'd nuzzle him with her nose. Her eyes would talk mischief in those moments, and he knew a kiss would make them laugh again.

'I'd warned you, Rahul,' Aarti had disrupted his fantasies, as the two stood on a busy railway platform during their last meeting, 'And I waited for you, I did. I cannot hurt my parents anymore.'

Rahul assumed it was just another argument over his career, but when he reached for her hand, he spotted a diamond ring.

'Are you engaged?' he shouted, not noticing the sudden rise in his pitch, as commuters stopped to listen.

'Take care, Rahul.' She smiled, tears now trickling down her cheeks. When she turned to leave, Rahul went after her. He was miffed. This was no Bollywood film. She could not walk out on him with that open-ended drama. They had spent years together. He deserved the courtesy of more words.

'What do you want from me?' she turned around when Rahul grabbed her arm.

'Almost everything," he said, "For starters, why don't you get married on my birthday?'

Rahul realized he was no better than a filmy jilted lover, but he also knew the statement would sting. His birthday was the first time they had kissed, and she'd made sure that each of his birthdays thereafter was as special. She would organize parties and invite all his friends. She would write him poems, and she'd promise forever.

'Forever,' he muttered as he walked away, the noise in his head as loud as the clamour of a train's siren in the background.

Three days before he reached Aarti's apartment to kill her father, Rahul had spent his twenty-eighth birthday scouring reception halls across Dombivli. For fourteen hours, he visited wedding after wedding – forty-seven of them – reading the welcome boards outside venues, looking for Aarti's name on one end of the arrow-stricken hearts. He didn't know what he'd say to her if he found her. He could walk up to her, and end that sham of a ceremony. Or he could take to a corner, and just watch, *believe* it was over.

'I couldn't find her, you know,' he said to his friend, Machmach, as the latter arrived outside Aarti's apartment. 'Machmach,' which means 'complaining', was his friend's underworld pseudonym, awarded on account of his constant badgering.

'Those rightists are right. Valentine's Day from the West has fucked our youth up,' Machmach grumbled. 'It's because of yesterday's 14 February that you drank this shit amount of alcohol and lost your mind. Now, get up. Let's go home.'

'Do you think she got married on my birthday, Machmach?' Rahul snuggled up to him. 'Do you think she could do that to me?'

'No, I don't,' Machmach said, putting Rahul's pistol away. He pulled the gangster up, and wrapped Rahul's arm around his own shoulder. As they descended the stairs, Machmach continued,

'She'd have to remember you on each of her wedding anniversaries. Imagine that, Bhai – a little bit of heartache, which corrupts her most memorable day every year – year after year, until she dies. Forget you, she won't do that to herself.'

Machmach's words soothed the gangster. It was years before he learnt that she did tie the knot with another man on his birthday. It wasn't just to punish Rahul. It was also a life sentence on her own heart.

———||———

On 15 September 2000, in one of the most ambitious attacks in the annals of Mumbai underworld, four D-Company gangsters entered an apartment in the Thai capital of Bangkok. The hit squad was looking for Chhota Rajan – their don, Dawood Ibrahim's erstwhile Man Friday. After pumping thirty-two bullets into Rajan's bodyguard, they proceeded towards his bedroom. The shooters unleashed indiscriminate firing on the locked door, and when they kicked it open, they discovered their target had escaped.

Rajan survived the attack with three bullets lodged in his intestine, thigh and lowerback, which left him partially paralysed. As he recovered, he suspected his own men of sharing his location with Dawood's hit squad.

'Only a handful of men, including Reddy and Mahajan, knew of his whereabouts, and a paranoid Rajan started looking at them with suspicion. When the doubts escalated, Reddy and Mahajan split up from Rajan, and started their own gang,' says an officer from the Mumbai crime branch.

After news of the fall-out reached Rahul, he started hoarding pistols. He was anticipating a reign of terror, where rival gang members would bump each other off – just like they had when

Dawood and Rajan parted ways. Over a hundred gangsters were killed in that turf war.

Like every lieutenant who worked with Rajan and Reddy, Rahul had to pick sides. Since he had never spoken to Rajan, Reddy was his obvious choice. He did not know that the breakup in leadership meant that Reddy would go incommunicado. Within days, the don's numbers went off, and he did not reach out to any of his handlers in Dombivli. Rahul also tried to get in touch with Mahajan, but in vain. Although concerned, the gangster was confident that Anna would resurface. Now that he was no more with Rajan, he might be busy shifting base, establishing a new criminal empire.

As he waited to hear from his don, Rahul found a great deal of free time to mourn over Aarti and drown himself in alcohol. As opposed to the single quarter of whisky at the local bar, Green Court, he started drinking a bottle every night – until he blacked out. He would summon Machmach and other boys from the naaka, and he'd buy them drinks. As the whisky ran through him, brick by brick, his walls would tumble and he'd start with his sorry saga.

When his friends were missing, he would gather bar staff around his table, and tell them his story. He would laugh at times at how things had panned out. At times he would cry, his stifled sobs gradually breaking his defences, forcing the waters out of his red eyes. That full-grown man, that gangster, in that dimly lit bar, his chin trembling, every inch of his muscular six feet shaking.

As weeks passed, with Reddy and Mahajan still unreachable, Rahul started frequenting dance bars with his friends. He had visited one with Bhaijaan many summers ago. The sharpshooter could not stop laughing after returning from the establishment.

'This boy has no balls,' Bhaijaan had said to his wife, Inayat. 'He's scared of those beautiful dancers. The idiot won't look at them. What do you fear, Rahul? Will they bite you? No, they will not. That's five hundred bucks extra.'

'Shut up,' Inayat defended Rahul. 'He has a girlfriend.'

'So? What's with this "all rights reserved" business? I have two wives! You're one of them, and you're okay with it.'

'Not all men are as fortunate as you.' She smiled.

'But all ladies are definitely as demented in love.'

Inayat had no qualms about her husband's visits to dance bars or brothels – as long as she knew where he was, as long as he returned home to her. She was a strong woman who was in love with every bit of her man, even his guns, grenades and sex workers.

Once, an encounter specialist from the Mumbai Police arrived at their home, pushed Bhaijaan to the floor, sat on his thighs, and shoved a pistol into the sharpshooter's mouth. Inayat begged for his life, offering to barter her jewellery and money. She would have ornaments made from the bundles of notes her husband gave her. They were easy to exchange for cash when he was in trouble.

'If I try to cage him, he'll flutter away. He's a gangster, and gangsters do not take instructions,' Inayat once told Rahul. 'Yes, he's a little difficult to love at times. But if love were easy, the world would miss out on some of its greatest art.'

———※———

From innocent hesitance during his first visit, Rahul graduated to being a loyal, overenthusiastic patron of dance bars. The first time he visited such an establishment after his breakup with Aarti, he occupied the farthest table, and kept his stacks of hundred and five hundred rupee notes on it. The bar was located in a dark, secluded building on the outskirts of the city, a special establishment – 'a disco, not an old, orthodox dance bar'.

'Those dance bars are very conservative, Bhiku Bhai,' the gangster's friends, a group of five, explained before the visit. 'Here, you can dance with the girls. Women parade before you, as in a fashion show, and you're free to touch them, lick them, bed them, whatever you like, anyhow you like.'

Rahul noticed that each of the four walls of the establishment was covered with mirrors from floor to the ceiling. A colourfully lit dance floor stood in the middle of the 500-square-foot space. A disc jockey occupied a makeshift chamber at one of the corners, while disco lights fluttered, alternately illuminating and blurring the swaying figures on the dance floor.

As Rahul sat watching, Machmach called out to one of the girls, and handed her two hundred-rupee notes. He pointed to Rahul, and the girl sat next to the gangster. She brushed her hand along his thighs, and ran her fingers on his neck.

'What's your problem?' Rahul threw her a murderous stare.

'Nothing,' she tucked the notes in her bra, and left. When Machmach protested, she turned around: '*Dhande ke time pe khoti nahi.*'

A few hours and many more drinks later, Rahul spotted a girl who looked a lot like Aarti – tall, happily healthy with a round face and scarlet cheeks. He quickly summoned the bar manager, and asked him for a garland of one-hundred-rupee notes. Once the festoon arrived, he walked to the dance floor and put it around the girl's neck.

'You're beautiful,' he told her.

She blushed, grabbed his hand, and the two started dancing. As their bodies moved sensually to a romantic Bollywood number, Rahul caught their reflections in one of the mirrors. Dressed in a black lehenga and blouse, she had pressed herself against his body. The gangster gawked at their images as he ran his hand through her long hair, and grabbed her naked waist. He was happy, he told himself – he had cigarettes, alcohol, money, guns and pretty women. He'd be greedy if he asked for more.

'Get a room, get a room,' encouraged Machmach, who was dancing with another girl on the floor. When Rahul shook his head, he said, 'Do you think Aarti isn't fucking, you idiot? Do you want to die a virgin?'

His head suddenly splitting with the image of his lost flame and her husband, Rahul asked the disco girl if she would like to leave with him.

'One thousand rupees for the night,' she whispered in his ear. 'As many times as you want, room tariff extra.'

'What's your name?' Rahul asked.

'Kareena,' she said, and grabbed his crotch. 'Come, let me show you what a real woman feels like. Whoever she is, you'll forget her in minutes.'

As the gangster walked away with the girl, his friends clapped, whistled and cheered. She took him to a room on a floor above the establishment, and latched the door. The air tasted stale and the space smelled musty from a lack of ventilation. Rahul noticed that the eighty-square-foot room was nondescript – just a bed, two chairs, a mini fridge, a white tube light and a wooden table with packets of condoms. The air conditioner started with a jolt as Kareena switched it on, and wrapped Rahul's arms around her waist. The two melted into each other with a passionate kiss, and the gangster started undressing her.

'Let me get you a condom, seth,' she broke away from his lips.

Rahul was suddenly alert. She had called him 'seth', the term for a rich man, one which sex workers typically use to address clients. He touched her skin, and it did not have Aarti's satiny texture. He looked into her eyes, and he spotted a pair of green artificial lenses. She wasn't Aarti. She had looked similar in that poorly lit bar, but she wasn't her.

'Are you hungry?' Rahul asked abruptly. 'Can we call for some beer?'

'What's wrong?'

'Nothing. I'm really hungry, and we do have the whole night.'

Kareena rang a bell next to the bed, and a boy, not older than thirteen, knocked on the door.

'Two Kingfisher bottles, one chicken biryani,' she told him.

The boy soon returned with the order, and Kareena poured beer for the duo. They started talking and she told him her real name was Pouru. An immigrant from West Bengal, her alcoholic husband had forced her into the flesh trade.

'My daughter is three years old,' she said. 'I want to make money quickly, and start a beauty parlour of my own – before she grows up, and begins to understand what I do for a living.'

'Let me know if you ever need help,' the gangster offered.

Rahul did not have sex with Pouru that night. But when he returned to his friends, he boasted of repeated intercourse and the hooker's multiple orgasms. He spoke of his exceptional performance in bed, and how he made her grab the sheets, bite her lip to keep from shouting out his name. His friends didn't need to know that the gangster was still seething, that his crushing grief had cut to his very core.

Over the next few months, Rahul's life turned into a carnival of longing. Loneliness danced relentlessly in his mind, and his refuge, his bottle of whisky, was barely able to keep up with the obscene moves. It wasn't just Aarti. More than a year had passed since the attack on Rajan. Yet, Anna hadn't called. Now, with his money drying up, Rahul was desperate to make a decision – quit crime, or start his own syndicate.

'I can't leave the underworld now,' Rahul told Machmach when the two were drinking in Green Court Bar one afternoon. 'I'm good at this, and what else would I rather do? Travel in those stuffed trains like my father, slog for eight hours, and still not have enough to eat?'

'I'm selling cigarettes for a new brand, Bhai. I can get you a job there if you want,' offered Machmach, who had taken up the stint to support his gambling addiction.

'Waah,' Rahul laughed, 'Don't you have two cases of half-murder against you?'

'Yes, of course,' Machmach boasted, 'Even today, when my victims cross paths with me, neither of them has the gall to look me in the eye.'

Without Rahul having asked, Machmach started with his story. Born in 1975, he was a year older than Rahul, and had committed his first crime when he was twenty. A drunken political party worker had beaten up Machmach's friend. To avenge him, Machmach gathered a group of boys, and attacked the worker with cricket stumps and choppers.

It was chaos, that assault inside the crowded booth of a local politician who had been campaigning for an upcoming election. It led to a stampede inside the shamiana on the busy Dombivli street, but Machmach and his friends remained undeterred. They stopped beating the worker only after he collapsed to the floor, froth oozing from his mouth, his body covered in his own blood.

'We assumed he was dead, but the bastard lived. It took a bribe of Rs 60,000 to get out of that case, Bhai,' Machmach informed, '60k in 1995 was a fucking lot. But it worked. Instead of registering an attempt to murder case, the cops only charged us with a bailable case of assault.'

His next crime was within a year. The victim was his landlord. Machmach, a school dropout, lived in a cramped 100-square-foot home with his parents and two siblings in a Dombivli chawl. With his father unable to pay rent on time, the property owner would abruptly disconnect water and electricity lines of the household, leaving Machmach fuming. One such afternoon, after the power cut woke him up from his nap, he went to a saloon nearby, where he ran into the landlord. Words translated into weapons, and the landlord, like the party worker, was also left to bleed to death.

'But that maderchod lived, too,' Machmach complained. 'I was arrested, and given bail again. A year later, both of them agreed on an out-of-court settlement.'

'Great,' said Rahul, 'Next time, finish the job. Corpses can't call cops.'

Rahul knew that since Machmach had committed his first crime to defend a friend, he could be banked upon. Friendship, not money, is the root of most evil in the underworld. If he ever started a syndicate, Machmach would be one of his first recruits. But this wasn't the time for a gang of his own. The gangster did not have the money or resources to afford a criminal proprietorship, so he spent his days drinking and dreaming.

After the excruciating wait, Reddy resurfaced in early 2003. The don was looking for flagbearers for his new company. With his relationship with Reddy, Rahul was offered a position of esteem in the new syndicate. He would be the Area Head for Dombivli, ensure the city kneeled before the new don. An elated Rahul returned to his life of organized crime after a lull of two years. This time, fiercer.

8

Their Guns and Their Fears

———◦———

4 July 2005, 9 a.m. Noted criminal lawyer Majeed Memon walked out of his Mumbai home for his daily round of courts. As the sixty-year-old defence advocate boarded his vehicle with his son, two men on a motorbike opened fire at them, shattering the rear glass of their car. Memon's security guard fired back, compelling the assailants to flee.

About forty-five minutes later, Memon received two calls at his residence, where ganglord Jaidev Reddy claimed responsibility for the attack, threatening that the lawyer, who escaped unhurt, 'might not be as lucky the next time'. The don also called television reporters, branding Memon a 'traitor' for defending over thirty accused in the 1993 Bombay blasts case, and earning acquittals for eight men in the 2002 Mumbai bus blast case, which left two dead and forty-nine injured.

'I will surely have him killed,' Reddy reportedly told television channels after the attack. 'I want to finish all those connected to Dawood. They are anti-India and connected to the ISI [Pakistan's Inter Services Intelligence].'

Memon, usually a media-friendly lawyer, still refuses to comment on the attack. 'They arrested some people, but I didn't pursue it. I won't be able to talk about it,' he says.

After his split from the D-Company, Rajan went on a killing spree, systematically eliminating Dawood's men who were alleged to be part of the 1993 blasts conspiracy. In the violent process, Rajan, who is said to have been hired by the Indian Intelligence Bureau for the job, carved the identity of a Hindu don. After he parted ways with Rajan, Reddy furthered the narrative, also positioning himself as a warrior for the Hindu cause – a 'patriot don', vociferous in his dislike for Pakistan-linked ganglords and those party to the jihadi terror infrastructure.

After Memon, Reddy went on to intimidate Hindu real-estate developers who paid hafta to Dawood. He also threatened Syed Ali Geelani, a Kashmiri separatist Hurriyat leader, for inciting students of the Delhi-based Jawaharlal Nehru University against the nation. He issued death threats to lawyers representing Indian Mujahideen operatives and, most recently, he has targeted activists, students and MLAs for criticizing the Narendra Modi government.

'It was a popular storyline – Hindu don, challenging the mighty Dawood conglomerate and Islamist terror outfits, which were rapidly gaining momentum at the time. It added purpose to the brazen killings,' says an officer from the Mumbai Crime Branch. 'Many gangsters – small and big – still try to forge the same narrative, using it for their defence and to gain favour with right-wing politicians, businessmen and cops.'

When investigators tried to trace the phone number used to call Memon, they were left baffled. The number was traced to Monaco, while Reddy was believed to be in Australia. It was much later that the technically ill-equipped cops realized that the don was using Voice over Internet Protocol – a service that Rahul had introduced him to – to issue threats.

'Bhai, I've discovered a fantastic hack,' Rahul told Reddy over a video chat on Yahoo Messenger two years before the attack on Memon. The don, barely a few inches over five and half feet, was dressed in a yellow, sleeveless ganji, with oversized headphones on his ears. He had a commanding, even attractive, set of eyes – elliptical, almost always bloodshot, a naturally drunken pair. Although his voice was that of a foghorn, he had the perfect horselaugh – he would throw his head back, and break into loud, contagious guffaws.

'Tell me,' the don replied as Rahul tried to make sense of his location from the scenery outside a window behind him. Endless stretches of green.

'The police are getting serious about cracking down on the extortion business. They've increased the number of anti-extortion cells in Mumbai from three to twelve. They're running wild for blood, and I've been thinking of ways to dodge them,' said Rahul.

'Hmm.'

'I've been researching on Voice over Internet Protocol. VoIP in short. Basically, you can make calls via the internet for a fraction of the cost of traditional telephone lines. For example, a call to the US now costs $1 per minute. With VoIP, it's ten cents per minute.'

'Good, we'll save some money.'

'Yes, but that's not the most interesting part, Anna. What's even better is that VoIP service providers also offer numbers with anonymity. There are two types of numbers – CLIR, which is Caller Line Identification Restriction, and CLIP, which is Caller Line Identification Presentation. With a CLIR number, if you call someone, your number won't show. Instead of the digits, it'll say 'unknown' or 'withheld number'. We can use these CLIR numbers for extortion calls.'

The don listened intently as Rahul continued: 'We, Indian gangsters, are way behind our counterparts in the US, UK and Russia, Anna. They're using proxy servers to make untraceable calls.

The terrorists are using private networks. What are we using? Only email and messenger. We need to hire tech. It's way more loyal than the uniformed dogs on our payroll.'

The don laughed. 'Where did you learn all this?'

'I got really interested in that computer class.'

'Good, good. What do you need to get these numbers?'

'We'll get one number for $30. We could go for a CLIR number, but even a CLIP number would work. For CLIP, they give out phone numbers belonging to countries like Monaco or the UK. There are some services that ask for documentation, but there are many others that give out numbers without asking for IDs.'

'Do what you think is right. Note down my credit card details if you want to buy the numbers. And don't wait in the cybercafe for too long after you make the extortion calls. Do your work, and leave.'

'But Anna, I've never made a real extortion call.'

'You found the service; you'll have to use it. We have no tech-literate gangsters in our company, or in the underworld.'

'I'll learn.'

—◦—

'Anthony *bol raha hoon*, Jaidev Reddy *ka aadmi*. I hear you're producing a new film. Hmm, Salman Khan *hero hai*. How much does he charge for a movie? One khoka? Or three? And that's only his fee. Looks like you've made a lot of money. Your daughter's studying in that school at Juhu, right? And your wife loves that spa on Khar Link Road. Have a crore set aside. I'll have it picked up from your office tomorrow. Do it, or you know the consequences.'
— Rahul 'Bhiku' Jadhav to one of his extortion victims, an eminent Bollywood producer, over a VoIP extortion call, 2004

The only thing more dangerous than an underworld gangster is a jilted underworld gangster. After Aarti's 'ruthless exodus' from his life, Rahul returned to the world of organized crime with a personal vengeance, the relics of his broken heart fuelling his aggression. His grandiose sense of self at guard, he did not blame himself for the split. The culpability was Aarti's – the reckless heretic who attacked and killed love. Reddy, meanwhile, held Rahul in high esteem, and deserved his loyalty. Anna will rule Mumbai and all its neighbouring cities, the gangster promised himself.

Rahul's day would start at 10 a.m. in Green Court, where he'd down three 90 ml pegs of whisky with his five morning newspapers and television news channels. He would follow crime stories with the alacrity of the sincerest student, reading reports about extortions and murders, kidnappings and contract killings. He would study crimes of his rival gangs and the literature around their victims and lieutenants.

Once he had gauged the pulse of his business for the day, he would shift base to a local cybercafe to make his extortion threats. He would pay twenty rupees for an hour of internet access in the air-conditioned space, playing online Road Rash when the underworld didn't need him.

Over the next three years, with an average of twelve calls a day, Rahul made thousands of extortion threats, and earned crores of rupees for his boss. With the internet assisting him with anonymity as well as contact data of potential targets, he was able to target some of the most influential men in the country. The VoIP calls told his victims that he wasn't an ordinary gangster. They made him look sophisticated, even important. Many of Rahul's targets paid up, a few did not. The conversion rate was still better than for other gangs.

When he first forayed into extortion, Rahul had been the brain behind the threats. He was the invisible technician who worked backstage, ensuring that the curtains never came down for his troupe. Now, the underworld enforcer was beginning to shed all inhibitions. It was his heartbreak and the intermittent distance from Anna that pushed the budding alcoholic to tread uncharted territory. It was also his success; it was making him morally insane.

'With each call, my aggression grows manifold,' Rahul once told Machmach after a little whisky and water, having acknowledged the budding monster inside of him. 'When I bark those threats down the receiver, I genuinely feel angry at those men. I've never known these men, and yet, when I abuse them, I can feel my blood boil. My skin heats up with rage.'

'Good na, Bhai,' Machmach replied. 'These extortion calls are like workouts for your brain; like mental yoga, the perfect outlets for your frustration.'

'Yes, but what if I need more colossal outlets? What if the aggression makes me kill someone?'

'It won't,' Machmach appeared confident. 'You're brain over blood.'

With Rahul's calls bringing in crores of rupees, he quickly brushed the inkling of ethics aside, and continued with the brazen dialling. One Bollywood director, whom the gangster had threatened on multiple occasions, also modelled a character around him in his subsequent films, giving him the same name that Rahul would use while threatening him. The director was probably trying to demonstrate his intrepidity against the underworld, but for the gangster it was a moment of pride. As a child, he had always wished to see his name in newspapers. Now, a part of him was on celluloid.

There is a popular saying in the underworld – If you do not wish to be killed like a dog, develop the instincts of a cat. Unlike many others in the universe of organized crime, Rahul was quick to develop these instincts. He could tell who would pay, who wouldn't; who could be convinced over phone, who required violence; whose life would be an asset, and who had to be bumped off.

One such prospect, who merited a sterner treatment, was veteran filmmaker Mahesh Bhatt. On the afternoon of 14 June 2006, an armed man barged into the director's office in Juhu, Mumbai, and enquired about Bhatt. When the staff said he wasn't in office, the man fired two rounds with an automatic weapon and escaped with his accomplice, who was waiting on a motorbike outside the office.

Filmmaker Ashoke Pandit, a close friend of the Bhatts, happened to reach the director's office soon after the youth had fled. He fielded a phone call. The caller identified himself as Jaidev Reddy. Through a bunch of expletives, he said, *'Abhi bach gaya, agli baar nahi chhodega.'* Reddy then made a second call to Bhatt's residence, and delivered a similar message to the domestic help who answered the phone.

About a month after the attack, Pandit too received a call from Reddy. The filmmaker had been all over the press following the firing, standing by Bhatt, and criticizing the rocketing threat to Bollywood personalities from the underworld.

'Reddy called my office landline, and started hurling abuses. Between the filthy words, he threatened to kill me. He was probably irked because I had been so vocal about the attack. I disconnected the line after a minute or so,' says Pandit. Although Bhatt was given security cover, Pandit refused it.

Following the firing in Bhatt's office, Arup Patnaik, Additional Commissioner of Police (Crime), told the press that Reddy had orchestrated the crime to 'create fear in Bollywood'. Around this time, Reddy is also said to have threatened other renowned figures in the film industry, asking them to pay as much as five crore rupees as extortion money. In most cases, the contact numbers were sourced through Rahul.

With a prominent Bollywood personality, Rahul went a step ahead. The new extortionist was conducting his ground research for an attack on a Bandra-based producer. To ensure smooth execution, he stayed guard outside the producer's office for days, noting security, possible escape routes, and patterns of the producer's visits. One such afternoon, Rahul was rattled – he had defecated in his pants. The gangster would drink a bottle of whisky each day, barely eating food. He had shed many kilograms of weight, and would keep falling sick, plagued by an incessant cough and cold. Worse, his intestines would remain agitated, leading to severe diarrhoea each day.

Rahul knew his health was deteriorating, but the faeces in his trousers were the most embarrasing alarm. He did not realize when he soiled his pants – not until he sat in an autorickshaw to return home. When he figured his pants were wet, he asked the driver to stop at a public urinal. He washed his clothes with water, turned them inside out and wore them again.

After that instance, Rahul realized he was losing control. He tried to add food to his intake, but his body would immediately reject solids, passing them out as involuntary stools. Doctors told him that his intestines had swollen, but he was addicted to the bottle already. He had also grown increasingly fond of his evenings at the local bar – the inebriated haze, his carefree, semi-naked dances, and how his friends, in exchange for free alcohol, made him believe that he ran the world.

Rahul started taking three, instead of one bar dancer, to rented rooms. His friends would look at him with pride and envy, even while the gangster still had difficulty copulating. All he would do was treat the women to food and beer, and talk. It wasn't just thoughts of Aarti that kept him from having sex with the women. By now, the alcohol had started preventing erections.

'Seth, before we do anything, please take a shower,' a sex worker once told Rahul. She was one of many who had raised the request. The women could not bear his stench – he wouldn't shower for days, his clothes smelt of smoke, and his breath of ethanol.

Despite his insanitary appearance, the women were never impolite to Rahul. He was a kind, even generous, client. Bar staff say that while other patrons exchanged their money for stacks of ten rupee notes to splurge on bar girls, 'Bhiku bhai wouldn't have denominations lower than one hundred rupees. He'd shower the women with notes – tens of thousands of rupees in a single night.' Rahul's generosity at the establishments is not unheard of in underworld circles. Abdul Karim Telgi, main accused in the multi-crore stamp paper scam, famously showered Rs 93 lakh on a bar girl in a single night in winter, 2002.

When Rahul became a faithful patron, the culture of dance bars had peaked in Maharahtra. Mafia operatives would routinely frequent the establishments, looking for ego boosts in the fleeting eye contact with bar girls, their pointing, gesturing and suggesting. The dances often led to prostitution in cramped rooms nearby, where mighty gangsters like Rahul revealed their passion and their vulnerabilities, their guns and their fears.

'They are nothing but armed, egotistic children,' says a thirty-seven-year-old dancer, who spent many nights with Rahul, 'It usually takes a few visits before gangsters like Bhiku seth start trusting you. But once they do, you know they're no different from other men – just a little more broken, and way more generous.'

––|––

As the years passed, Rahul grew to be an invincible part of the Jaidev Reddy–Daya Mahajan syndicate. Towards the end of 2005, however, the company witnessed a break-up in its leadership – Mahajan and Reddy decided to part ways. It was a sour split. While Mahajan claimed to have kicked Reddy out as he was using Mahajan's name to make money, Reddy stated that he had chosen to walk out on his own.

'Daya is nobody to throw me out of his gang. I have bigger clout, both in terms of men and money, than Daya. I need not use his name for anything,' Reddy told a *Times of India* reporter over the phone, and then asserted his Hindu don philosophy: 'My mission now is to eliminate both Dawood and Shakeel. I am targeting for extortion only those businessmen who are close to these two gangsters.'

With the break-up, Rahul was again compelled to pick sides. Although Mahajan had granted him entry into gangland, he had worked with Reddy for most of his criminal career. Rahul liked Anna. The don was a man of his word. He was materialistic, but never denied cash to his boys. He was a megalomaniac, but kind to his lieutenants.

'The best part is, Anna never forces a job on me,' Rahul reasoned with Machmach while making his choice, 'He cares about his men. He gives thousands of rupees to arms deliverers from Uttar Pradesh so the poor boys can see Mumbai. He's also a devout man. Do you remember that time when his relative was unwell? He asked me to make a video call from Mumbai's Siddhivinayak Temple so he could offer prayers. I told him my phone didn't have a camera, so he bought me a new one.'

Rahul was almost convinced about pledging his loyalty to Reddy. Soon, a medical crisis affirmed his decision. Rahul's father had to undergo an urgent surgery on one of his kidneys, and the procedure required Rs 40,000. With no other source in sight, Rahul called Anna and Mahajan. While the latter did not deliver, Reddy had the cash sent within hours.

Having chosen Reddy, Rahul was ecstatic. A new syndicate meant more influence for him. But within weeks of the split, Reddy's wife was arrested in a fake passport case. The development hit the new don hard, and he again went incommunicado. Rahul could not reach any of his international phone numbers, nor was he replying to emails. The gangster enquired with handlers in Dombivli and

Mumbai. No one had been able to establish contact with Reddy, the new king who went into hiding within days of his coronation.

After the don went missing for a second time, Rahul continued with his lifestyle. He was again certain that Anna had sought temporary refuge at a secret hideout, that he would emerge, and bring him closer to his underworld dream. Soon, he started running out of money. As hope does not pay bills of bars or bar dancers, he would extort money from local developers, and play the lottery. At times, he would loan the cash from his mother.

Rahul's parasitic lifestyle had become a cause of worry for his family. The extortionist would return home inebriated and pass out on the floor after brawling with his brother. Most mornings, he would wake up with his face covered in his own saliva, his limbs shivering, his senses distorted, and his head throbbing with a hangover. His parents worried that he would develop a serious ailment if he didn't quit the bottle. When they expressed their concern to Rahul's brother-in-law, Kishor got him employed as canteen staff with a bank in Mumbai's Bandra Kurla Complex.

'Take the job or leave the house,' Shalini told her son.

Although reluctant, Rahul could not protest: he had no money to afford rent if his parents threw him out, and the don hadn't emerged from his hiatus for months. The last time Anna went missing, he took two years to return. Rahul could not wait that long. He needed cash to pay his vices.

The extortionist spent seven months at the bank, working for a monthly salary of Rs 3,850, serving food to bank employees and clearing their dishes. His ego had taken a substantial hit – he no longer saw himself as the invincible ganglord he had hoped to become. He felt vulnerable, even small.

Rahul despised the throw of the dice that had trapped him in that office and his thoughts often drifted to his life with the underworld. He would ache to return to his gangland, but Anna was still unreachable. Gradually, Rahul gave up on his don. Within months, fate intervened to steal his disappointment. One noon in mid 2006, a close friend of Reddy called Rahul, looking for the don's number.

'I haven't been in touch with him. All his numbers are off,' Rahul told the caller. 'But wait, I have one email address, which he might respond to. Let me try.'

'Good to hear from you, Rahul,' the don wrote back immediately. 'This is my new number. Please share it with my friend. And give me your number as well.'

Rahul was elated. The don had probably responded only because his close friend was in need, but the gangster did not care. He immediately shared his office landline number with Reddy, who insisted on that number as the Intelligence Bureau tends to track international calls on cell phones. The don called him within seconds. The receptionist, who transferred the call to the canteen, was surprised at the international call for a low-rung employee.

'Foreign number?' she asked him before switching the line.

'So? Can't poor people have rich relatives?' Rahul said curtly, acutely aware that he needn't be kind to anyone anymore.

Rahul was pleased to hear his don's voice. Not only did he love his Anna, the ganglord's return also meant an end to all his troubles – the demeaning work, humiliating pay and the cheap alcohol. After the two enquired about each other's families, the don got down to business.

'Are you working at this bank?' he asked Rahul.

'Yes, Anna. Look what's become of me.'

'Don't worry,' said Reddy, 'My friend needs one lakh rupees. Pick the money up from Andheri and give it to him.'

After delivering the amount, Rahul still had Rs 50,000 left. When he called the don, Reddy asked him to keep the cash.

'It's for you,' the don said. 'I've missed you.'

Rahul was thrilled. The amount was thirteen times his monthly salary, and all he had done was pick up a bag.

'Thanks, Anna,' he replied. 'Now, let's get you that underworld throne.'

9

Twelve Bucks and a Bullet

—◆—

6 July 2006. 6.05 p.m. Rahul stood at a cigarette stall on Shaheed Bhagat Singh Road, Dombivli (East). The street, lined with shops on both sides, was home to a local market with busy shoppers buying groceries, vegetables, fruits and other essentials. Some savoured delicacies from street vendors, others strolled about for their evening walks. Rahul lit a cigarette, wondering if his boys would disrupt the market's annoying chirp, replace it with the soothing quiet that follows a bullet.

The gangster had his doubts. His lieutenants – Machmach and another recruit, Kaalya – had tried to fire at their target, twenty-six-year-old businessman Anish Shah, at least thrice in the recent past. Each time, they had returned with excuses instead of blood – 'There were too many people in the store, even women and children. The road was crowded, we couldn't have escaped after. He's six foot five; the fatfuck would have knocked us down with his pinkie.'

'If they don't fire today, they're fired,' the gangster blew out a cloud of smoke. He had spent countless hours preparing the duo. The job was simple. All they had to do was hand the man a chit with Reddy's name and number on it, gun him down and run. The hitmen had been conducting recces at the spot for the past four days. Only a few minutes ago, they had called Shah's store, Gem Electronics. The target had answered the landline himself. He was available to die.

'Thokenge,' Rahul assured himself, and pulled another drag.

The gangster stood a few feet from the store, on its right side. He could see the door to Shah's shop, but not the action inside. He saw Machmach and Kaalya enter the shop after two nervous strolls.

'Come on, come on,' Rahul blurted out, his closed fist punching the air.

The gangster decided he needed a fresh cigarette to douse the mounting tension. Before he could light another one, he had his coveted silence. The street and its industry had hit a pause.

Shah, in his statement to the police following the shootout, recorded the murder attempt as follows:

Evenings are quite busy at the store. Since we don't have enough staff, I went to the store myself on the evening of 6 July 2006. I was sitting on the chair behind the cashier's desk, which is right next to the entrance door.

6.10 p.m. Vicky Sachdev, who works with our neighbouring Kohinoor Electronics, walked into the store and stood before my desk. He had come to collect a cheque for a few items we'd bought from his shop.

6.15 p.m. As Sachdev stood next to me, explaining the bill, two unidentified men walked into the store through the half-open glass door. One of them, a twenty-seven or twenty-eight-year-old man in a yellow shirt, had a revolver in his hand. He didn't say anything, and pointed the weapon at my chest. Before I could react, he opened fire. Since I quickly ducked, the bullet hit the left side of my stomach. As it left my body, it penetrated Sachdev's leg. Both of us collapsed in pain. The two men ran out of the shop.

I have never seen the assailants before, and I do not know why they are after my life. But should I see them again, I'll be able to identify them.

Rahul narrowed his eyes to view the developing chaos. He saw his boys rush out of the store, and split up at a crossroad a few metres ahead. He saw hordes of people emerge suddenly from the silence, as if someone had unfrozen them. Some went after the boys, while a few panicked shoppers reached for their cell phones to dial the police helpline.

'Let's drink,' the gangster announced to no one, and headed to his bar.

As soon as Rahul reached Green Court, he called Machmach. The hitman was clearly out of breath. He told Rahul he was being trailed, and that he would meet him at the bar.

After he split with Kaalya, Machmach ran into a narrow by-lane, hoping to dodge the chasing crowd. Although he managed to leave the mob behind, he was confronted by two men on a motorbike, who stood before him, only fifty feet away.

The by-lane was crowded with hundreds of uniformed children aged six to ten, walking home from a nearby school. Machmach pulled out his revolver to fire at the bike-borne duo. As soon he raised the weapon to take an aim, the children went into a tizzy, and started running berserk. The mayhem lent brief invisibility to the shooter. He cashed on the few moments by hailing an autorickshaw and fleeing the spot.

When Machmach reached Green Court, Rahul sat smiling with Kaalya, sipping his drink.

'Where the fuck were you?' a panting Machmach asked Kaalya, and handed the revolver to Rahul.

'I just ran until I reached here.'

'Good job,' Rahul patted their backs, and examined the weapon. 'Where's the fucking magazine?'

'Bhenchod,' exclaimed Machmach. 'I think I dropped it while running.'

'What *chutiyagiri, yaar*, Machmach,' Rahul was irked. 'Are you a fucking novice? Even a fucking amateur won't lose the fucking magazine.'

Machmach was embarrassed. After a few moments of silence, he quietly reached out to his pocket, pulled out his pint of palm toddy, and began to pour himself a drink. Rahul grabbed his hand.

'Did you or did you not shoot Anish dead?'

'I took a shot on his chest.'

'Did you or did you not hand him the chit with Reddy's number on it?'

'Yes, of course I did, Bhai. How could I forget that?' said Machmach. As he saw Rahul breathe, he quickly poured his drink and downed it. Wiping his wet lips with his palm, he added, 'I bought a new pen to write that chit, Bhai.'

'Why are you drinking this desi nonsense?' Kaalya tried to lighten the mood, 'Drinks are on Bhiku bhai tonight.'

'It's my mom, yaar,' bickered Machmach. 'Since I've been drinking too much, she mixes some shit in my food, some powder she got from some fakeer baba. I don't know what's in that. But the moment I drink imported liquor, or even Indian ones with English names, I immediately turn red, start vomiting.'

'And desi daru is fine?'

'Yeah, yeah. Arrack, palm toddy, molasses-based – the baba can't do shit to them.'

As Machmach poured another round, Kaalya turned to Rahul, who was staring at his whisky glass. 'Don't worry, Bhai. We saw the fatfuck fall. The job is done,' he assured Rahul, and added, 'Why Anish Shah though?'

'He's a businessman and a real-estate developer, one of the wealthiest in Dombivli,' replied Rahul. 'If he's brought to his knees, all of Dombivli will follow. I want this city to shudder at Anna's name.'

'But there are many others like him. Why him?' Kaalya, who earned the underworld pseudonym owing to his dark skin, persisted. He was twenty-eight at the time with one murder and many extortion threats to his credit. Unlike Machmach, he was well built, and even polished in his speech and mannerisms. While Machmach was attached to the underworld for money, mainly to feed his compulsive habit of gambling, Kaalya would tread legalities for repute. He sincerely hoped to make it big in the underworld. Rahul, he believed, could be his mentor.

'Because the maderchod deserves to die,' Rahul once again looked irked. 'Anna has been threatening Anish since 1998. Once, he asked him for two lakhs, and the bastard gave the cash in denominations of ten and twenty. Bhai was pissed. What was the asshole thinking? Is Bhai some small-time chor? Anna asked the bag boy to keep the money, and decided that Shah had to be shown his place. With his new company and the fresh bid to rule over Mumbai and Thane, the revenge plan just fit in.'

'I almost laughed when I entered the store, that rhino of a man on that tiny chair,' Machmach intervened. 'And when we fired, you should have seen how he was howling, Bhai. It was hilarious. When the bullet hit him, he instantly went from rhino to poodle.'

'Cheers to bullets,' Machmach raised his glass.

'To poodles,' said Rahul.

When newspapers arrived the following morning, Rahul was left fuming. He had expected the press to sing glories of his Bhai's terror, create fear for his name, and crown him the don of Dombivli. To his dismay, neither the news channels nor newspapers mentioned Reddy. The reports stated that two unidentified dacoits tried to burgle Shah's electronic store. Since they were unable to rob, they left after firing at the two victims.

'Why the fuck is he still alive?' Rahul kept thrusting his right forefinger on the newspaper before throwing it on Machmach's face. 'And dacoits? What the fuck do they mean by dacoits? Didn't you leave the chit with Reddy's number on it?'

'I threw it on the desk just before I left, Bhai. I swear I did,' said Machmach, seated in the same bar, trying to nurse his hangover from the night before.

'You fucking idiot,' Rahul was furious. 'You should have shoved it in his fucking hand, told him very clearly that you're Reddy's men. Only then should you have fired. The staff and visitors would have taken note. You fucking, *fucking* idiot.'

'But we left the chit on the table, Bhai. They were supposed to pick it up, and see Anna's name and number. We did our job. How's it our fault if the cops didn't do theirs?' Machmach argued.

'Listen to yourself,' Rahul said, not convinced. 'There's a man with a bullet-shaped hole in his stomach, and you expect cops to bother with a piece of paper on his desk. I'm sure no one even saw you drop the chit.'

'Arre, but they should have at least found it when they conducted the panchnama. Or maybe they didn't examine the store at all. Cops have become really lazy these days, Bhai.'

'They'll find the chit now,' Rahul barked, the tip of his revolver touching Machmach's forehead. 'When I pump bullets into your brain, and leave a note behind.'

Reddy echoed Rahul's anger. The shoot-out was a waste – Shah was alive, and the don had failed to make headlines. No one would fear a name they didn't know.

As he tried to calm his boss, Rahul had a brainwave: 'Bhai, call Anish Shah and own up. That's what terrorists do. Just make it sound like another threat. Say: "Gandu, Reddy here. You got away with an injury this time. Pay up, or next time, the bullet will be in your heart." He'll tell the police, who'll fart it to the press, and we'll have the publicity we want.'

Convinced, Reddy made the call. The following day, the press allotted generous footage to his advertising campaign.

———||———

With hits on prominent Bollywood personalities like director Mahesh Bhatt and producer Vashu Bhagnani, Reddy had successfully created a fear psychosis in Mumbai. The don was now looking to extend his reign of terror to important cities in neighbouring Thane district – Kalyan, Dombivli, Thane city and Navi Mumbai. These cities, rapidly urbanizing and witnessing population booms, were now home to fresh, flourishing businesses and new extortion targets.

Rahul was the front man for Dombivli, and the bullet on Anish Shah had marked the don's arrival in the satellite town. It was quite grand, that entry. It had the cops panicking, left the rich alarmed, and compelled the local press to sit up and take note of Reddy. Rahul was elated. He had laid the perfect foundation. Now, to build on it, the company required some important deaths.

After a few weeks of research, Rahul came up with a name – Rajabhau Patkar, President, Block Congress Committee, Thane district. One of the richest landowners in Dombivli, Patkar had multiple ventures across the district – from diagnostic centres and malls to schools, charitable trusts and housing societies.

'Patkar's family is probably the most esteemed one in Thane, Anna. They have fucking roads named after them! If we get him, all the rich fucks in the state – politicians, developers, businessmen – will piss their pants,' the gangster explained.

'That's way too ambitious, beta.'

'No risk, no reward, Anna.'

'But we can't afford stupid mistakes this time. Tell your boys, I don't forgive twice.'

'I'll shoot him myself.'

'Bajao!'

Rahul had never fired at a man before, but he had handled weapons on numerous instances – with Bhaijaan, and while procuring and delivering consignments for shooters in his company. He wasn't hesitant before he offered to take the hit on Patkar. He knew he would deliver. Also, the crime paid well – Rs 50,000 a strike for other boys, a lakh for Rahul.

'Are you sure you'll pull the trigger?' Machmach was sceptical.

'Yes, why not?'

'Because you're brain over blood. I'm the killer, not you.'

'Who said killing isn't about the brain? Killing is a mindset, not training, not anything else.'

One major thing that went wrong with the Anish Shah shootout, apart from the fact that he survived it, was that Reddy's role in the attack did not become immediately evident. To avoid the blunder with Patkar, Rahul asked his don to call the target before he fired his gun. The evening prior to the attack, Reddy made the call. As expected, Patkar reached out to the police, who immediately offered him protection. The following morning, Reddy's name was all over the press. Reports spoke about how the don, a Chhota Rajan mentee, had extended his criminal prowess to Dombivli, now targeting the top brass in town.

'Fantastic,' Rahul exclaimed as he saw the newspapers, and gulped his large peg of whisky. Turning to Machmach and Kaalya, he announced, 'Chalo, it's time.'

On a September afternoon in 2006, the trio reached outside Patkar's newly constructed City Mall in Dombivli (East). The mall, one of the first in the city, was located on an important crossroad with multiple educational institutions, corporate offices and industrial complexes nearby. Labourers walked next to formally dressed men and women, while students appeared busy with local food-vendors along the promenade.

'You stay here,' Rahul told Kaalya when they reached the mall's entrance. 'Hail an auto as soon as you hear the gunshot. No running like mad dogs this time. This is going to be nothing like the disaster that Anish's firing was.'

'Not one mistake,' he warned Machmach, and broke into a bout of spot jogging. 'Come on! Come on! Energy, energy.'

As the duo entered the mall, a security guard stopped them.

'I'm looking to host this one's wedding here,' Rahul told the guard, pointing at Machmach.

'Very nice, sir. World-best wedding hall we have, Mauli Hall. It's on first floor, sir. World-best catering also,' the guard was exuberant.

'Perfect,' said Rahul.

'Come, sir. I will take you.'

'No, we will manage. We've seen the hall before.'

As they walked the few metres to the staircase, the duo noticed that most of the shops were unoccupied. Work was still ongoing, and labourers were busy with painting, tiling and furnishing. The air tasted powdery from the dust while drill machine sounds echoed in most of the 10 x 15 foot spaces. A cake shop, a travel agency, a computer hardware store – Rahul read their signboards.

'The baldy is making a lot of money from this already,' Machmach told Rahul, speaking of their target. 'This mall has three floors: ground plus two. Twenty shops on each floor, so sixty shops. He's selling each for five lakh. Plus, his two wedding halls.'

'Good,' said Rahul. 'The more he makes, the more we make.'

As the two climbed the deserted stairs to the first floor, Rahul pulled out a pistol from his back, and loaded it. Machmach followed suit. The hitmen were certain that Patkar was at the hall; an informant had confirmed his presence only a few minutes ago. In addition, days of reconnaissance had told them that the eminent businessman typically visited the mall between 12 noon and 1 p.m. on alternate days. He would attend to the sales office on the ground floor, and spent at least thirty minutes at the wedding hall office before leaving the premises.

Seeing Machmach load his weapon, Rahul instructed, 'I will fire. Use your pistol only if he resists, or if someone comes to his rescue. He could have protection – private guards, cops, or both. Stay near the door, and make sure no one leaves the office. If they raise an alarm, there'll be trouble.'

'Are we going to kill him?' asked Machmach.

'It's necessary.'

With Rahul in the lead, the duo walked the few steps to Mauli Hall's bookings office. They opened the glass door and noticed that Patkar was missing.

'How may I help you, sir?' a male receptionist enquired. The office was an elaborate air-conditioned space with contemporary furniture and a fancy glass chandelier. Leather sofas lined the sidewalls, and a couple occupied one of them, probably waiting to make enquiries about the wedding venue.

'Where's your boss?' Rahul asked, the pistol still in his right hand.

The young receptionist stared at the weapon in response, beads of sweat now gathering on his forehead.

'*Aye bhenchod*, don't you understand?' Rahul barked. 'Where is Rajabhau Patkar?'

'Boss hasn't come in today, sir,' the receptionist offered. 'Should I call him?'

'No, tell the motherfucker to call Bhai,' said Rahul, suddenly angry. He handed over a chit with Reddy's name and three international numbers to the receptionist. 'Tell him Anna is waiting. If he doesn't call today, he won't see tomorrow.'

As the couple watched in silence, Rahul took an aim at the receptionist. He did not want to kill the man. The action was to scare him. Once he saw that the weapon had had its effect, he fired a bullet in the air.

'It's been more than twelve hours since Bhai called your boss, and he still hasn't paid up. *Samaj jaao, aur sudhar jaao. Nahi toh* the end.'

Upon hearing the gunshot, the couple tried to flee from the spot, but Rahul grabbed the man by his collar, and held the pistol under his chin. 'Gandu, stay. *Nahi toh thok dalega idhar hi.*'

Rahul and Machmach walked out of the office after locking the trio inside. Aware that they would take a while to find their way out, Rahul called Reddy as he descended the staircase. He informed that their intelligence had been flawed, that Patkar wasn't in office. The businessman either left early, or didn't show up because of Reddy's threat the previous evening.

'Since the receptionist had already seen the pistol in my hand, I couldn't have returned without firing,' Rahul explained.

'I'm glad you fired,' said Reddy. 'As long as you've killed the receptionist.'

'No, I didn't. He's a poor man, Anna. What will his murder get us?'

'What will mercy get us? Murder brings money, mercy doesn't do shit.'

Rahul did not agree with his boss, but stayed quiet.

'You've disappointed me, Bhiku,' the don said and disconnected.

As the two walked out of the entrance, they spotted Kaalya near the bus stop opposite the mall. Machmach asked if the autorickshaw was ready. Kaalya pointed to the one waiting in front of him.

'There's a couple inside, you chutiya,' Machmach complained. 'It's a share auto.'

'You're so fucking stupid, Kaalya.' Machmach was miffed. 'Who takes a share auto after a fucking firing?'

'Meet us at the bar,' Rahul told Kaalya, and boarded the rickshaw, paying twelve rupees to the auto driver for the two gunmen.

Twelve bucks and a bullet – that's all it took to drag Dombivli to its knees.

10

The Kingdom of Scotch and Tits

———•|•———

Cops gun down dreaded gangster

A dreaded gangster who had created havoc in the Kalyan–Dombivli belt by carrying out a series of shoot-outs on businessmen, builders and politicians [including Congress leader Rajabhau Patkar] was shot dead in a police encounter by the property cell of Thane police.

Acting on a tip-off, the police team laid a trap in Dombivli, where gangster Bobby Nair, 28 and one unidentified person were wating for someone. On identifying Nair, the police team asked them to surrender. Instead, Nair stood behind his motorcycle and fired two rounds towards the police. In retaliation, the police claim they fired three rounds, and injured Nair.

Nair was rushed to Rukmini hospital, where he was declared dead.

– A *Times of India* report
20 October 2006 (a month after
the firing at Patkar's office)

Rahul looked at the press report and smiled. The cops had become desperate. Immediately after the attack on Patkar, politicians in Thane district had called for an all-party meet, headed by Home minister R.R. Patil and the Thane Police commissioner. Authorities faced severe flak over the law and order failure, and Patil declared a day-long bandh in Dombivli. He also issued transfer orders to the senior inspector, under whose jurisdiction the crime took place. The press bawled, stating that if such a high profile leader of a national party could be targeted, no one was safe.

The mounting pressure left law enforcement agencies running wild. Cops were now trigger-happy, willing to shoot any gangster dead and slap allegations on his corpse. They just needed one man's blood to announce the case solved. After Nair became the casualty, to consolidate their position further, the Thane district police also arrested eleven of Nair's gang members. The real culprit, meanwhile, was sipping whisky with a bunch of cops, drowning in conceit.

'Tonight, I'm going to drink till I can't tell cops from crooks,' said one of the two police constables attached to Thane Crime Branch's detection unit as they sat with Rahul and Machmach in Green Court. It was the evening following the firing at Patkar's wedding hall.

'Why?' Rahul enquired as the cop downed his rum and coke. The police officers, like the gangsters, were regulars at the bar, and acquainted with each other. 'What's so special tonight?'

'Didn't you hear?' replied the other constable, who was relatively slow with his peg, 'Some maderchods opened fire at Patkar's office today. We spent the whole day digging up old files, noting down names of history sheeters.'

'Patkar is the builder–politician, right?' Rahul feigned naivety. The cops did not know he was a gangster – the man they had been searching their files for.

'Yes, who else?' said the quick drinker, refilling his glass. 'Tomorrow, we've to round up all the gangsters in our records. Netas are really pissed. There's going to be no sleep, no food.'

'That reminds me, let's call for some chicken tikka,' added the slow drinker.

Rahul rested his back on his seat, and parked his feet on a chair in front of him. 'Let's call for two.'

———◦———

Spurred with his success, Rahul decided to cash in on the chaos. He started readying a gang of shooters who could orchestrate firings in his don's name and maintain his glory on news headlines. Over the years, Rahul had made notes about many boys like Machmach and Kaalya, who could make for reliable extortionists with some guidance. The boys already revered Rahul. He would buy them alcohol worth thousands of rupees every night and sponsor their dates with bar dancers. Now, he had grown to be Reddy's top lieutenant in Dombivli. He was responsible for the bandh in their city, a senior cop's transfer, and for alarming every authority, every rich man in the district.

Apart from Machmach and Kaalya, Rahul had identified eight potential recruits. One evening in November 2006, he invited them to a friend's apartment. The men, all aged twenty-four to twenty-eight, occupied three sofas in the nondescript flat as Rahul took centre stage. A table stood between him and his audience, holding hard-liquor bottles, glasses, iceboxes, mixers, stirrers and fried snacks.

'There's a reason why you're here,' Rahul addressed the group. 'The underworld is in desperate need of daring men, men with some real courage. You, my friends, have balls, and I'm here to rent them out.'

As the group listened in silence, Rahul noticed that most of their eyes were fixed on the liqour bottles. 'Help yourself,' he said. 'The girls will be here soon, too.'

Once the men settled in their seats with their drinks, Rahul continued. 'Majnu, isn't your mother unwell? Don't you want to have her tumour removed? Tochan, hasn't your father just retired? Don't you need money for your sister's wedding? Birju, since when have you been planning to get that television set for your wife? My friends, each of these wishes can come true. Dons are desperate for shooters. They'll pay anything.'

Rahul wasn't lying. Not just his gang, the entire underworld was reeling with an acute shortage of gunmen at the time. Earlier, ganglords would handpick shooters from the wild plains of Uttar Pradesh, Konkan and Mangalore – loyal men, who would orchestrate audacious killings for as little as Rs 5,000. Over the years, resentment had replaced loyalty. Shooters had realized that although they would put their lives on the line, the dons paid them a few thousands. The bosses, meanwhile, earned lakhs, even crores from the shootouts.

The seven-year-old law – the Maharashtra Control of Organised Crime Act – had also established its draconian strength by the mid 2000s, acting as a strong deterrent to shooters. The legislation had extended unprecedented powers to cops, who gunned down dozens of gunmen over the years. The surviving shooters languished in prisons with little room for reprieve.

'And we won't be an ordinary gang of shooters,' Rahul continued, 'I've spoken to Anna. We plan to have sleeper cells in each of the major cities across India – only for your security. Say, if our gang member in Mumbai bumps off a man, he can immediately seek refuge with a sleeper cell in another city. You'll keep shifting locations.'

'What about our families here?' one of the boys asked.

'We'll take good care of them. You have my word.'

Tochan raised a concern. 'But, Bhiku Bhai, I already have a criminal record. I'll be caught within days if I went about firing pistols.'

'Everybody here has a criminal record,' said Rahul. 'Those are our achievements, but ones that haven't paid well. I'm talking about crime that'll fulfil your wildest dreams. The world has deprived you of your dues, told you that you're worthless. I say fuck the world where you do not have a standing. Come with me to the kingdom of organized crime – the land of scotch and titties, where you'd be the princes.'

'What about the training, Bhai?' asked Majnu. 'I don't know how to fire.'

'I'll have sessions arranged for whoever needs them. Pistols are easy.'

'But I don't think I'll be able to kill. I don't have it in me.'

'He's right, Bhai,' a potential recruit spoke for Majnu. 'The chutiya cries when he sees Tom hit Jerry.'

'That's perfectly okay,' said Rahul, ignoring the laughter. He then turned to Majnu, 'If you don't like killing, there's no pressure. Tell me what you like. I will have you trained for that. Only one thing, dream big. If you like stealing bikes, go after the Kawasakis and Harley Davidsons. Steal those, and don't sell them in the Indian market. Go global. We will help you with the buyers. Earn lakhs, not hundreds.'

When he saw his audience convinced, Rahul continued: 'All of us have known each other for years. I, too, come from the same naaka, but look at me now. You can be here with me. Each of you has so much potential. Have faith in me. Have faith in yourself, and you'll never have a thing to worry about.'

That evening, Rahul did not ask the boys for a commitment. He just offered them a dream, expensive alcohol, and even expensive sex workers. He did not realize that unwittingly, he had used the same tactics – flattering and motivational words – to lure the potential recruits to him, just as Mahajan had when Rahul first committed to the underworld. He did not know that somewhere between those manipulative words, the drunken haze and the skimpily clad women, he had taken his first step towards becoming a don.

———✦———

Seated in a bar on a Thursday afternoon in November 2006, Rahul struggled to lift his whisky glass off the table. It was banal, that inability of his limbs after a long night at the bar. Today, however, he could not afford the incapacity. The gangster had work to finish. If he wished to get it right, he would have to gulp at least three of those large Bagpiper pegs before his body agreed to join forces with him.

'Maderchod,' he barked at the waiter, 'didn't I tell you to get me a straw?'

The attendant, a young boy, rushed to the thirty-year-old gangster, and put the plastic tube in his beverage. As Rahul sucked up his whisky, the waiter glanced at his only client's table. In the dim lights of the tavern, he saw two pistols kept carelessly next to a bundle of five hundred rupee notes. He would be quicker with his service, the boy decided – the table had given him two reasons.

As soon as Rahul finished his first drink, the attendant poured another one. Without an order, he also refilled the bowl of bar snacks – no salted peanuts, no chips, no salad, only a teaspoon of rock salt with a lemon squeezed into it. Rahul could not bear to eat. His alcohol-dependent body was still revolting at the sign of food. Right then, it was especially pissed – ten hours had passed since the extortionist put down his glass. Withdrawals had rushed in.

Rahul felt better after the first drink. His face had stopped sweating, his eyelids were gradually giving up on their needless fluttering, and the tremors in his hands were slowly losing rhythm. With the fresh grease in his bearings, he threw the straw, lifted the glass with his hand, and gulped down his second drink in a single go. He still had his throbbing head and palpitating heart to fix.

As the attendant helped Rahul with a third serving, Machmach walked into the bar. Hungover, too, he quietly sipped his first drink of palm toddy. Having downed 180 ml by now, Rahul could think straight.

'The boys seem useful,' the gangster told Machmach. 'I had sent them out for a couple of recces – a yesteryear Bollywood actor's bungalow in Bandra, a bar owner in Andheri, one director's Khar office, and an under-construction site in Navi Mumbai. They've returned with some good information.'

'But do you think they'll fire?'

'Six of them are willing.'

'Good.'

'Next target is Mavani,' said Rahul, staring at his glass. 'But we're not using the boys yet. They need time and we need to get Mavani in a day or two. We have to cash in on the panic we've created through Patkar."

After a few seconds, he added, 'And we need to kill Mavani. Despite the success we've had, Anna is really pissed because we let Patkar's receptionist live.'

'We must kill Mavani.' Machmach was exuberant. 'This firing won't just be heard in Dombivali. It'll echo in fucking Mumbai.'

'We're not shooting him today, you blood-thirsty animal,' said Rahul. 'Today, we're only conducting a recce. Drink as much as it takes for you to get sober, and we'll be on our way.'

Rahul knew reconnaissance required vigilance. They were planning to shoot at Mohan Mavani, the owner of Durian furniture store in Dombivli (East) – a wealthy businessman, whose murder was bound to make headlines. Many things needed to be surveyed before they pulled the trigger – the furniture store where he was to be shot at, location of the victim's cabin in the showroom, number of staff members and security guards, busiest hours of the store, if it was equipped with CCTV cameras, if there were cop stations or police outposts nearby, and the easiest escape route from the place of crime.

As the gangsters drank their withdrawals away, Reddy called Rahul.

'Mavani is in the store right now. We have to kill him today,' Rahul said, rising after the call, renewed with a fresh purpose. The six-foot-tall man tied back his long hair, tucked one of the two pistols into his trousers, and threw a couple of notes from his stack of 500s on the table.

'Kill him or scare him?' Machmach was still ambivalent.

Rahul smiled and threw the second pistol at him. 'This one will be heard in fucking Mumbai.'

———◦———

16 November 2006, 3.35 p.m. As Rahul and Machmach approached the four-lane road outside the Durian furniture store in Dombivli (East), they noticed the thoroughfare was barely crowded. Everyone seemed to be at leisure that cosy winter afternoon – vehicles were in no rush, trees swayed with an easy grace and street dwellers napped peacefully on pavements, resting before the evening rush hour. Escaping after the shootout will be easy, the gangsters mulled, until they noticed a politician's office on one side of the store, and an octroi outpost on the other.

'We'll have to be very quick,' said Rahul, reading his accomplice's mind. 'Damn, I should have worn my sports shoes.'

As soon as the hitmen entered the basement store, a saleswoman greeted them with a smile, 'How may I help you, sir?'

'We're looking for computer tables,' Rahul said as he glanced at the sprawling, 1,000-square-foot showroom. The retail outlet offered readymade household furniture, and the store was full of furnishing ensembles for various rooms – bedroom, living room, study and dining room. 'Quite fancy,' he thought to himself when the attendant interrupted.

'Here, please follow me,' she said.

'Oh, we'll manage on our own, thank you. Could you get me a pen and a blank paper, please?' Rahul requested.

As the woman left to fulfil the odd request of her only clients that afternoon, Rahul put his hand on his right hip to confirm his 9 mm pistol was with him. He then turned to Machmach, 'I'll fire the first round. You shoot when I nod at you. Go for his heart. He's right there on his desk, extreme end of the store, centre.'

A happily buzzed Machmach simply smiled in response, admiring the teakwood finish of a study desk. Rahul reached for his shoulder. 'Machmach, come on, try and look angry. We've to kill this motherfucker. You look like you're going to go and hug him. Come on. Anger, anger.'

When the sales clerk returned with a piece of paper, Rahul scribbled a thirteen-digit ISD number, and wrote his boss's name under it.

'Thank you very much.' He smiled at the woman, returning her pen.

While the woman stood, Rahul and Machmach walked to the storeowner, Mohan Mavani's desk.

'Are you Mavani?' Rahul sat on a recliner facing his desk.

As the perplexed owner searched his wits for the right answer, Rahul made himself comfortable, resting his calves on Mavani's desk. His fingers, meanwhile, ran along the length of his pistol, as if adoring it, as if it, too, had that glorious teak finish.

'Yes,' said Mavani, and Machmach, who was standing next to Rahul, let out a coy 'maderchod'.

'*Gaand mein daat aaye hai tere*,' said Rahul, banging his left fist on the desk. 'Why didn't you return Bhai's call? *Teri maa ka bhosada, maderchod.*'

Even before Rahul could wrap up his curses, Machmach, who was now suddenly active, whipped out his pistol, held the trigger with both his forefingers, and took aim on Mavani's chest. As soon as he fired, the storeowner moved to his left, and dodged the bullet. But before he could get off his chair and escape, Rahul, who was only a few feet away from him, fired another round. A loud screech was followed by silence, with only the sound of a bullet exiting the man's body and hitting the ground.

As the gangsters began to leave, they saw a young boy standing behind them, his eyes wide with horror, and his jaw dropped open in shock. The boy, a peon at the store, was carrying a tray of teacups, which collapsed to the floor when the hitmen turned to him. Looking at his stunned face, and the glass ruins on the floor, Rahul laughed.

'*Arre chutiya*! Have you pissed your pants as well?' he tapped the boy's cheek, still laughing.

As the two walked out of the showroom, the sales representative rushed to her boss. In her statement to the police, she recounted, 'His shirt was stained red with his blood, and he had passed out. He had a bullet injury on the right side of his navel. I looked at him once, and I felt a shudder. He wasn't a young man, at least fifty years old. When they rushed him to the hospital, I saw that the bullet had exited from the rear side of his left hip.'

Rahul and Machmach walked out of the door, and climbed the ten steps from the basement store to get to the main road. Once on the street, Machmach stood with his hands on his hips.

'What the fuck? Run!' commanded Rahul.

'There's no rickshaw, Bhai. You didn't even get the damn bike.'

Rahul stood scratching his head with his pistol, trying to think of an alternative, when the peon emerged from the store.

'Catch them, catch them,' the boy shouted at no one, as the armed gangsters took to the road, and ran.

——⊹——

As the peon chased after them, the foolishness of the plan dawned upon the shooters. They should have at least had a getaway vehicle ready before they set out to kill a man. *Never doing this drunk again*, the two vowed as they rushed through the Dombivli street.

Ahead of the Durian store, a divider on the road split the two. While Rahul ran on to the left side of the road, Machmach stayed on the right. The peon was still after them, his 'Catch them, get them' prayerful and consistent.

'*Bhak maderchod*,' Rahul spat in the boy's direction. Firing at him would attract too much attention.

After a few hundred metres down the road, Rahul turned around, and saw that the peon wasn't alone anymore – at least fifteen men were running with him, repeating his chants. The group was led by six men on three motorbikes, quickly pacing in the gangsters' direction. To deter them, Rahul fired a round. The bikes had a sudden drop in their speeds, and the chasing men relaxed their frantic strides. Attendants at the nearby octroi outpost froze in their spots.

'No stopping, Machmach,' Rahul shouted in his accomplice's direction. 'No stopping for nothing.'

Rahul, who had lost one of his slippers in the rush, was now running next to a vacant auto rickshaw. He climbed into it, and yelled at Machmach, asking him to jump in. Rahul then put his pistol on the nape of the driver's neck, and told him that if he stopped, he would be killed. His life dependent on the gas pedal, the auto driver accelerated.

While in the auto, Machmach turned around, and saw that the crowd was still chasing after them. Rahul leaned out of the rickshaw and fired another round. The mob dispersed briefly, but only a few metres ahead, the hitmen saw a police patrol van racing in their direction. Rahul asked the auto driver to turn left into a narrow, adjoining lane. With the diversion, the van passed them by, its occupants unaware that the speeding auto was hoarding the gangsters that they were out looking for.

Inside the lane, the duo got off the rickshaw, and Rahul paid the driver five hundred rupees. Machmach protested, mostly because Rahul was wasting time by paying the man, but he knew his friend, and his untimely benevolence. As they ran inside the lane, they noticed that one of the bikers was still following them. The chaser had got off his bike and was now running behind them.

For hundreds of metres thereafter, Rahul and Machmach ran through the maze of old chawls, jumping over water tanks and parked scooters. They dodged the few people in their way – women washing clothes, and old men who slumbered on stone pavements outside their homes. The hitmen refrained from using their pistol, but when a dog kept barking at them, threatening to bite, Rahul couldn't resist. He shot at the canine. The dog retired to a heap of sand, cowering.

When the gangsters turned around to run, the biker stood in front of them.

'Aye, wait,' the man commanded. 'Even I have a pistol.'

Machmach attempted to run, but his feet slipped over some sand, and he fell to the ground. Rahul begged him to run. If he didn't, the biker would pounce on him. Too exhausted, Machmach was unable to get up. Rahul saw no other option. He fired at the biker and the man collapsed.

The gangsters, who were now close to Dombivli railway station, ran across the footover bridge. Once they reached Green Court, they washed Mavani's blood off their shirts. While Machmach left to tonsure his head to evade cops, Rahul ordered his whisky.

'The job is done,' the hitman called his boss.

11

Double Zero

———◆—◆———

Hoping to assemble a homemade bomb, Rahul headed to an abandoned building on the outskirts of Dombivli after gathering the paraphernalia for his pyrotechnics project. The half-constructed, dilapidated structure stood in the middle of a wasteland with mountains of trash for neighbours. Its developer, in the midst of construction, had declared bankruptcy, turning the property into an ideal joint for gangsters, lovers and drug addicts.

As he climbed the stairs of the three-storeyed building, Rahul wondered if, like the Al Qaeda terrorists, he would be successful in creating the flawless shrapnel bomb. *Perhaps, an ammonium nitrate one would have been easier*, he thought to himself. The chemical, often used by farmers as fertilizer, was readily available and cheap. He would use it the next time, he decided – after he had his prototype in place.

As the afternoon sun blazed, Rahul parked his duffle bag in a corner of the terrace, and laid its contents on a bed sheet he'd borrowed from his mother – ping-pong balls, thick strings, duct tape, gunpowder, steel ball bearings of about five millimetres in diameter, stainless steel razor blades, thin nails, a small spoon, a candle, a screwdriver, a cup and nail polish.

'So what if Anna refused to buy me apples,' Rahul told himself. 'I'll make my own bombs. Like Captain Ray Quick in *The Specialist*. Sylvester Stallone was a hitman like me in that movie. He built his own bombs, and fucking good ones.'

Rahul liked his idea of using a ping-pong ball. Less space meant more pressure. Smiling, he punched a hole on top of a ball with the screwdriver. Right opposite the hole, he cut a bigger one, using the blade. He lit the candle, and dipped a five-inch piece of string in the melting wax to harden its tip. He then threaded the string – the bomb's fuse – through the smaller hole.

After blowing the candle off for safety, he made a mixture of gunpowder, a few ball bearings and thin nails in the cup, and used the spoon to add the blend to the ball through its blade hole. Stuffing it to the brim would be excessively catastrophic, he mused, and stopped after filling half the canister. He then sealed the blade hole with duct tape, and painted the canister with nail polish. The paint wasn't for aesthetics, it made explosions louder.

As the polish dried, Rahul carefully cleaned up the gunpowder, then smoked a cigarette. About five minutes later, he walked to an open space outside the building. Using his lighter, he lit the tip of the fuse, threw the canister as far as he could, and ran to a spot a few metres away. The bomb exploded, and Rahul smiled. The perfect golden blast, the triumphant sound of ball bearings hitting the ground. 'Beautiful,' he said out aloud.

'I've figured the perfect apple recipe, Anna,' a thrilled Rahul phoned his boss. 'All we need now is close-ended steel pipes to replace the ping-pong balls. I've also found the manual for a terrorist organization. It has their code of conduct – some brilliant tips on dodging suspicion and evading arrests.'

'Are you out of your fucking mind, Bhiku?' Reddy was not impressed. 'I told you this a few days ago. We do not need bombs or jihadi guidebooks. We're gangsters, not terrorists.'

'But wouldn't it be easier if we just hurled bombs when people chased us? Like in Mavani's firing. That run was exhausting.'

'Do not argue with me, child. You're drinking too much, too much. This is not something a sane man would do.'

'But, Anna…'

'Your job is to pump two bullets into your target and leave.' The don was irritated. 'What's the reaction to the Mavani firing?'

'As expected, Bhai. Special teams have been formed to identify us. Security has been beefed up for important men. Your name is all over the press.'

'Good,' said the don. 'There's a new consignment coming in. I'll email you the details. These are special, expensive weapons. I've scored them for you.'

Rahul was surprised. Anna was a staunch businessman, who believed in economics more than vanity. He did not waste money on imported pistols for extortion gigs. He would procure the duplicate ones from Uttar Pradesh, available for Rs 25,000. They did the job, bringing a minimum of five lakhs per bullet.

As instructed, Rahul picked up the consignment from a Dombivli bus stop. They were gorgeous, those weapons – sleek, light, American steel, Bulgarian make – but wrapped in a plastic bag. Unhappy with the disrespect towards his pistols and revolvers, the gun enthusiast visited a leather showroom, and purchased a bag for Rs 4,000. He then went to a stationery store, and bought carbon paper. Black carbon, he had learnt, blurs contours, making weapons undetectable under x-ray scanners. His hands soiled from the paper, he called his boss, and narrated the consignment's contents – three 9 mm pistols, two 7.65 mm pistols, six magazines, and about five hundred 0.38 mm bullets.

'Good,' said Reddy. 'Keep what you like, and have the remaining sent to our shooters in Mumbai.'

'Noted, Anna.'

'And don't waste your time on bombs and other such shitty ideas. Don't drink that much. It's the alcohol that is doing this to you.'

Hearing Rahul's silence, the don added, 'You've done great work so far, beta. A few more hits, and I'll bring you here, on double zero. You don't have to be in a city to rule it. You can sit with me, and manage the city through your ground network. I've made investments for you. There's money in your name; you'll have nothing to worry about. Just don't lose your mind until then.'

Rahul was elated. In terms of layman appraisals, he was offered the job of his company's vice president. An underworld jargon for gangsters settling abroad, the 'double zero' is indicative of ISD numbers. A don who is sitting on double zero is in the safest position, far from the reach of cops and the law. There is no arrest for him, no jail. He works without hindrances and without direct repercussions.

'I'll finish up here and be with you soon, Anna,' Rahul could barely contain his grin, eager to be his Anna's Chai Pau.

'Do you have a passport?'

'No.'

'Get one made, and let me know who's going to be your next target.'

—||—

A critically injured Mavani spent two months in hospital after Rahul shot him. Doctors did not expect him to live, and investigators were able to record his official statement only a fortnight after the attack, once he was able to speak.

Desperate to control the reign of extortion, the police had experts draw sketches of the two gangsters. Apart from the storeowner and his staff, many locals had seen the duo as they rushed through Dombivli by-lanes, trying to escape the chasing mob. The police had vital clues.

It was the speed at which Rahul was orchestrating his shootouts that alarmed the police infrastructure the most – three hits in five months on some of the most prominent men in Thane district. Based on the sketches, the Crime Branch locked up a man who looked strikingly similar to Rahul. He, too, was a gangster – and tall, fair, lean and muscular. The lookalike languished in prison for three months before the case against him was quashed for want of evidence.

As for Machmach, the cops questioned him thrice during the month after Mavani firing. Since he had shaved his head and carried a forged ID card, they had let him go. But although unharmed, Machmach was beginning to realize that if he did not wish to be killed in an encounter, his days in the underworld would have to be numbered.

'They're picking me up randomly, Bhiku,' Machmach told Rahul. 'They're searching my clothes, my bag, everything. We are lucky that so many boys here know about us, and haven't ratted us out. If the cops offer good money, they will do it. I think we should lie low for a bit.'

'Don't be such a fattu, Machmach. What are these guns for? If someone comes after us, we'll just fire at them.'

'Bullets cannot be the answer to everything, Bhiku. Lately, you've been proposing the same solution for every problem. You were never this trigger-happy egomaniac. You were mind over violence.'

'Do not lecture, Machmach, please,' Rahul said, bored. 'Think logically. How will they get you? The cops went digital in the late 1990s. Your crimes are from 1994, 1996. You aren't even on their records.'

'I have a strong feeling, Bhiku. We had a very narrow escape with Mavani. We can't get lucky each time.'

'*Bhak, gandu*. I knew you'd chicken out,' said Rahul, too proud for fear.

The underworld's wisdom preaches that gangsters should thrive in the dark, appear only to do their jobs, and then crawl back into the shadows. Rahul refused to heed the insight even as Machmach distanced himself from the world of crime. The alcoholic gangster continued frequenting his bars, enjoying the dread he had spread among the highest echelons of the district. With two pistols tucked into his trousers at all times and his don's blessing, Rahul felt powerful, almost imperishable – even as the cops were closing in.

It was his bar girls, who first noticed that something was amiss. 'Strange men' had started visiting the establishment a few weeks after the Mavani shootout.

'Seth, don't stay here for long,' Pouru, Rahul's first bar dancer, once told him during a visit. 'We're noticing new faces. The regular cops – humare hero log – they haven't visited in a long time. There are these other Crime Branch officials, who come instead. They occupy tables, but don't call for beer, food or girls. No flirting, not even a wink. They just keep observing everything in the bar. Once in a while, they corner us and ask questions about some patrons. If we speak, they tip us a few hundred rupees and leave. I know they're up to something, and it can't be good for you.'

'Have they asked you about me?'

'No,' said Pouru. 'Not yet.'

'Then don't worry, my love.' A confident Rahul grabbed her by the waist and kissed her. 'I'm no petty thief. I'll be riding the double zero flight before they get to me.'

Rahul took cognizance of the threat only by the end of 2006 when he started noticing unfamiliar faces in the bar. Some of these men had trailed him a few times. Some even stopped him, asked his name. Rahul had replied confidently each time, certain that the weapons tucked in his back would rescue him if needed. And if not the pistols, the stacks of notes in his pockets would.

'If you don't want to be careful, at least take care of your health. Your body shouldn't give you away,' Reddy once told Rahul over a chat on Yahoo Messenger.

'Who told you I'm drinking too much, Anna? Was it Machmach? The paranoid rat!'

'Doesn't matter,' said Reddy, and sent topless pictures of his own. 'Look at me. Look at these abs. I too drink a lot, but I also work out. I swim so much. It keeps me fit. Stop drinking so much, beta, and get some exercise.'

'Okay, don't give up on alcohol,' the Bhai conceded when Rahul appeared unconvinced. 'At least stop sitting in the same bar for too long, and stop hoarding weapons. Avoid going home too often. Or they'll hunt you down and kill you in an encounter. Just stay safe until I bring you here.'

With dreams of settling in an exotic locale with his Anna, Rahul agreed to the precautions. The first thing he had to do was get rid of his weapons. He knew he was getting careless with them. The two pistols would fall off his underwear every time he attended to his frequent loose motions. Once, when he returned from the bar washroom, he realized he had kept the pistols on his table before he left – a spectacle for curious patrons.

To lose the weapons, Rahul called Tochan, one of his eight fresh recruits. The newbie was happy to help. Tochan took the pistols home, unscrewed a wooden tape recorder, put the weapons in it, and screwed it back. The recorder sat pretty on the display unit in his living room, far from suspicion.

Although his drinking did not decline, Rahul stopped spending his days at Green Court, switching taverns every few hours. As more and more people started warning him – bar dancers, waiters, managers and his boys – he stopped going home, sleeping in bars, their kitchens, and local hotels and lodges. One of his friends, Mallik, then offered him a security guard's cabin on his building terrace. Rahul moved into the vacant space. He brought a mattress, a pillow, a few clothes and a radio, falling asleep to romantic Bollywood songs every night, alone.

One night in early February 2007, around 2.15 a.m., an inebriated Rahul went home. His mother opened the door, and he enquired if she had cooked dinner for him.

'You're home after weeks,' she said. 'How was I to know?'

Barely able to walk straight, Rahul collapsed on the floor next to his father's mattress. He hadn't showered in days. His breath smelt of alcohol, and his clothes reeked of smoke. His father, without a word, rolled over to the other side. Rahul grabbed his arm, and fell asleep. He woke up two hours later, curled up beside his father. The gangster left quickly, worried that cops would track him down. As he walked to his friend's terrace, he wished he could have stayed home longer. With his father next to him, he had felt safe – the last time he would feel that way.

———

Rahul's fourth target was Deepak Mejari, President, Kalyan–Dombivli Builder's Association. One of the wealthiest real-estate developers, Mejari had lobbied for the all-party meet after the firing at Patkar's wedding hall. He was the one who had taken to the rooftops, proclaiming that developers and businessmen needed protection. He was the rich men's spokesperson in the district, and if he were killed, the entire builder brigade would cower in panic.

In preparation for his fourth shootout in February 2007, two months after he targeted Mavani, Rahul ensured he had changed his look. He would wear the same collared, casual t-shirts, which were still in vogue from Aamir Khan's character in the popular 2001 film *Dil Chahta Hai*. But to mislead investigators, he started donning the stereotypical appearance of a Muslim man – he let his beard grow, kept no moustache, and wore the white skullcap.

Since Machmach had refused to take part, Rahul approached Kaalya, Tochan and another underworld hopeful, Durga. The fresh recruits were elated – it wasn't just the pay of Rs 25,000 each, it was also the excitement of witnessing a 'real shootout'. While Kaalya would accompany Rahul for the firing, Tochan and Durga would be the watchers – men who remain at the spot for hours after the firing, gauging the public and police reaction.

'The firing is pointless if it doesn't create panic,' Rahul explained to his boys. 'This is why shooters have accomplices. While one fires, the other gauges the reaction. If the shootout is in public, we plant several watchers whose only job is to make note of the reaction.'

With the Mavani firing, where crowds had chased after Rahul and Machmach for kilometres, the gangster had realized the importance of a getaway vehicle. A few hours before the firing, the quartet went to a garage six kilometres away from Dombivli, and picked up two stolen bikes from a local thief. They then rode to the creek near Rahul's home and test-fired the two pistols.

'They're perfect. Let's go!' Rahul announced.

On two motorbikes, the four headed to Mejari's showroom, Unique Automobiles in Dombivli. Rahul's boys, who had conducted a recce minutes ago, told him that their target was at the store.

As in the previous three shootouts, this spot, too, was located on a busy street – a bus stop, vegetable market, grocery stores and many housing societies. Since Rahul had a bike, fleeing would not be difficult. The challenge in this crime was different – getting past the display of cars, and gaining entry into Mejari's cabin.

By now, Rahul had developed a preference for perpetrating his firings during the first half of the day – between 10 a.m. and 1 p.m. on weekdays, when most employees were at work and the impact of the firing was greatest. With this in mind, he arrived outside Mejari's showroom around 12.30 p.m. From the glass windows, he could see at least ten employees – men and women – moving about the cars parked inside. Three more staffed the reception.

As the group pondered over an excuse for Rahul's entry into the showroom, the gangster noticed a paper bill stuck on a wall outside, announcing vacancies for automobile salespersons. Having spotted the perfect pretext, the gangster bought a pen and an A4 sheet from a nearby stationery store. He wrote down Reddy's name and three international numbers. He then wore his skullcap, and asked Kaalya to wait outside the showroom.

'Keep the engine running. As soon as I get on the bike, start racing. If someone follows us, I'll turn around and fire,' Rahul instructed.

He then turned to Tochan and Durga, 'Do you see that tiny restaurant opposite the showroom? Here's two 500s. Get yourselves some food and keep observing.'

The Thane Police recorded the subsequent events as follows:

On 9 February 2007 at about 12.45 p.m., when complainant Rajesh Mejari and his brother Deepak were sitting in complainant's showroom, one unknown person came from outside and approached one of the employees, who was at the reception counter. The person informed him that he wanted to submit his biodata. Hence, the said person was diverted to the Sales Counter, where he asked one of the employees, Aruna, for Deepak Mejari. Aruna told him that Deepak was not there. Thereafter, the said person handed over some papers to Aruna and asked her to hand them over to Deepak Mejari.

Thereafter, the said person went out from the Sales cabin, and headed towards the front door. However, just before he reached the front door, he turned back and removed a gun concealed in his clothing and fired towards the mezzanine floor, where one of complainant's employees, Sanjay Gawade, was sitting, under the impression that the said Gawade was Deepak Mejari.

Throughout this time, one other unknown person was waiting just outside the front door. Said person had kept the engine of the bike running, and was sitting on it. The assailant ran outside and got on to the said bike, and ran away from the spot.

Sanjay Gawade did not receive any injuries as the bullet from the gun passed through the table and hit the chair. Thereafter, the complainant checked the papers that the assailant had handed over to Aruna, and found the words 'To Deepak Mejari'. Below that, 'Reddy' and three different numbers were written on it.

Following the shootout, Rahul and Kaalya reached Green Court. A few hours later, Tochan and Durga joined them.

'It was complete pandemonium after you left, Bhai. The employees rushed out shouting. Cops barricaded the whole stretch. The Thane Police commissioner was there himself! Imagine! The cops looked like they'd shat their pants.' Tochan was ecstatic.

'Was there an ambulance?'

'No, why?'

'So the bullet didn't hit the bastard?'

'No, I don't think.'

Rahul was disappointed. He knew he had panicked; it was the large number of employees at the showroom. His mood changed only after his boss called him, congratulating. Reddy's name had once again made headlines on news channels, and the overseas don was watching the developments, elated.

'Bravo, beta!' the don said. 'I saw the showroom's broken glass pane on TV, the haggled cops. This is enough to scare him. We'll kill Mejari if he doesn't pay up.'

'Who would you like me to target next, boss?' Rahul was still upset.

'No one, not immediately at least. Four firings in eight months is an underworld record! We don't have to set the district on fire,' the don said. 'Cool off for a few weeks now. Go on a holiday. I'll send you some cash.'

'Thank you, Anna,' said Rahul. 'Once I return, we'll turn the cyclone towards Mumbai.'

——◦||◦——

On 11 February, two days after the Mejari firing, Rahul celebrated his thirty-first birthday at his regular bar. His parents hadn't wished him, and the day, as it did every year, reminded him of Aarti.

Inebriated, he called her parents' home. When her father answered, Rahul launched into expletives and demanded to speak to his estranged love. The man disconnected the line, but Rahul dialled again. Three such calls later, Aarti's father put the receiver on the side. The call still on, the lonely gangster listened to the silence in her home for twenty minutes – the closest he had felt to her in years. When he finally disconnected, realizing the futility of it all, his Bhai called.

The don had remembered his birthday. After the wishes, he said, 'Now, go home. Do not loiter around. I want you to have a long, healthy life.'

'I haven't been home in weeks, Anna. I miss home.'

'Imagine my plight, child,' the don replied, 'I haven't been home in ten years, ever since I fled the country. My mother is still there, all my family. Missing loved ones, I'm afraid, is part of the job description.'

Responding to Rahul's silence, Reddy continued: 'It's your special day, Bhiku. Don't be sad. You have done some phenomenal work in the past few months. I've monopolized all of Thane because of your four firings. After your last shootout, dozens of extortion calls have been made. Not one fucker has refused to pay up. You are going to rule Mumbai, beta. I can see it.'

Rahul felt better with the don's praise. Each of his childhood dreams – money, fame, respect and recognition – had tasted reality. After the call, he returned to his friends and downed another drink.

A few days later, the hitman called Reddy again. Despite two weeks since the shootout, the ganglord hadn't paid him. This was unlike Rahul's usual jobs, where cash reached him immediately after the crime. Often, before.

'My money is drying up, Anna. I also need to pay the boys,' Rahul told Reddy.

'There's a cash-flow problem, Bhiku. It's stuck in transit. I'll have it sent as soon as I can,' the don promised.

The gangster trusted his boss. He knew it wasn't a cause for concern – not until the evening of 27 February. Rahul was standing outside Green Court, speaking on his phone when a stranger accosted him.

'Rahul?' the man, dressed in a white shirt and trousers, enquired with the gangster.

'*Haan, tu kaun?*'

The stranger hugged Rahul. Before he could react, another stranger hugged him from behind, locking his body between the two men. Within seconds, the first man handcuffed the gangster, while the other held a pistol on his back. The bar manager, who was standing nearby, tried to intervene, but was ordered to keep away. The two men then shoved Rahul into an SUV and drove away.

12
The Real Bhai of Mumbai

––◦I◦––

27 February 2007. 8.30 p.m., Kalyan–Shilphata Road. Rahul stood off the deserted highway, his palms on the nape of his neck, his eyes staring at the dark wilderness before him. These could easily be the final moments of his life. The team of six police officers who had picked him up from outside Green Court stood a few feet behind him, their revolvers facing his back. The investigators had created the perfect scene for an encounter – they would fire at his back; and when confronted, they'd justify the kill, saying the gangster was attempting to flee.

Within seconds, Rahul heard the familiar sound of a revolver being hand-loaded, and considered shouting for help. It was futile, he soon realized. Not one car seemed to pass by, no concrete structure visible in miles, no sign of life – just the gentle sound of bees, buzzing among dense trees. The gangster's heart raced, like a ticking time-bomb in his chest, matching the swift pounding in his head. His limbs shivered, and he sweated abnormally on the winter evening. It isn't fear, the alcoholic hitman assured himself. *My body is just craving alcohol.*

'Trust me, sahib. I am more valuable to you than my corpse,' Rahul responded to the weapon's sound. 'Just give me one drink, and we'll have a sensible conversation. I can sort each of you out.'

'Of course, you can sort us out, maderchod,' one of the cops now stood next to him, and hit the side of his forehead with the revolver's grip. 'How much did Reddy pay you to terrorize Dombivli? To get the home ministry on its toes?'

'I don't know any Reddy.'

Two cops now held Rahul, and a third kicked his knees. Once he dropped to the floor, an officer held the revolver on Rahul's forehead.

'Where's your chappal? I hear you lost one recently,' the cop was referring to the Mavani shootout, where Rahul lost a slipper while escaping the crowd. 'And where's the taqiyah? The Islamic skullcap suits you well.'

The gangster did not respond. The cops had figured that he was involved in the Mejari firing as well, where he had worn the white cap to fool investigators. His trick had worked. The Mejari police complaint did mention that a Muslim man had perpetrated the shootout. Investigators were derailed, but only briefly.

'Talk, bastard. Don't you want to strike a deal anymore?'

When Rahul stayed quiet, the cops started searching him. All they could find was a Nokia mobile phone, a railway pass, and a ten-rupee note. Anna had been right. Not hoarding weapons was a good idea.

'Fucking pauper,' the armed cop spat at the grass. 'How the fuck will you sort us out? With ten rupees?'

'No point keeping this beggar alive. Shoot him here and finish it off,' suggested another.

Without looking at any of the plain-clothed officers, Rahul reiterated, 'I'll sort each of you out.'

Rahul's white flag received no takers. The officers lost their cool instead, and started hitting the gangster with fists and blows.

'Do you even know who we are? We are encounter specialist, Vijay Salaskar's squad. We are the Mumbai Crime Branch, you arrogant fuck. We'll shoot you dead right here, and no harm's coming to us. Killing strays is state-sanctioned.'

Amidst the rain of blows, Rahul realized his bargains wouldn't work with these cops. Too proud, they needed to believe he was petrified, that they had broken him. If he feigned cooperation, he could also buy time before the bar manager told his friends of his arrest, and word reached Anna.

'I'll tell you everything, sahib,' the gangster feigned submission.

The cops put Rahul back in the police Bolero. During the two-hour ride to the Kurla Crime Branch headquarters in eastern Mumbai, Rahul was more worried about his withdrawal than the upcoming assault. He mulled over the ways he could convince his escorts to get him a quarter of whisky. While on the road, he pointed to several wine shops, and argued that his choice of spirit was quite cheap.

'I speak out of necessity, sahib.' Rahul made his case, his voice now breaking from the withdrawals. 'I need three quarters every night to get my head in place, and you picked me up after I'd finished one. I was just about to go for the second one, but you had me. It really isn't as frivolous as it sounds. If I don't drink, I'll pass out. I won't be able to answer your questions.'

The officers, who had dealt with several alcoholic criminals, knew the gangster wasn't lying. His withdrawals were real. Once they reached Kurla, one of the policemen handed Rahul a pack of ten Gold Flake cigarettes.

'You're not getting alcohol,' the cop stated. 'Smoke as much as you want.'

The gangster sat in a corner of the room as the six cops occupied two wooden benches, which lined the walls of the 300-square-foot space. With his trembling hands, Rahul smoked cigarette after cigarette, hoping to chase the fleeting high. A few minutes later, a policeman brought him a plate of noodles. The evidently famished gangster required energy for his interrogation.

'Sahib, I eat one idli in the morning and one chapatti with egg curry in the afternoon. That's it. I cannot eat this. My system doesn't accept anything but alcohol. If I force the food down, I will either puke or shit,' Rahul tried to explain. 'Just bring me a drink, please.'

'Will you shove it down your throat? Or do you want me to do it for you?' the cop with the noodle plate asked.

Rahul took the dish, and vomited within minutes. When he tried to stand to get away from the filth, his feet gave in, and he collapsed on the mess.

'What have you done to yourself, you drunk fuck?' one of the cops barked, as others dragged him to the bathroom to wash him. 'You'll kill yourself before we do.'

———◆———

As Rahul sat in his drenched clothes, inspector Vijay Salaskar walked into the crime branch's office. Head of Mumbai's anti-extortion cell, Salaskar had joined the force as a sub-inspector in 1983, and scaled up the police hierarchy swiftly. With a scorecard of over 75 gangster kills across Mumbai, he was famed for his unparalleled ability to sniff out and hunt down criminals. He did not have specialized officers working under him; he was a one-man show.

As the star encounter specialist occupied the only chair behind a desk in the room, the six cops stood in unison, and raised their arms in smart salutes.

'Do you know who he is?' one of the police officers pulled Rahul up, forcing him to his feet.

'Yes, of course. He's Salaskar sahib,' said the gangster, his gaze fixed at the senior officer. Rahul noticed that Salaskar did not look like a killer. He didn't have the eyes for it. Dressed formally, his built was athletic, barely muscular. And his smile, it was a gentle, endearing one. *Too kind a face*, Rahul mused. *Maybe, he should grow a beard to look a little villainous.*

'Good,' said Salaskar. 'So you must also know that I'm the real Bhai of Mumbai. Not cowards like your underworld baap, who've fled the country.'

When Rahul did not respond, the encounter specialist turned to his subordinate, and asked him to give his pistol to the gangster.

'I hear you're good with guns. You have three firings to your credit.'

Slightly nervous now, Rahul turned his gaze to the floor. The officers knew about three, not two, of his shootouts.

'Come; let's see some of your skills,' Salaskar continued. 'Show us how to load and unload this pistol.'

'It's a semi-automatic. I don't know how to use it,' Rahul said after examining the weapon, which was missing its magazine.

'Really? Which ones do you use?'

'Automatic only. Italian and Bulgarian make,' the proud gangster, although unwell and shaking, tried to belittle the Mumbai Police. 'They're much more expensive than these.'

'Really? And where are they?'

'I don't have them.'

'So what do you have? Ten rupees?' Salaskar asked. 'No cash, no weapons, only your Bhai's number. All this arrogance on the basis of one number.'

The encounter specialist then turned to his men: 'Get each of his gangmates here, first thing tomorrow. And take care of him. I need him to survive his withdrawals.'

The extortionist was given a pillow and a bed sheet, but he barely slept that night. Two of his limbs – right hand and right leg – were chained to iron hooks on the floor, and his health was rapidly deteriorating.

Rahul spent the night alone in the room, reaching out to his cigarettes, smoking, coughing, vomiting, passing stools, and trying to get away from his own filth. He had slept only for a few hours when morning arrived, and with it, the same set of officers, clean and bright for a fresh round of questioning.

'*Chal aye*, Bhiku Mhatre, get up,' one of the officers kicked Rahul. 'This isn't your Bhai's brothel. We've got work to do.'

The cop saw the dirt around him. He started dragging the gangster by his hand to the bathroom when he noticed that his body was ablaze with fever. Rahul spoke incoherently when questioned, and soon passed out. The officers rushed him to a hospital. He spent the day in a hospital bed, the in vitro saline working hard to keep the frail gunman alive.

Late evening, as soon as doctors declared him stable, the cops bundled him in an SUV, and started driving towards Dombivli. They had intelligence on three of his friends – Machmach, Kaalya and Mallik.

———•———

The Mumbai Crime Branch squad first visited Machmach and Kaalya's homes. Since both had already fled, the cops ordered their families to get in touch as soon as they had word on their whereabouts. The search party also informed Salaskar, who then commissioned teams to look for the duo in Thane, Mumbai and other neighbouring cities.

Hoping to get hold of Rahul's third friend, the officers then drove towards Mallik's home. During the short drive, Rahul tried to explain that Mallik was innocent, and that he had only offered him shelter on his building's terrace.

'I'm telling you, sahib. I've shot three people for Reddy. Mallik has nothing to do with any of these firings,' Rahul tried to convince. Having worked with lawyers to secure bail for gangsters in his company, he knew that courts hardly accepted confessions as admissible evidence. He could easily refute his statement, saying he was beaten into it. The officers, however, were in no mood to relent.

'Sahib, Mallik's brother is getting married tonight. If you do have to get him, make this visit tomorrow,' Rahul persisted in vain.

All of this will be over soon, the exasperated gangster told himself. The don would leave no stone unturned to secure his release. He had won Thane district for his Bhai. It was only reasonable that Anna would show up for his rescue.

As they neared the street outside Mallik's home, the cops saw that his bungalow was decorated with thousands of colourful lights and flowers. Mallik, son of a prominent industrialist, was a wealthy man. About 450 guests had gathered for his brother's nuptials. The wedding band blasted saucy Bollywood numbers, as the groom watched the dancing crowd from atop his horse. Soon, he spotted two police SUVs rush by, and turn to block his baraat on the narrow road. Thirteen men jumped off the two vehicles, armed with carbines and pistols. The loud music came to an abrupt halt, and revellers froze in their respective dance steps.

'Mumbai Crime Branch,' one of the police officers announced.

Mallik's father rushed to the cop, and proposed there might have been a mistake. He explained he was a respected businessman, who had always lived by the law. As the crowd inched closer to the conversation, the groom got off his horse.

'It's about your son. We're here to arrest him,' the cop informed the old man.

'For what, sir?'

The cop, in response, asked his subordinate to bring Rahul from the car. The gangster, whose wrists were handcuffed to two policemen, was pushed to the centre of the crowd. The cop took off his veil, called for Mallik, and asked him if he recognized the gangster.

'Yes, sir. He's my friend, Rahul Jadhav,' said Mallik.

'Great,' replied the cop. 'You should come live with your friend. He's held a special spot for you in prison.'

As the officers grabbed Mallik's arms and began to drag him towards the vehicles, his father begged them to let him go, 'I'll bring him to you tomorrow, sahib – first thing in the morning. Please, let us get done with the ceremony.'

'Kurla Crime Branch, 8 a.m. tomorrow,' the cop dictated, put Rahul's veil back on, shoved him in the car, and the two vehicles sped off.

In Rahul's SUV, the cops laughed, recounting the dramatic confrontation, mimicking Mallik's pleading father. The gangster sat shivering with rage. He did not blame himself for the trouble he had brought upon his friends. He blamed it on the cops. He knew that Mallik wasn't important to them. Their theatrics at the wedding were only to break him. He would have to be strong, the hitman told himself – *the motherfuckers are yet to get to my family.*

———•|•———

After Mallik's home, at around 10.30 p.m., Crime Branch officers drove Rahul to his naaka. Although most of the shops were shut, the street was busy with local goons and gangsters moving about restaurants, taverns, cigarette stalls and dance bars. The cops stopped the car outside Green Court, and made Rahul kneel on the road.

'You're the don of this area, aren't you?' A cop kicked the gangster in his stomach as passersby watched. 'Now, tell me, who are your cronies here?'

The police officers knew that they weren't going to get much information in the middle of the street at that hour. Rahul's accomplices had already fled. The sole purpose of that assault was to crush the gangster's pride, destroy his ego, and shame him in front of men who looked up to him. Their plan worked: the gangster was deeply embarrassed, but he couldn't do much with his hands cuffed on his back. He just got up each time they kicked him to the floor, desperate to assert his esteem through his erect posture.

After the street corner, it was time for Rahul's home. The cops were looking to find concrete evidence on the gangster's involvement with the underworld, and were certain that his home would hold some clues. Rahul's mother answered the door, and saw her youngest son after weeks – veiled, handcuffed, dishevelled.

'Is that Chotu?' Shalini asked the plain-clothed officers.

The cops entered the apartment, and pulled off Rahul's veil. Perturbed, Shalini turned around to look at her septuagenarian husband, who sat quietly on the cot in the the living room.

'Can we shut the door, sahib?' Ramakant requested. 'I don't want the neighbours to know.'

'There's no point now, uncle,' one of the cops replied. 'This boy is going to bring you a lot more shame. Do you know what he does for a living?'

'Yes, he did a computer course, and does something related to that,' said Ramakant.

The cop laughed. 'He threatens people and pumps bullets into their chests in broad daylight, that's what he does. He's a Bhai with the underworld.'

As Rahul's parents stood in silence, three cops started searching the apartment. The cupboard and trunks yielded nothing. The officers then turned to the cot. Within minutes, they had a vital discovery – a folder with at least 200 A4 sheets. The printouts contained names, personal phone numbers and addresses of the most distinguished personalities in Mumbai and Thane, including film producers and distributors, real-estate developers, diamond merchants, businessmen and hoteliers. The stack was Rahul's database of extortion victims.

'Maderchod,' the cop slapped Rahul across his face. 'How many people have you threatened? And how many more were you planning to gun down? Good we caught him. The bastard would have unleashed a bloodbath.'

As the cops started dragging Rahul away, his mother went close, hugged him and wept.

'I'll send you some food and clothes,' she said.

'Don't bother, aunty,' the cop replied for Rahul. 'Jaidev Reddy took care of him earlier, and the Maharashtra government will take care of him now.'

During the drive back to the crime branch, Rahul sat quietly. The events of the evening – Mallik, the naaka, his parents – had left him disturbed. He wondered if the Bhai knew about his detention, if Machmach and Kaalya had managed a safe hideout.

'You look so much like your mother, you know,' the cop seated next to Rahul interrupted his thoughts. The policeman was older than other officers, his eyes kinder. 'They say children who look after their mothers are really fortunate. Your parents are old. You should take care of them instead of wasting your life on crime and alcohol.'

When Rahul didn't respond, the cop softly rubbed his cuffed hands. 'I had a son as old as you,' he started over. 'He was as tall, as fair, as good-looking – an army man. I still remember the day of his induction. He got me his uniform and said, "Baba, this is for you. It was my dream to serve the country, and you were my inspiration." I had tears in my eyes.'

'You know, fathers and sons don't talk emotions,' the cop continued after a pause. 'Somehow, we feel that would lessen the men in us. But I can never forget that moment, how proud my son made me feel. After he was killed in the 1999 Kargil War, whenever

I miss him, I go back to that moment and tears fill my eyes. There's nothing worse than seeing your son's mutilated body, you know. Nothing worse than carrying him to the funeral pyre on your shoulders, setting him ablaze. I'm glad my colleagues didn't kill you. I wouldn't wish that fate upon your father.'

Rahul sat with his eyes shut, his face turning red, and his hands desperate to attack.

'Talk to me, boy,' the officer went on, 'Crime Branch officers are ruthless. They don't think before pulling the trigger. Talk to me, and I promise I'll make everything right – not for you, for my son. You remind me so much of him.'

'Ahhh, shut your fucking trap up, you old fuck,' Rahul said, his fists clenched in rage. The veins on his arms stood out. 'Shut the fuck up. For one. Fucking. Minute.'

An officer, who was seated on the front seat, turned around and slapped Rahul in response. The frail gangster's body collapsed to his right. After he pulled himself up, he stared at the cop, his eyes blood-shot with murderous glee. The officer slapped him again.

'Maderchod,' the cop barked. 'Animals like you deserve the bullet, no niceties.'

The gangster laughed. 'You're Mumbai Police, sahib. You're nice to no one – unless they're offering you cash or their cunt.'

'Stop the car,' the cop ordered the driver as the SUV moved along the dark, secluded interpass connecting Kalyan and Mumbai. 'I'm going to gun this bastard down right now.'

'Don't let your blood boil over such men, sahib,' the old officer tried to soothe the enraged cop. 'Such men kill themselves. He's lucky we arrested him. If he'd stayed out, his alcohol would have murdered him.'

'I'm very lucky, yes,' Rahul stayed committed to his arrogance. 'I've been thanking the gods ever since we met.'

13
The Wayward Pawns

―――◄I►―――

Two members of Jaidev Reddy gang arrested
March 2007
DNA Mumbai

Two members of notorious gangster Jaidev Reddy have been arrested by the Ulhasnagar Police in Thane district.

Acting on a tip-off that the two would come near Sahar Railway crossing to loot a businessman, the cops laid a trap and nabbed the gangsters. They were identified as Ramesh Sutar a.k.a. Machmach and Vinay Bedekar a.k.a. Kaalya. Police seized three weapons, two pistols and one revolver from their possession.

The gangsters were wanted in several cases like extortion and attempt to murder in Thane district.

Minutes after Rahul's arrest, as soon as the development reached Machmach, he caught hold of Kaalya, and the two spent the night on a friend's terrace. The following morning, after borrowing

Rs 5,000 from Mallik, they headed to Mumbai and called Reddy from an ISD booth. Since Machmach had given up on crime after the Mavani shootout, he did not have the don's number. Desperate, he called one of the numbers that Reddy would give out to his extortion targets.

'Who arrested him?' the don asked, concerned.

'Must be the Thane Crime Branch. I'm not sure,' said Machmach, unaware that Salaskar's squad was behind the arrest.

'I'll look into it.' Reddy assured, 'Don't call on this number. The cops monitor this one. Write down Bihari's number. He's my hawaladar in Mumbai. Pick up some cash from him, and leave the state immediately.'

Machmach was aware that cops, in order to trace criminals, immediately put their phone numbers under surveillance, tapping their movements through their network providers' tower locations. He threw his SIM card away, and also got rid of Kaalya's. He then went to a public phone, and called Bihari, who said he would need a day to arrange the cash. For temporary refuge, the duo went to one of Machmach's friends in Mumbai, and stayed the night at his home. The following morning, Machmach took a copy of his friend's address proof to get a new SIM card.

'I called Bihari, and gave him my new number. He asked me to meet him at Andheri, and said he would call with the exact meeting point in a few hours. I reached Andheri railway station, where Kaalya and I waited for eight hours. He did not call. His number was off, too,' said Machmach. 'I didn't know that as soon as I left my friend's place, he heard that cops were looking for me. He immediately went to the mobile shop, and asked them to revoke the service. My SIM was blocked. There was no way Bihari or Anna could get in touch with me.'

As Kaalya and Machmach stood at the railway station, they wondered if Rahul was alive. They could not call their families, friends or Rahul's kin to check. It was obvious those numbers were being monitored, too.

'Had they killed him in an encounter, the press would have reported it. There's been no such news,' said Kaalya. 'I think he's safe. I really hope he is.'

'I'd told him, you know,' said Machmach, 'I'd told him, rent a room, and call your girls and alcohol there. I even told the bar manager not to let him sit at Green Court for too long. Had either of them listened, none of this would have happened.'

'Do you think they'll get to us?' Kaalya asked nervously.

'I don't know.'

'I have a friend who's a cop. Do you want me to check on Bhiku Bhai through him?'

'Is he a good friend? Can you trust him?'

'Yes, absolutely. Childhood friend.'

'Do it then.'

Kaalya called his friend, who informed that the Mumbai Anti-Extortion Cell had picked Rahul up. The duo was shocked. They wondered how the elite Salaskar squad got involved, and discussed that their arrests were inevitable. They could, however, minimize the subsequent assault. Hopeful, they asked Kaalya's friend if they could surrender with him.

'Yes, of course,' said the cop, 'This will get me a promotion! In exchange, I'll take good care of you.'

'But you're with the Ulhasnagar Police, and our cases are from Dombivli,' said Kaalya.

'That's no problem. Look at the profiles of the men you've shot. Plus, the Reddy connection. You are prized catches. Doesn't matter who arrests you.'

'But we also have weapons. Do you think we should destroy them before we turn ourselves in?'

'Not at all, bring them along. I'm here, I'll handle everything.'

On 4 March 2007, the day of Holi, the duo entered Dombivli after covering their faces with gulal. They went to a local bar, had their favourite drinks and food, and took an autorickshaw to the police station.

———◆———

'It is alleged that on 1 March 2007, the complainant [an officer with the Mumbai Crime Branch] received intelligence that in Mulund, north-east Mumbai, one person was coming, who was involved in many serious offences and always carried firearms. Accordingly, a trap was laid down to trace the said person.

At about 18.05 hours, one person with a red plastic bag was walking around at the said spot. On questioning, he told his name as Rahul Ramakant Jadhav @ Bhiku r/o Dombivli (West).

Thereafter, the police took personal search of the accused. They found a country-made weapon and two live cartridges of 1.5 inches in length, brass make. The pistol's bar was 6.5 inches with a wooden grip.

It is further alleged that the accused was found carrying firearms and ammunition without the requisite license. An offence was thus registered against him.'

– Mumbai Crime Branch's report to the Metropolitan
Magistrate Court following Rahul's arrest
2 March 2007

The police's version of Rahul's arrest hurt the hitman's pride. The gangster wasn't bothered that cops had lied about the sequence of events leading to his arrest, or that they hadn't informed the court that he had been in their custody for almost three days, beaten and hospitalized. His thoughts remained fixed on the desi katta – the country-made pistol, which officers claimed to have retrieved from him. The cheap weapon would hurt his precious image in the underworld, make him look like a novice shooter.

Country-made? he thought to himself as the cops listed his criminal achievements before the court, *A chopper would have been more respectful.*

The court remanded Rahul to the Crime Branch's custody for two weeks. After the hearing, a lawyer rushed to the gangster, and asked him to sign the waqalatnama – a document that would authorize the advocate to represent him. Rahul was doubtful, but when the lawyer mentioned that Reddy had sent him, he quickly signed. Word had finally reached the don.

'Because a lawyer was sent for Bhiku, we were further convinced that he was no ordinary gangster,' says Arun Jadhav, a.k.a. Bhau, the officer who arrested the gangster. 'Help arrives only for the most indispensible in the underworld. There are two reasons – they're important, and they know important secrets.'

Rahul was arrested on Bhau's intelligence. A local from Dombivli had informed the policeman that a gangster – 'Reddy's main handler in Dombivli, and also his right hand man' – was to arrive at Green Court. Since Rahul's capture was an eminent one, the informant was paid an unusually high remittance of Rs 20,000 from the Mumbai Police's secret fund. The officers were felicitated with departmental awards.

'Initially, Salaskar sahib wasn't convinced that this was an important arrest,' adds Bhau. 'Bhiku was an alcoholic, could barely stand straight. He barfed at the sight of food, kept soiling his pants. But when the skeletons slowly started tumbling out, everyone – from our squad head to the Joint Commissioner of Police (Crime)

– was impressed. The police were diligently trying to control the bloody reign of extortion at the time, and Bhiku's arrest had brought us significantly closer. Four shootouts in a few months was unheard of in the underworld as well as police circuits.'

After Reddy's lawyer showed up, Rahul turned confident that his Bhai would bail him out. To feign cooperation, he started sharing select pieces of information with the officers – enough to save him from torture. In turn, investigators went easy on him, tending to his withdrawals, trying to rebuild his fragile health. But when his accomplices surrendered, Crime Branch officers were left fuming.

Rahul was eating from his plate of idli one morning when the cops flung the door open and barged into the room.

'*Tujhya aaichi gaand, maderchod.*' A cop kicked him when he was about to take a morsel, spilling his food over the floor. 'Gandu, we've been nothing but nice to you, and you've been fooling us.'

When another cop, who was already seated in the room, enquired what the matter was, the assaulting one kicked Rahul again.

'Bastard,' he said. 'While this son of a bitch has gained three kilos from the delicacies we've been serving him, his accomplices have surrendered at Ulhasnagar Police Station. Ulhas fucking Nagar in fucking Thane. We've lost credit for their arrests. Plus, they've taken in pistols and revolvers with them, while we're looking foolish with only this nincompoop to show for our work.'

'But how could I have prevented their surrenders, sahib?' the gangster asked softly, wiping the sambhar off his face. 'I was here with you.'

'Maderchod.' the cop kicked Rahul again. The investigation credit meant much to him. 'You didn't take us where they were. Of course, you knew where they were, and you bought time for them while we took care of you.'

'I took you to their homes,' Rahul persisted.

'You need to be shown your place.'

As one of the police officers bolted the door, four cops surrounded Rahul. One of them opened a desk drawer and pulled out a conveyor belt used in traditional Indian rice mills, a weapon commonly used by the Mumbai Police to maim suspects. The belt grips the skin on impact, causing maximum pain but leaving no marks. Rahul knew he was in for a long session of beating.

'Gandu, you told me you were involved in three firings. What about the fourth one? Why didn't you tell me you were also involved in the Anish Shah shootout?' one of the cops barked as his colleague landed the belt on Rahul's back. The gangster, who was seated on the floor, wanted to cover his head with his arms, but couldn't. His right limbs were chained to iron hooks on the floor.

'Tell me. What were you waiting for? And who's Tochan? Who's Durga? You said there was no one except for Machmach, Kaalya and you.'

With every statement, the officer assigned belt duty thrashed the gangster on his back, palms and calves as Rahul yelled in acute pain.

'No, no. Don't you even think of denying these facts. We got this information from your cronies.'

The gangster did not know what to say. Until then, he had been leading the investigations in the direction he liked, at the pace he desired. His withdrawals, which were still with him, had helped him buy time. Now, his accomplices were blurting out important information, probably assuming that Rahul had shared the details already. His pawns were no more under his control. Wayward, they were all over the place, making mindless moves of their own.

Worse, Rahul did not know what the two had already told the cops, and what they hadn't. He couldn't decide if he should share details about Tochan and Durga or protect them since they were still training and had little to do with the crimes.

'Take me to them, sahib,' the gangster pleaded amidst the blows. 'I don't understand what you're saying. Maybe they can explain.'

Without an instruction, the officer with the belt landed another lash on the gangster's back. The cops could now see through him.

'Maderchod,' the interrogator roared. 'The cross-examination has you panicked, isn't it? You want to be questioned with your cronies so you can weigh your answers. Don't worry, boy. We will put the three of you in the same room – only if you survive us today.'

—·|·—

'Real-estate developer Narendra Bhatia has been running a construction company, Raja Builders at Santacruz (West), Mumbai since 1975. On the day of the incident, the company's work was ongoing at 14th Road, Khar, Mumbai to build a new residential building named "Kishan Abode".

'Around 4.30 p.m., two unidentified men arrived on a motorbike, and parked the vehicle outside the construction site, where security guards Rajbhuvan Sharma and Aniruddha Shukla were on duty. While the rider stayed on the bike, the man seated pillion approached Sharma, and asked if the site engineer was available. When Sharma said yes, the man pulled out a white envelope from his shirt's breast pocket and put it in the guard's hand. The man said that the envelope contained Jaidev Anna's phone number, and that Sharma should hand it over to the engineer immediately.

'As Sharma walked towards the engineer's office, the man pulled out a pistol, and fired at the second guard, Shukla. Upon hearing the gunshot, Sharma turned around and saw that the assailant, who was still holding the pistol, had shot Shukla on the left side of his stomach. Sharma tried to return to the gate to help his colleague, but the man warned him. "If you come any closer, I'll shoot you, too."

'The man returned to his bike, and the duo fled the spot. Shukla collapsed, and was rushed to Bhabha hospital. The police also recovered the envelope that the assailant had handed to Sharma. It contained a white paper with the name "Jaidev Reddy" written on it, and three international numbers in big, black letters.'
    – Excerpt from the First Information Report registered in the shootout at Raja Builders' under-construction site
January 2007

On 12 March 2007, the Mumbai Crime Branch produced Rahul before a special court meant to adjudicate cases under the stringent Maharashtra Control of Organised Crime Act (MCOCA). The officers argued that Rahul deserved to be tried under MCOCA as he was the shooter in the Raja Builders firing, which injured the security guard. For the first time after his arrest, the gangster experienced fear. If convicted under MCOCA, he would face either death or life imprisonment.

'He's a close operative of fugitive ganglord Jaidev Reddy,' the cops informed the judge, as Rahul sat on the farthest bench in the courtroom. 'He threatens and extorts money for Reddy, and is also involved in his money laundering and hawala operations. He also collects data on noted personalities in the film industry and the business world. He has five cases of shootouts against him. Taking the gravity of these offences in consideration – and the evidence we've recovered from his home – it's imperative that we interrogate the accused further.'

The judge turned to Rahul, 'Do you have anything to say?'

'False case, sir,' Rahul stood up. 'They're framing me.'

'And why would they frame you? Do they have any personal grudges against you?'

'I don't know, sir. I live and work in Dombivli. I have no business being in Mumbai. These allegations are unfounded.'

Rahul's investigating officer intervened, 'We have strong preliminary evidence of his role, sir. We've retrieved about 200 sheets from his home with contact details of prospective extortion targets, most of these from Mumbai. Bhatia's details are also mentioned in those papers. The Raja Builders guards have shared descriptions of the assailant, and they perfectly match Rahul. With further interrogations, we will have more evidence in place soon.'

The judge remanded Rahul to the Crime Branch's custody for another fourteen days. The gangster, for the first time, was booked under various MCOCA sections, which established he was part of an organized crime syndicate. His other five cases so far – four firings and one concerning illegal possession of weapons at the time of his arrest – pertained to the Arms Act and Indian Penal Code sections like 307 for attempt to murder, 120B for criminal conspiracy and 506 (2) for criminal intimidation. They could be dealt with. MCOCA was the real blow.

The extortionist knew that being booked under one of the toughest Acts in the country would strip him of bail privileges, and make it much harder for him to escape the charges. The stringent law had a conviction rate of almost 60 per cent at the time as opposed to 25 per cent in cases under the Indian Penal Code. The Act was also adopted by New Delhi and states like Tamil Nadu after it brought about a significant drop in the number of shootouts in Maharashtra – from 203 between 1995 and 1998 to sixty-three in 1999–2000 after MCOCA was put into place to ninety shootouts between 2001 and 2009. Ninety shootouts in nine years across the state, of which, 5 per cent belonged to Rahul.

After MCOCA, the gangster faced another setback. His lawyer, whom Bhai had sent for him, refused to defend him.

'Anna told me that I must have you bailed out, but he hasn't sent any money,' the advocate told Rahul. 'Send him a message, tell him I need cash if I have to represent you. MCOCA is a lot of work.'

'How will I get in touch with Anna? None of my friends or family have visited. Why can't you tell him yourself?'

'No money, no attorney,' the lawyer stated. 'If I defend any more gangsters on charity, I'd have to move my kids to a government school.'

'Please, sir,' said Rahul, the courtesy being a first in years. 'You know I'm innocent, at least in this MCOCA case. You cannot do this to me.'

'It's like Satan complaining against evil,' the lawyer laughed, and left after handing Rahul a five-hundred rupee note. 'Get something good to eat today.'

A few hours after the hearing, the Mumbai Crime Branch hosted an elephantine press conference, announcing the hitman's arrest. The police, by then, had also picked up Tochan. The veiled, handcuffed gangsters stood inside the pressroom at the Mumbai Police commissioner's office, as photojournalists clicked pictures and reporters ringed in questions about their crimes. From the clamour, Rahul could tell he was standing before a packed audience.

Soon after the press conference, television channels carried reports about Rahul, branding him a '*khunkhar gunda*', 'a dreaded gangster', and 'an infamous shooter'. They expressed their amazement at how the gangster, who had been with the underworld for a decade, had managed to stay off the police radar for so long.

A news agency carried the following report:

In a major breakthrough, the Anti-Extortion Cell (AEC) of city police has arrested a close associate of underworld don Jaidev Reddy. Addressing media persons here today, Deputy Commissioner of Police (DCP) Dhananjay Kamlakar said acting on a tip-off, the AEC team, headed by Vijay Salaskar, arrested Rahul alias Bhiku Ramakant Jadhav (31), who was associated with Jaidev Reddy for last ten years but apprehended for the first time.

As for Tochan, they wrote, 'In another prized catch, AEC team nabbed another Reddy associate, Nilesh alias Tochan Nikalje from Kurla yesterday. Police seized two revolvers and three live cartridges from his possession.'

As the cops paraded the duo before the press, Rahul felt like a caged beast. He had last felt as helpless many years ago, when Aarti had left him. He thought of his lost love and smiled. A lonely smile in the darkness of that black veil.

14

Oblivion Is Golden

———◦|◦———

Despair crowded Rahul's mind as he entered a Mumbai Central Prison on 28 March 2007. The gangster had spent four weeks in the Anti-Extortion Cell's custody, and investigators had been rigorous with their interrogations as well as beatings. The officers, who had closely studied the pages retrieved from Rahul's home, came up with a list of targets mentioned in his database – men, who had been threatened or attacked in the recent past. These included Indian steel magnate Lakshmiprasad Mittal, journalist-politician Pritish Nandy, director Mahesh Bhatt, producer Ronnie Screwvala, and Cyrus Mistry, Director, Tata Power.

'I didn't threaten these men,' Rahul tried to explain to his interrogator. 'I don't know if Reddy did.'

'Who else is likely to be targeted in Mumbai? Give me every name on your don's hitlist.'

'I don't have that information.'

'Good then. Mittal, Nandy, Bhatt, Screwvala and Mistry – these are some of the biggest names in the country. That stack of papers is enough evidence against you. We'll add these cases to your portfolio. They'll be the end of you.'

'This isn't right, sahib. I told you, I haven't threatened these people.'

'Of course, you did, maderchod,' the cop started with the conveyor belt again. 'You got the contact details of all these men, and many more. You're Reddy's chief handler. All his phone numbers have been switched off after your arrest.'

'I didn't threaten these people,' Rahul repeated amidst the assault.

'Not killing you in an encounter was a mistake. Talk, or I will shoot you dead right here. Give me each of Reddy's phone numbers. Apart from the three he's been giving out to his victims.'

'I know eleven other numbers from five different countries,' Rahul gave in, and dictated the numbers he had memorized. Sharing those VoIP numbers wouldn't bring any harm to his Anna. Also, he knew that resistance would mean death. The Mumbai Police had got down to real business after pressing MCOCA charges against him. Thirdly, although his body was recovering from the alcohol abuse, it was not ready to sustain heavy assaults.

'Where is Reddy now?'

'I don't know. He'd call me from a number with 00377 as the dialling code earlier, which is Monaco. Lately, 00277, which is South Africa. He must be in South Africa, I'm not sure.'

'When was the last time you spoke to him?'

'A few months ago, over video chat. It was 10 p.m. here, but I could see the sun from the window behind him.'

'Could he be in Australia?'

'I don't know.'

'How would he call you?'

'International SIM cards, Yahoo Messenger, and satellite phone at times.'

'Why satellite phone?'

'That was when he was on the ship, somewhere in the sea.'

'Why sea?'

'It's safer. If a search party comes for you, it can be spotted from a distance, attacked and neutralized.'

'What sea?'

'I don't know.'

'How did you call him?'

'Global System for Mobile Communications (GSM) SIM card, one called Easy Roam.'

'What's that?'

'It's a pre-paid card, which allows you to make international calls at a flat rate anywhere in the world – a little more than one and a half US dollars per minute. Swisscom, a Swiss telecommunications provider, launched the GSM card Easy Roam a few years ago. The company found distributors in India, and aggressively marketed the product in the early 2000s.'

'Who told you about these cards?'

'Research.'

'Why didn't you use Indian cards?'

'Cops, as you can see, don't know about GSM numbers, and Indian SIM cards have much higher rates for making and receiving international calls – as high as Rs 1,500 for ten minutes of talk-time. Easy Roam was much more economical.'

'Where did you get the card from?'

'It's easily available in the bazaars of Masjid Bunder, or any other area in Mumbai with a high gangster population. It's used extensively in the grey market, mainly for smuggling and extortion.'

After many such rounds of interrogations over four weeks, Rahul was left apprehensive. The Crime Branch had threatened to book him in five fresh cases, pertaining to Mittal, Nandy and others.

With six offences already registered against him, his only way out of prison was bail or acquittal in all his cases. Neither seemed likely.

———◆———

On his first day in Mumbai's Arthur Road Jail, Rahul felt the way he did when he was a child – desolate, vulnerable and prone to being bullied. Life had obscenely turned a full circle, pushing the star extortionist to his lowest. His guts, intelligence and criminal instincts, which earned him great esteem in the underworld, were insignificant here. In prison, respect is bartered exclusively for money, and he did not have any.

'Which company?' the jail warden asked Rahul as two of his subordinates stripped the gangster soon after he entered prison. 'Haila! Where's your underwear?'

Rahul wasn't wearing one. During the month after his arrest, only his maternal uncle had visited him once. Although he had brought him two pairs of clothes, a toothbrush, toothpaste, soap and a towel, Rahul's mother had somehow forgotten to pack his undergarments.

'Gangster going commando,' the warden laughed as his subordinates asked a naked Rahul to bend, squat and jump to make sure he wasn't smuggling drugs in his anus.

Once he came out clean, the warden repeated himself: 'Which company?'

'Jaidev Reddy.'

'Hmm. Rahul Ramakant Jadhav aka Bhiku Mhatre. One Arms Act case, five cases of firing, MCOCA accused,' one of the jail officials read from Rahul's papers submitted to the prison.

'*Kya baat hai*, MCOCA! Should we put him in anda?' the warden mulled aloud, referring to the egg-shaped, bomb- and bulletproof cell meant for high-risk criminals.

'No, no,' replied one of the subordinates, 'Why waste a private room on him? He cannot afford it. Chutiya doesn't have money to buy chaddi.'

'Oye, don sahib,' the warden turned to Rahul, 'Hasn't your Bhai come to your rescue? Where's the moolah?'

The gangster did not respond. He was infuriated, evident in his penetrating gaze.

'*Achcha, achcha*, relax. *Baap re*, he looks like an angry young man. Listen, Sunny Deol, what company are you compatible with? Which company gangsters are you least likely to kill?' the warden asked, trying to identify a suitable barrack for Rahul. With the warring gangs in Mumbai, prisons often reported violence when lieutenants of different companies were confined in the same space.

'Dawood doesn't work.'

'Will Chota Shakeel do?'

'Yes.'

'Good. Circle six, barrack four. Have a pleasant stay.'

———◦||◦———

As Rahul walked to his barrack, he was left amazed at the sprawling compound spread over 2.83 acres. The prison, Mumbai's oldest and largest, was divided into twelve circles. Each circle housed two one-storey buildings, and every floor was home to one barrack. When Rahul was shown to his, he noticed that the 500-square-foot rectangular space looked like a cheap rest house. Only one tiny ventilator on one of the twelve-foot walls, and even ceiling fans bawled in protest. A bathroom and three toilets stood at one end of the barrack, while the other hosted a thirty-two-inch, wall-mounted television set. Old songs played on the old TV, just like in Rahul's home. *Dekha ek khwab toh yeh silsilay huve...*

Since his escort hadn't allotted him a spot, Rahul occupied an empty space next to the bathroom. It was 6 p.m. Inmates had been locked in for the day, but they were in no mood for bed. In fact, the party only seemed to be starting. The inmates, nearly fifty of them, sat in groups they had chosen based on their syndicates, criminal allegiances, political beliefs, religious faiths and love for hashish. The men smoked, played cards, cooked, sipped tea, prayed, argued, sang and laughed – all together in that cramped jailhouse, dwelling by Mahatma Gandhi's dictum as the Father of the Nation smiled upon them from a portrait: *Live as if you were to die tomorrow.*

About two hours later, at 8 p.m., inmates started laying down their mattresses along the walls – four columns with ten mattresses each. The space in the centre remained free for men to move about. Later in the night, it would house a single line of ten beds for the lowest rung criminals in the barrack, who would lie down only after every other inmate had called it a day.

Rahul did not know where he would sleep. His criminal résumé made him eligible for a bed next to the wall, but no one seemed to be acknowledging that. This was Mumbai. No one knew of his accomplishments here. Worse, the jail staff hadn't given him a mattress, bed sheet, pillow or blanket. His missing underwear had told the officials too much about his financial status.

'Oye, new boy, where do you plan to sleep?' the barrack in-charge, also an inmate, approached Rahul.

'I'm wondering, too.'

'What case?'

'MCOCA.'

'Waah, waah. Wait, I'll sort your bedding.'

Rahul realized that if not in the world outside, the MCOCA charge was a boon in prison. Authorities as well as inmates assume that MCOCA accused, who are closely connected to organized crime syndicates, are loaded, and much wealthier than regular criminals.

The barrack in-charge soon returned with Rahul's sleepware, and assigned him a spot in the middle column. Around 11 p.m., the gangster retired to his mattress, only to be woken up with a kick on his head. It was the man sleeping behind him.

'Bastard, mind your foot, or you won't have one to mind,' Rahul sat up.

'Who the fuck are you, bhenchod?'

'Your fucking pop, maderchod,' Rahul said, voicing his frustration of weeks. 'One more word, and I'll fuck you harder than I fucked your mother.'

Agitated, the inmate sprung to his feet, his closed fists ready for a tussle. Rahul jumped up too.

'Oye,' an inmate patted Rahul's shoulder. The gangster turned around to punch, but lowered his arm when the man asked, 'Jaidev Reddy na?'

'Yes, how do you know?'

'I also work with Reddy, Mahesh Bhatt firing. Our other colleagues, ones in the Majid Memon shootout, are in the ground-floor barrack. They told me that a Reddy gangster was coming in today. I looked for you everywhere, but no one knew.'

'Yes, I didn't tell anyone that I'm with Anna.'

The inmate laughed. 'Stay far from modesty here. It'll get you killed.'

The inmate, Raghu Diwakar alias Gabbar, was three years older than Rahul. He was fair, of average built, and married. Rahul learnt of his marital status within minutes of their introduction.

'After Reddy split with Rajan, I left with Anna,' said Gabbar as the two walked to the bathroom end of the barrack. 'It was for my wife. Rajan's work involved too much blood. I had to stay in hiding all the time. With Reddy, you can fire a round in the air and go home.'

'Why? Didn't you kill anyone for Reddy?'

'No, not really. Anna is protective of his boys that way. He knows that if a bullet in the air can do the job, why make a corpse. Murder means longer jail time for his shooters, graver sentences.'

'With me, he'd insist on killing,' said Rahul.

Gabbar laughed. 'Yeah, that's because he's been reconsidering his bullet policy lately. Everyone's saying he's all fart, no shit.'

'Are you in touch with him?'

'No, still waiting to hear from him.'

'I wasn't paid for my last job. I'm hoping he'll pay the lawyer so I can get out of here.'

'You've done some good work in Thane. He will get in touch soon. Meahwhile, I'll make sure you have a good time here,' said Gabbar, who earned the underworld sobriquet after he chopped off one of his victim's hands. 'Come, I have a bed for you next to the wall.'

Rahul was only settling in when a week after his arrival at Arthur Road Jail, a police team took him to Dombivli's Manapada Police Station, and dumped him in a thirty-square-foot lock-up with six other men. Rahul did not like his new cell: Mosquitoes feasted on him. A narrow stream of waste ran along one of the walls, and a makeshift toilet in a corner of the cell, although with ample water, stank. The only redemption was the lock-up's floor, which was tiled instead of hard stone. The ceramic earth made Rahul happy – investigations required a healthy relationship between the two for five weeks.

During his first round of interrogations with senior inspector Babul Deshmukh at Manpada Police Station, Rahul stated he had nothing to say as he had detailed every fact to Salaskar and his team. Deshmukh, a softer cop, told him he would have to repeat the details for his police station's records.

'Mumbai is only filing two chargesheets – your Arms Act case, where you were arrested with a country-made pistol, and the Khar MCOCA firing case. Manpada will file three chargesheets for your three firing cases here,' the cop explained.

'And the Anish Shah firing?'

'Ram Nagar Police.'

'*Maa ki choot*!' Rahul cursed to check if he could take the liberty. He could. 'Six cases is a lot.'

'You deserve every one of them,' the cop smiled.

Although it wasn't a compliment, Rahul didn't mind it. Words were easier to handle than conveyor belts. The gangster was happy to cooperate, repeating details he had already shared with the Mumbai Crime Branch – from how he established contact with Jaidev Reddy to his arrest. He'd accompany the Manpada cops on their evidence-gathering trips, gladly offering tours of his regular bar, cybercafe, his SIM card vendors, the street corner, the firing spots, and the areas where he'd pick up arms consignments and hawala money from. He waited patiently as cops recorded the same statements as the Mumbai Crime Branch, turned to him with the same enquiries. The Manpada Police were easy, the gangster was convinced – until he had a visitor from the Thane Anti-Extortion Cell (AEC), Inspector Shailesh Kumbhare.

'Should I tell the court to grant me your custody?' Kumbhare asked Rahul. The two, accompanied by Deshmukh, sat in an interrogation chamber at Manpada Police Station. The room lived up to its Bollywood stereotype. It was dark and dingy with one yellow bulb in the centre and, under it, a chair to chain the accused.

'Why?' asked Rahul.

'Because you've done such great work in my area. I've heard of your terror monopoly in Thane. I say, we slap MCOCA on you, and make sure you're fucked for the rest of your life,' the officer threatened, his face now inches away from Rahul's.

'I already have MCOCA,' the gangster looked away, the distance making him uncomfortable.

'Look here, maderchod,' Kumbhare slapped Rahul. 'That's MCOCA with the Mumbai Commissionerate. I can lodge a fresh case here, under the Thane Commissionerate. You'll be irretrievably fucked.'

'But why would you do that? What do you have against me?'

'Nothing, and I will continue to have nothing if you answer all my questions. Now, tell me. How does your company work? Who is financing it? Who are Reddy's cronies in Thane? Who is he planning to attack next? Where does he recruit his shooters from? Where does he source his arms from? Who are his supporters in Bollywood, business and politics? Where are his hawaladars based? I want the whole network.'

'These details are known only to the don. Pawns like me are not aware of such intricacies. You're a senior officer. You must know this much.'

Kumbhare lost his cool, and started beating Rahul with his bare hands. His assault lacked system – he would hit any part of Rahul's skin that caught his eye – his mouth, neck, chest, buttocks, calves and stomach. Soon, two other cops joined Kumbhare. The gangster wailed as they grabbed his testicles, twisted his legs after stretching them to their maximum, beat his body with the conveyor belt, and punched and kicked his face.

Amidst his cries of pain, Rahul turned to Deshmukh. 'This is not right, sahib. You know it. I'll complain to the MCOCA judge. I'll tell the court that this cop, who has no right to question me, tortured me while I was in your custody.'

As the assaulting cops got even more violent with Rahul's threat, Deshmukh panicked.

'Please let him go, sahib,' the officer told Kumbhare. 'If he has bruises on the day of his hearing, I'll be in serious trouble.'

Kumbhare was in no mood to relent. He called for his case files and sat on a chair in front of Rahul.

'Listen, gandu,' he told the gangster, referring to his mobile phone records, 'On 20 January you got a call, where you spoke for twenty five minutes. Who was this person?'

'My friend; it was her birthday.'

'*Waah, Bhai ki* item. What's her name?'

'Reema.'

'Reema weds Bhiku. *Waah, waah.* But the baraat will only have cops,' said Kumbhare as the two officers, who had also been beating Rahul, laughed between their panting breaths.

'Don't go there.'

'Why shouldn't I? Is this one's pussy exclusive? If she likes your little sepoy, she's going to love my warrior,' Kumbhare stated, once again grabbing the gangster's genitals.

'She's not my girlfriend.'

'Then who is? Is it the one you spoke to a week before your arrest? Thirty-minute call, and I see that you kept talking to this person every few days,' said Kumbhare, and read out the caller's number.

'That's my neighbour's wife, Priya. She has a four-year-old daughter, Sakshi. The child and I are very close. She grew up in front of me. She's the youngest in the building. Since she'd have no one to play with, she'd come to our home. I would play games, colour books with her. A year ago, they moved out of our building, so I called her mother to speak to her.'

'I'm sure Priya has big tits, and this bastard has been suckling on them.'

'She's like a sister to me,' Rahul looked Kumbhare in the eye.

The gangster was irked, which encouraged the officer. Within minutes, more torture successfully culled out the women's full names and address. The cops also managed to get details of his ex-girlfriend, Aarti. They took him to her building, and beat him up as residents watched.

Over the next few days, Kumbhare's team reached out to the three women for enquiries. Since Aarti had moved abroad after her wedding, she couldn't be reached. Priya, meanwhile, was repeatedly questioned. The cops suspected that she had hoarded the criminal between his firings, offered her residence for gang meetings, even allowed Rahul to use her SIM card to connect with his boss. The women weren't charged for want of evidence, but the questions were sufficient to leave them petrified.

Although the cops did reach out to the women, Rahul does not know the fact. The women and investigators never told him, and he never asked. Oblivion, he knew, offers more hope than knowledge.

———◦———

Over two months after his arrest, it was at the Manpada Police lock-up that Rahul met Machmach and Kaalya – his friends, accomplices and, now, co-accused. The Manpada Police, who had also taken the duo's custody, confined them to the same lock-up as Rahul. As the iron door opened, the gangster saw the two walk in. For once, he did not get into a skirmish with his emotions, and reached out to hug them.

'Dekho, dekho, Bharat milap!' The cop, who locked the door behind them, remarked, 'Lord Ram's reunited with his brothers! Just that the fourteen-year exile is yet to begin.'

The three settled in a corner of the lock-up, and the gangster observed his boys. Like Rahul, their hair and beards had grown to the brink of insanitation, their clothes smelled with weeks of frozen sweat, and their bodies were covered with rashes from incessant itching. The three looked different from when they last saw each other, perhaps younger: The distance from alcohol had acted like varnish on their pale skins, detoxified them, and added considerable kilos to their body weights.

'If nothing else, jail is good for health,' Rahul smiled.

'My father's no more,' Machmach stole the grin.

'What?'

'A few days after I was arrested, he read about it in the newspaper, saw me on news channels. He suffered a heart attack and died.'

Stunned, Rahul hugged his friend.

'He was a good man, you know. He was an honest mill worker, who did not deserve this end. The worst part is that I didn't even get to say goodbye,' Machmach's lips shivered on Rahul's chest. 'I found out fifteen days later from Kaalya's family. I was his only son, and I couldn't perform his last rites. When we lost my brother to kidney failure five years ago, my father would keep saying that he had to shoulder his son's coffin, that his pallbearer was gone. He counted on me, you know – to see him off, to escort him on his final journey. It wasn't much of an ask, but I didn't deliver. I failed, Bhiku. I killed him.'

'But why didn't your family tell you? The cops would have allowed you leave for the funeral.'

'My mother said she didn't want me near my father, not in handcuffs, not with armed cops accompanying me.'

After a few moments of silence, Kaalya added, 'Mallik is dead, too.'

'What the fuck?' Rahul was flabbergasted.

'Yes, he died a month after the cops took you to his brother's wedding. Doctors concluded it was chronic alcoholism, which led to a complete organ failure, claimed his life. But his family holds you responsible. They say he started drinking mindlessly after you took that cop cavalcade to his brother's wedding. Mallik's father would keep cursing him for bringing shame upon the family. He could never get over it, and before the family could help, he was dead.'

Rahul's heart sank. He leaned his head against the wall, and shut his eyes. 'I told the cops not to go to his place on the wedding day, I fucking told them. The maderchods just wouldn't listen,' the gangster's grief quickly turned into anger. 'Fuck.'

'Everyone's fucked, Bhiku,' said Machmach, 'Your eight new recruits, even they've been picked up, beaten and interrogated.'

'But they have nothing to do with our shootouts.'

'I know,' said Machmach, 'The cops claim that since they'd spend so much time with us, they obviously knew about our underworld connections. They knew, and they didn't alert the police.'

'What proof do cops have?'

'That's to be debated in court,' replied Machmach, 'They're at the investigation stage now. Suspicion is ground enough for torture. And most of our boys have been picked up in false cases of arms possession. The bar manager at Green Court, he was threatened with a police complaint, too. He paid up some four lakh rupees to get out of it. Some of our other friends – richer ones like Mallik – they, too, paid the cops. But the other boys didn't have money.'

'Fuck,' Rahul repeated, unable to believe the repercussions. There were more.

'Tochan's wife also left him,' Kaalya informed. 'After the cops picked him up, and paraded him at the press conference with you.'

'But didn't he just get married?'

'Yes, they'd been married only for a week then. So it was easier for her to let go. She said she didn't want a hitman for a husband,' Machmach explained.

'But he wasn't a hitman, damn it. He was a watcher. He was just gauging the public reaction. That too only in our last firing.'

'Yes, but the cops have named him as a co-accused in our shootouts, slapped cases of attempted murder,' said Machmach. 'We've not just fucked our own lives, Bhiku. We've destroyed many others.'

15

The Cheap Philosophers

---◆---

Shootout at Sanpada
Underworld returns with a bang in city, gangsters fire shots
at builder's office
DNA, 25 September 2006

Rearing its ugly head in Navi Mumbai, criminals acting on the behest of gangster Jaidev Reddy opened fire inside the site office of Bhoomi Constructions Builders and Developers in Sanpada.

At around 2.30 p.m., two persons walked inside and thrust a chit to two employees of the developer, sitting at the reception. 'The criminals said it was the Australian mobile number of gangster Jaidev Reddy. However, before we could dial, they opened fire,' said one of the employees.

Four rounds were fired with a 32 mm pistol of foreign make. While one of them hit the glass pane behind the reception desk, the other three were fired in the air. The duo then fled the site office on a motorcycle.

After five weeks at Manpada Police Station, when Rahul returned to Arthur Road Jail, he believed the worst had transpired. Apart from his victims, he had the onus of two deaths, and many other fractured lives. He may or may not have accepted his culpability, but he did believe he had hit rock bottom. The extortionist was to sink further.

Within minutes of his arrival at the Mumbai Central Prison, Rahul was bundled off in yet another police SUV. It was the Turbhe Police, wanting his custody to investigate the Bhoomi Developers firing in Navi Mumbai. The gangster was a prime suspect. He was Reddy's Man Friday, and his extortion methodology was strikingly similar to the shootout at Sanpada.

Rahul was shown to a lock-up cell at Turbhe Police Station, and given two vada pavs and bottled water. Since he was picked up before lunch, the gangster was hungry and swallowed most of his food. Once he was done, he started thinking about the shootout he was freshly being investigated for. He remembered having discussed it with Reddy. The don had offered him the job, but Rahul had declined. He was preparing for the Rajabhau Patkar firing at the time. He recollected he had called Anna after the shootout at Patkar's mall, and the boss seemed elated.

'Fantastic,' the Bhai had said. 'Bhoomi's done, too.'

Although he hadn't perpetrated this firing, Rahul was tense. The Mumbai Crime Branch had falsely booked him in the Khar MCOCA case, and threatened to charge him in extortion bids against many distinguished personalities, including Lakshmiprasad Mittal and Pritish Nandy. Rahul expected the Navi Mumbai Police to do the same with the Bhoomi Developers case. There was no reason why cops would listen to him. More belts, more kicks, and more blows were to follow. All he could do in those moments was choose his dignity over weakness, his pride over wails for mercy. He had the freedom to not cry, he told himself – the freedom to not kneel before the enemy. It does not seem much, this little liberty. To the gangster, it was liberating. His fear had given birth to courage.

'Assault is the extent of it. They aren't allowed to kill me,' Rahul told himself, 'I'll take it. And the day I walk out, each of them will pay.'

As Rahul sat thinking of ways he would torture his investigators, two SUVs skidded to a halt outside the police station. About ten officers led by DCP Prayag Tyagi jumped out of the vehicles, and took Rahul to the police in-charge's office. The DCP sat on the leather chair behind the table while his men lined the walls. The handcuffed gangster, who stood in front of the senior IPS officer, knew the drill and started narrating his life story.

'All that is great,' the DCP remarked, 'Everyone knows all that. You've missed Sanpada. Tell me, where did you get the weapons for this firing?'

'I haven't done it, sahib.'

'Tell me the truth, Bhiku. I do not believe in torture. All it does is replace the truth with the truth we seek. I'm not going to torture you, provided you do not lie to me.'

The gangster was surprised at the officer's reasonability. He said, 'Sir, I'm responsible for four firings in Dombivli, I won't deny that. In fact, I accept the blame with utmost pride. I wanted to rule Dombivli, those shootouts were good steps in the direction.'

'Aye, you're talking to the DCP here,' one of the subordinates interrupted Rahul's speech, and pulled out his pistol. 'Drop your boastful banter or you'll drop dead.'

The DCP, in response, raised his right forefinger to his lip, asking his officer to shut up. 'Let him talk *re baba*, and put that pistol back in its case. I've told you, you're overenthusiatic with it.'

Rahul continued, 'I wasn't involved in the Sanpada shootout, sir. I had fired at Patkar's mall the same day, only an hour before the Bhoomi firing took place. I could not have travelled the distance between Dombivli and Navi Mumbai in an hour. You can check the timings of the two shootouts.'

When the DCP still looked sceptical, Rahul continued, 'I have four other ways for you to confirm this – check the CCTV footage of the Bhoomi construction site, match my handwriting with the paper with Reddy's number, check fingerprints on the paper, and, lastly, take me to the spot and ask the guards to identify me. Even if one of them says I'm the shooter, slap another case of MCOCA against me.'

'Another reason, sir, is that Navi Mumbai is not my area. As you know, gangsters work hard on monopolizing domains. We try to create a fear psychosis in one particular place so that money rolls in whenever our names are dropped. This region of influence is limited for some people while for others, it transcends borders. For me, that area was the city of Dombivli. A shootout in Sanpada is of no use to me. No one knows me there, no one will pay up.'

'You're firing in Reddy's name,' the DCP stated.

'I haven't done it, sahib. I'd be happy to own it up. It's a prestigious shootout; it'll look good on my profile. But I haven't done it. If you still want to slap a false case on me, I'll fight it out.'

'You've already been named as an accused in the Bhoomi Developers complaint. We'll take a call on your involvement following investigations,' the DCP said after a few seconds. 'If we find you're innocent, you won't be prosecuted.'

Rahul spent the next week in the Turbhe Police's Custody, reiterating details that he had shared with the Mumbai Crime Branch and Manpada Police. After Turbhe, Ram Nagar Police officers interrogated him for two weeks in the Anish Shah firing case. Over the next four months, at least five different police stations and crime branch units availed his custody. They suspected his involvement in five other extortion cases, where he claims he wasn't involved. These included three shootouts on eminent businessmen in suburban Mumbai.

Some of Rahul's interrogators tortured him, some did not. Each of them bled him of the little compassion he held within, left him a little more hardened. The slight regret, which had crept in after his confrontation with Machmach and Kaalya, was gone. The little morality, poof.

——◆——

Prisons often make cheap philosophers out of men. Rahul realized this when he was seated in his barrack at Arthur Road Jail in early 2008, speaking to his gang-mate, Gabbar. With their afternoons free, the gangsters would occupy a spot along a barrack wall and share their lives over hashish.

'This jail is a whorehouse.' Rahul offered his latest musing and lit his chillum.

The gangster was looking forward to smoking his freshly forged clay pipe. He had waited two days for its mud to dry under the faint sunlight falling on his barrack's ventilator. He had learnt the bit of pottery from other inmates, and soon, he was an ace at it. A good alternative for alcohol, it was simple, the art of making chillums – get wet mud from the prison's recreation ground, shape it into a conical pipe, make holes at both its ends, and let the pipe dry under the sun. Once it's ready, cover one of the ends with a tiny cotton cloth to make sure the burning hash doesn't hurt the smoker's throat.

'This jail is a whorehouse,' Rahul repeated, exhaling after a long pull. 'You, me, all these prisoners, we're all whores. The judge is the pimp, and the police are the sexed-up clients.'

'Explain.' Gabbar was intrigued.

'See, we're all prostitutes, locked up in overly cramped, dirty brothels for barracks. The clients, the cops, go to the pimp – the judge – asking for time with us, our custody. The pimp grants it, and the client comes to this whorehouse of a jail, picks us up, and takes us to his place, the police station. He violates our bodies and our minds, and then dumps us back in the brothel. Soon, another client comes by, then another, until we become indifferent, until we become immune.'

'You're right,' said Gabbar. 'And no one can agree more. I have eight cases against me. No gigolo here has been tossed between those dicks like I have.'

Rahul laughed and coughed, the smoke choking his throat. 'Good hash,' he said, passing the pipe to Gabbar.

'Chamber got it, the best forty bucks we'll ever spend,' said Gabbar, exhaling.

'How do they not catch these chamber boys?' Rahul wondered. 'Chamber boys' are usually undertrials held in multiple cases. They procure the charas during their frequent court hearings, and sell it in prison. The term 'chamber' refers to the boys' anuses, where they hide the plastic with hash balls.

'They shove it way up,' Gabbar offered. 'Or they just swallow the plastic with water, and shit it out the next day.'

'What if they get caught?'

'They bribe their way out. Some cops like charas. All cops like money.'

'Hmm,' said Rahul, the chillum back with him. 'But at forty rupees a pop, do you think they make any money on the asses they're risking?

'Not everything works on money in prison, Bhai,' Gabbar stated. 'Power is key. If a don gets charas from a chamber boy, he may not pay him in cash. But he might speak for him to the circle officer, who is paid well by the don. The circle officer will then ensure that the chamber boy has a bucket of hot water to bathe every day, gets some good rice from the prison godown, and is safe from prison brawls and beatings.'

'That is true,' said Rahul. 'I like the hashish sessions. I've met some of the most interesting men here through charas.'

'That'll be true anywhere in the world, Bhai. The most interesting people in the world are smokers – from the Godfather to some of India's greatest politicians,' Gabbar smiled, and rested his back on the wall behind him. Rahul was already comfortable, his legs stretched, his palms on his thighs, and eyes turning red. The cannabis had found its way to their minds and their bodies, tickling their senses, and slowly numbing them.

'Prison isn't all that bad, you know,' Rahul offered another musing after a few moments. 'Have you met Birju? He's forty-five. He just doesn't want to live outside the jail. He finishes his term, goes out and commits more robberies so he can come back in.'

'I know,' said Gabbar, 'He doesn't have a wife or children. In fact, the whack-job has created an entire surrogate family in here. He has given different roles to different inmates – an old thief is his father, a middle-aged murderer is his brother, and two young burglars are his sons. They are really tight. They eat together, pray together, sleep together.'

'Get the dry fruits,' said Rahul, the hashish making him hungry.

With Gabbar, Rahul was able to enjoy expensive dry fruits, and a comfortable stay at Arthur Road Jail. Although Gabbar did not have money, he had a close friend in prison, who was incarcerated for a financial scam. Having swindled crores of rupees from an airline in a ticketing fraud, the man had paid prison guards well, ensuring no luxury eluded him during his stay – chicken tikka, mutton kebabs, special canteen coupons, expensive toiletries, good hasish and the occasional scotch.

As days passed, inmates learnt of Rahul's criminal profile, and he started drawing respect. There were three reasons – his own work so far, his association with Jaidev Reddy, and the fact that Bhaijaan, an underworld veteran, had mentored him. The only problem, one he had not anticipated, was loneliness.

Rahul's family hadn't reached out to him, while all his friends and co-accused were at Kalyan's Adharwadi Jail. On the suggestion of his Arthur Road inmates, Rahul wrote to his MCOCA judge, requesting a jail transfer. He offered two reasons to justify the move to Adharwadi:

- Four of the six cases against me are being heard at Kalyan Sessions Court. My trial is suffering since prison officials do not take me to proceedings there. The court is more than thirty kilometres away, and not many prisoners at Arthur Road have hearings in Kalyan court. Officials do not want to waste resources on a single prisoner – special vehicle, four guards. This cannot be at the cost of my trial.
- My home is located in Dombivli. My mother is old and ailing. She has not been able to visit me since my arrest over a year ago. Arthur Road is too far for her.

The gangster's plea worked. The judge allowed the transfer, and Rahul was moved to Kalyan Jail in August 2008. He was home.

—————

The moment he set foot in Adharwadi Jail, Rahul felt better. It was the familiar faces that pleased him the most – Machmach, Kaalya, his eight recruits and many local gangsters from Thane, whom he had known over the years. They were murderers, extortionists, thieves, kidnappers and gunrunners – men from his street corner, taverns and dance bars. Even better, they knew him, too. Aware of his criminal achievements, many of them looked up to him. The gangster was relieved. Being a prisoner had been a lonesome job. No longer.

The first thing that Rahul's stable state of mind brought was the desire to break free from legislative clutches, and return to the underworld. The gangster was quick to realize that prisons were major networking events for underworld henchmen. He availed a tiny diary and pen, and started noting numbers of various criminals he met in prison. The inmates – especially arms dealers, bike thieves and independent extortionists from various geographies – would be useful when he returned to his criminal estate. With his dreams of 'double zero' still alive, he also noted contact details of African inmates who had been incarcerated for peddling drugs – one from Botswana, another from Tanzania.

'Indian gangsters can't survive in Africa,' the burly drug traffickers, who felt superior to their Indian counterparts, would tell Rahul. 'We don't do blood. And if we do, we only use machine guns and hand grenades, not pistols and choppers like here.'

'Why not blood?'

'There's enough money in drugs and cyber frauds, one needn't kill a man. Indian gangsters need to evolve a little bit.'

Although Rahul had no cash coming in from his kin or his don, his ten co-accused had their families visiting them, sending money orders. The boys were happy to pay for Rahul, who had footed their bills from bars and sex workers for years. Machmach, who was closest to Rahul, would go a step ahead, and arrange alcohol for the gangster during court visits.

'Please, sahib. My brain has stopped working,' Machmach would plead for alcohol with police escorts, who drove the group to the Kalyan Sessions Court for their hearings.

'Why do you need your brain in prison?'

'To plan my escape, sahib.'

The cop would laugh, and after Machmach had persisted for forty-five minutes, he would ask the driver to stop by a wine shop on the way. The constable would get out of the van as the undertrails waited in anticipation, each with one hand cuffed to a hook on the vehicle's ceiling. Depending on the group's budget for the day, the cop would buy vodka and bottles of Mirinda. With one hand free, the men would mix the spirit with the cold drink.

'You should not smell, you assholes,' the cop would instruct. 'If you reek of this shit, the judge is going to fuck your asses. Mine won't be spared either.'

'This is vodka, sahib. No smell, only game. Will you have some?'

'Too early in the day for me.'

Once in court, the men would buy chicken biryani for the constable and pay him after pooling in money from their kin. The gangsters had a special party in prison when Inspector Vijay Salaskar was killed in the 26/11 Mumbai terror attacks in 2008. As India mourned the martyr's death, a few inmates drank in celebration.

'Only if we had fire crackers,' Rahul told his co-accused.

Rahul would remain in high spirits at Adharwadi Jail. The only thing that creased his forehead was the fact that his don had abandoned him. Reddy had sent neither a lawyer nor cash. Whenever he met gangsters or attorneys even remotely connected to Reddy, Rahul would request them to take his message to Anna, to tell the don that his ace shooter required rescue. The messages either never got through, or the don never bothered acknowledging them.

'Why isn't he sending anyone for me?' Rahul would think to himself, 'Has he forgotten everything I've done for him? No, that's impossible. I'm sure he's trying to get in touch. Maybe he's assuming I'm in a different prison.' The hitman was being naive; his conviction blind.

—⊢—

As months passed, Rahul's faith in his don transformed into frustration. His co-accused, too, would complain, asking him to get Reddy to pay up for their last firing. They needed money to afford lawyers.

'We don't know Anna, Bhiku Bhai. We did as you instructed, and we ended up in prison,' they'd say, 'The least he can do is pay our dues.'

Rahul decided that if he could establish contact with his don, he would strike a deal: Send me money every month, and I will continue with your extortion racket from behind bars. Running a syndicate from jail required rolling cash – mainly to buy the circle officer's silence, and to distribute hash among barrack inmates so they don't tell on him to authorities. To make extortion calls, all he had to do was buy a cell phone from one of the prison guards. Thereafter, Anna's boys could pick up the cash from victims.

The closest Rahul came to his don was in October 2008 – one-and-a-half years after his arrest. During a hearing at Kalyan Sessions Court, he ran into advocate Nikhil Gavaskar, the lawyer who handled most of Reddy's cases in the Thane belt. Rahul had worked with Gavaskar often in the past, to secure bail and release for over a dozen of his gang-mates.

'You have to get me out,' Rahul grabbed the middle-aged advocate's arm in the courtroom corridor.

'I can't just take you on, Bhiku. The instruction has to come from Reddy.'

'I'm not able to get in touch with him. Have you spoken to him of late?'

'No,' said Gavaskar. 'He's been focused on his Mumbai boys, who've been arrested for shootouts there.'

'You know I've paid you way more than your dues in the past,' Rahul said, desperate. 'Once I'm free, I'll do it again. Just get me out this once.'

'I'll do it,' the advocate gave in, aware that the gangster had always lived up to his word. 'But I will need some money before I start. It's not just you. You have this whole jingbang of ten co-accused.'

'I'll have it arranged.'

Rahul was well aware that freedom requires cash, and the lack of money had now started taking a toll on his mind. When New Year's Eve, 2008–09, arrived, the concern graduated to a matter of pride. Most inmates in his barrack had called for imported alcohol to celebrate the occasion while Rahul and his gangmates had to make do with desi liquor. The hooch told other inmates he was broke, greatly rupturing his ego.

'Yaar, you boys have terrorized the city. How can't you afford a bottle of Black Label?' one of the politician inmates asked Rahul after the New Year party, 'Robbers are drinking wine, and you're from the fucking underworld. They have one case against them, you have six. Shouldn't you be loaded?'

'Boss, your wife visits you, brings you bundles of notes. Cops don't question or harass her. That's because you're not a professional criminal. You killed over personal enmity,' Rahul tried to defend his limited means. 'I am a gangster. I cannot allow my family to visit or to bring me cash. The don has sent money for me, it's with my mother.'

Although Rahul made the convincing argument, he did not buy it himself. Desperate, he wrote to his mother:

Dear Ma,

I'm at Adharwadi Jail in Kalyan. You might not care, but I
spent more than a year at the Mumbai Central Prison. Every
time they took me to police stations for investigations, I
called you. You didn't answer, disconnected the call, or lied
that you'd visit. I sent you messages through other inmates'
families – so many messages. But you didn't show up, not
in police stations, not in courts or prisons. I'd expected this
indifference from Baba. He never understood me. But not
you, Ma. Never you.

I need money in jail. Send a money order in my name.
Rs 1,500 is the maximum amount permitted. Also, ask my
brother to get me some clothes. I've been wearing the two
pairs you'd sent for the past year. And remember to send
underwear.

– Chotu
Kalyan District Prison, January 2009

Fifteen days after Rahul sent the note, prison officials summoned
him. When he reached the warden's office, he saw the circle officer
reading to his colleagues from a letter, laughing. The men sobered
up when they saw Rahul.

'Letter from your mother,' a jail officer handed him the note.

'Why are you reading it then?'

'To make sure your Bhai isn't sending love messages to you,' the
officer replied. 'And here, she's also sent a money order for Rs 1,500.
Deposit it in the canteen for credit.'

A smile appeared on Rahul's face. He took the letter, rushed to
the toilet in his barrack, and latched the door. He knew his mother
would answer. All other inmates had visitors – their parents, wives,
children, siblings and friends – who brought them clothes and

home-made food. She was the only one who hadn't showed up. Glad that his 'strongly worded' note had worked, Rahul opened the letter:

Chotu,

Your arrogance in your letter only shows how little remorse you feel. I didn't visit because I don't want to have anything to do with you. You've dragged our family's name through the mud. I cannot step out of the house because of you. I do not attend weddings or funerals, not even my daily visit to the temple. I cannot tolerate the murmurs when I walk by people.

No one calls or visits us – our relatives, friends or neighbours. Everyone knows you're a criminal, that you shoot at innocent people for money. I did not raise you to be this blood-thirsty hooligan.

Your brother will bring you your clothes. Your father and I will keep sending you money. Don't expect anything more from us.

Two days after the letter, Rahul's brother visited him at Adharwadi Jail.

'Here, your clothes,' said Mangesh, as the two met in the mulaqat room at prison. 'And stop writing to mom.'

'Fuck off,' said Rahul.

'You don't know what you've done to her, you ass,' Mangesh was vexed. 'She's already on so many medicines for her arthritis. Now, because of you, she wakes up in the middle of the night, panicked and shouting. She hears noises, like someone's under the building, yelling out your name, or someone's banging on the door, ringing the bell, ordering you to surrender. Baba tries to explain that you're in prison, that no one will come looking for you at home. She still stays up all night, crying. We've had to put her on sleeping pills. Her treatment is draining all our money and, now, your added expense.'

'Tell her I'll be back soon,' Rahul said, after many seconds of silence. 'I'll fix everything.'

16

Six Wickets in Six Balls

———◦❙❙◦———

As the days passed in prison, Rahul realized that his arrest was largely an occupational hazard. In fact, it was a reward. Jail strengthens criminal reputation. The day he would walk out, he'd be able to command more fear, more money. One threatening phone call and the affluent would be eager to kneel. The only barrier was his confinement.

Over two years after his arrest, the hitman had tried hard to keep faith in his Anna. He was certain the boss would send cash, rescue him. The don did not show up. Now, it was time to push blind conviction to the backdrop, and let reason take centre stage.

In January 2009, while in Kalyan's Adharwadi Jail, Rahul picked up the six chargesheets filed against him. He had been an avid reader since childhood, and started enjoying the documents that nailed his guilt – statements of victims and eyewitnesses, police's recoveries, descriptions of his weapons and evidence of his association with one of India's most wanted ganglords.

With the delicate dream of freedom in his eyes, Rahul attempted to understand the charges pressed against him. He could follow basic sections in the Indian Penal Code (IPC), like 307 stood for attempted murder and 120B for criminal conspiracy. He could not make sense of most other allegations – various provisions of the Indian Arms Act and MCOCA. Eager to understand the charges, Rahul approached a lawyer incarcerated in Adharwadi Jail for dowry harassment. The advocate advised him to read Justice M.R. Mallick's book *Criminal Manual.*

'Apart from IPC, it covers two major criminal Acts in India – the Code of Criminal Procedure (CrPC) and the Indian Evidence Act. It also has guidelines and precedents on criminal law from the Supreme Court as well as the Human Rights Commission,' the advocate told Rahul.

'My cases are under MCOCA, IPC and the Arms Act. Why do I need to read the other laws?'

'Because they'll help you defend yourself. The CrPC will tell you about the types of courts and magistrates, their jurisdictions, and the duties of police officers when they arrest and question you. You'll understand how your rights have been violated, and you can use these violations to make a case against the police.'

'And the Indian Evidence Act?'

'It'll tell you what kind of evidence is admissible in the court of law. It'll help you call out errors in the police's testimony, and will also guide you in gathering evidence for your defence.'

'But where will I get this book?'

'Ask your family to get it. It's easily available in bookshops.'

Over a month after his mother had replied to him, Rahul wrote to her:

Dear Ma,

Mangesh mentioned you're not keeping well. I just wanted to tell you that please do not spoil your health over me. I'm sorry if I've let you down and for all that you're going through, but I am innocent. All those allegations against me are false. The cops have put me in jail because they can't find the real men behind the crimes. I was a drunkard, an easy target. My arrest is not warranted, only a big cover-up.

I know you'll say the cops found those papers in our home. They weren't mine, Ma. Machmach had kept them with me. Please believe me, and please start taking care of your health.

I also need another favour from you. Since I do not work for the underworld, no one has come for my rescue. But I have to prove my innocence, and get out of here. For that, I need a book called 'Criminal Manual' by Justice M.R. Mallick. Please ask Mangesh or Baba to bring me the book.

Shalini did not reply to the letter, but she did send the book with her husband during one of Rahul's hearings. The gangster saw his father after two years. The old man looked substantially older, fatigue etched on his worn face. His skin was looser than Rahul remembered, and his back stooped some more. The gangster felt a rush of emotion, something his egotistic heart hadn't anticipated. He wanted to hug his father, but refrained from the show. He took the book, and thanked him.

'Please do not make things worse,' Ramakant pleaded with his son.

'I won't, Baba. I promise. But I need some more help from you. I have hired a lawyer, Nikhil Gavaskar. He is representing me in my four cases of shootouts in Kalyan Sessions Court. I'll pay him the full fee later, but he needs a token amount for now. Can you arrange Rs 50,000?'

'We don't have that much money, Chotu,' his father said, and added immediately, 'I'll see what I can do.'

While his family mortgaged his mother's little jewellery for the amount, Rahul started reading *Criminal Manual*, highlighting relevant bits and making notes. As his interest grew, he stopped loitering in the prison and immersed himself in the law book. He learnt that convicted men were not allowed visitors more than once a month. If proven guilty, he would have no access to the outside world, no source of reprieve except for filing appeals in higher courts. He had to work hard and secure acquittals in each of the cases against him, he told himself. This was his only time.

———◄►———

Seeing Rahul busy with *Criminal Manual*, an undertrial inmate once asked the gangster if he could help him write his bail application. Rahul had often seen the sixty-two-year-old in his barrack. He was assigned the dirtiest job – cleaning toilets. The senior citizen would also run errands for two dons – washing their clothes, brewing tea, storing buckets of water for their bath, and massaging their feet. In return, they would help the personal steward with delicacies and protection. Rahul had noticed that the old man barely smiled or spoke to other inmates – his social withdrawal an evident sign of despair.

'I've been here five years. I want to go home now,' he told Rahul. 'I have a three-year-old granddaughter. I've never seen her.'

'What are you here for?'

'House break-in theft. I broke into a neighbour's locked house, and stole some gold. I wanted money to treat my wife's breast cancer.'

'Okay, leave your chargesheet with me. Let me see what I can do.'

Rahul spent the next two days reading the charges filed against the man and mulling the possible arguments for his bail. Soon, he had a breakthrough – Section 436A of the Code of Criminal

Procedure (CrPC), which states that an undertrial can be realeased if he has spent more than half the maximum punishment for his offence in detention.

Rahul figured the maximum punishment for the man's offence was seven years. Since he had already spent five years in prison, he was eligible for bail. The gangster quickly wrote an application quoting the CrPC section. Within days, the old thief was released on a personal bond. Grateful, he requested his dons for some expensive hashish, and gifted it to Rahul.

'You're a good man,' he told the gangster as he left, 'Recognize that.'

The old man's bail boosted Rahul's confidence. A few weeks of study had armed him with considerable legal acumen. As word spread about the cleaner's release, more inmates started approaching Rahul for help with their bail applications. The gangster, in turn, was happy to offer his expertise. Quoting sections from legal dogmas, he filed dozens of bail applications, and was able to free many inmates who had been languishing in Kalyan Jail for years. He particularly remembers the 'Cough Syrup Bandits', a group of eight men from the Thane district, who'd chug bottles of cough syrup and commit robberies under the influence.

Encouraged by his success, Rahul, in May 2009, sent out letters to the three magistrates who were adjudicating his trials – one in the Kalyan Sessions Court for his four shootouts in Dombivli, one in the special MCOCA court for the Khar firing case, and a third in Mumbai's Qilla Court for his Arms Act case.

The gangster wrote: 'I have been in prison for two years, sans legal aid, for crimes I haven't committed. My parents are old, and need me to take care of them. I request you to kindly grant me bail, or expedite my trial so I can prove my innocence and reclaim my lost honour. Until you respond to my letter, I'm going to be on an indefinite fast. I'm not going to eat a morsel of food, or drink one sip of water. I may die, but it would be better than this underserved humiliation.'

Rahul was positive his theatrics would work. A day after he sent the letter, he started with his fast. A few hours into the morning, the jail superintendent approached Rahul's barrack. The gangster was surprised. It was unusual for high-ranking officers to visit inmates.

'Drop the fast, beta,' the prison in-charge told Rahul. 'Even if the courts do respond to your letters, it'll be days before you hear from them. I do not want a death in my prison, especially since you claim you're innocent.'

'I've made up my mind,' the gangster replied, almost curt.

Rahul hoped the officer would insist some more, but the superintendent walked out. The extortionist would have to stand by his proclamation. Within a day without food and water, he realized it was not going to be easy.

'I think I should have some water,' Rahul told Machmach on the second afternoon of his hunger strike.

'No, no, no, no,' said Machmach, licking the dal off his fingers as Rahul watched him having lunch, famished. 'You've given your word. No food, no water.'

'Yes, absolutely,' Kaalya agreed. 'A gangster's no gangster if he doesn't live up to his tongue.'

They're right, Rahul thought. Now that he had made a promise, he must put up with the thirst and hunger. Determined, he continued fasting for a few hours. When evening came, his body started wearing down. His dry lips tingled, his skin was turning pale, and he felt dizzy from the abstinence. He mixed a teaspoon of sugar in water, and gulped it.

'Water is fine. More than half the human body is water,' he said as his co-accused stood staring at him, shaking their heads in disappointment.

'And the remaining half is shit,' Machmach taunted, now busy with his tea and biscuits.

That night, Rahul got Machmach to sneak in a few chapattis and bhaji from the dinner spread. The gangster smuggled them to the bathroom, and ate heartily. Thereafter, he would make frequent visits to the bathroom, gobbling biscuits and other dry foods that Machmach would arrange for him. On the sixth day of his 'fast', the superintendent returned to his barrack.

'You must be feeling weak,' the officer said. 'We should have a doctor examine you to make sure you're stable.'

'No, I'm fine.'

'We'll get it done tomorrow,' the officer stated.

Rahul panicked. A medical check-up would bust him: A man who had abstained from food and water for six days could not be as healthy. To his relief, a few hours after the superintendent's visit, prison authorities informed him that the Qilla Court had scheduled a hearing in his Arms Act case, one pertaining to his arrest and recovery of a countrymade pistol. He could give up on his protest. The sham had worked.

On the day of the hearing, Rahul rubbed some saliva under his eyes before he entered the courtroom. Standing in the witnessbox, he quoted the same CrPC section as he had for the old thief. He argued that although the maximum punishment for his offence was three years, he had already spent two years in prison. The judge saw merit in his argument, and granted bail. The gangster was elated. It took two years, but he was slowly taking back control over his life.

To walk out of prison, Rahul would have to secure bail in each of the remaining five cases against him. Even as advocate Nikhil Gavaskar was working on his four Dombivli shootouts, the major obstacle was the Khar firing case before a special Mumbai court. MCOCA ensures that bail is difficult for those associated with organized crime syndicates. Worse, Rahul did not have legal representation in this case. Encouraged by his success in the Arms Act case, the extortionist decided to argue for himself. Although the idea sounded overly ambitious to him at first, he told himself that it was a false case and that he would certainly win. Truth, he reasoned, does not fret over criminal affiliations of its expounders.

With his MCOCA hearing approaching, Rahul started preparing his defence. He soon stumbled upon a provision in the Act, which said that an accused could be granted bail 'if there is reasonable doubt that he or she did not commit the offence'. He decided to focus on proving his innocence.

On the day of his hearing, Rahul refrained from alcohol on the way. Once past the metal detectors at the courtroom, he was shown to a bench on the farthest end, where he sat with his co-accused. The gangster observed the silent courtroom. His investigators from the Mumbai Anti-Extortion Cell were absent, but many other police teams occupied the benches with their respective offenders, including Dawood Ibrahim's brother Iqbal Kaskar and nearly a dozen accused from various bomb blast cases in Mumbai. About half an hour later, the judge summoned Rahul to the witness box.

'Are you still fasting?' the judge asked the hitman.

'No, sir. I quit after Qilla Court allowed me a hearing, granted bail.'

'Good. What case was that?'

'Arms Act.'

The special public prosecutor, who was representing the state against Rahul, stood up, and narrated the charges against the extortionist, pertaining to the Khar shootout.

'What do you have to say about these allegations?' the judge turned to the gangster.

'False case, sir. They're lying.'

'And why will the cops implicate you?'

'For promotion, increment.'

As the audience laughed over Rahul's brazen reply, the judge continued: 'You've demanded bail. Convince me that you deserve it. You have five minutes.'

Rahul looked at the clock, noted it was 11.05 a.m., and started speaking. He went on to deliver an uninterrupted monologue of close to thirty-five minutes:

'There is no circumstantial or prima facie evidence that corroborates the prosecution's story, or proves my involvement in this crime, sir. This case, and all the allegations herein, is completely false and baseless.

'The prosecution states that I was involved in the Khar firing, where a security guard at the Raja Builders construction site in suburban Mumbai was injured. I would like to ask, what is the basis of this allegation? Have they retrieved the pistol used in the crime from me? No. Have they recovered the shooter's motorbike from me? No. The victims shared description of the shooter's clothes with the police. Have they recovered these clothes from me? No. Even the letter, which was dropped at the crime spot, its fingerprints did not match mine, nor did the handwriting. The prosecution's own experts have affirmed this, but they never presented these reports before you.

'Check my cell phone location on the day of the crime. Every handset has an IMEI number. If you trace it, you will know the user's location. Check my location, and see if I was in Khar that day. The cops checked my Call Data Records (CDR), and because their findings did not match their allegations, they did not produce my CDR in court as evidence.

'If you consider the witnesses' statements, including people from my neighbourhood, not one has said that they had seen the bike or pistols in my possession around the day of the crime. Hence, under the Intention, Motive, Preparation Act, the prosecution's allegations do not corroborate with the evidence presented. In fact, there isn't one piece of evidence that proves their ridiculous claims.

'On 27 February 2007, the Mumbai Police arrested me from Dombivli. Although they are supposed to produce me before the court within twenty-four hours, they did so on 2 March, and said that I was picked up from Mulund on 1 March. These are blatant, blatant lies. Please check my mobile location for 1 March. If it shows Mulund, I'm willing to spend the rest of my life in prison. Even the country-made pistol, which they claim to have recovered from me, it's a figment of their imagination. And yet, despite all their lies, the court granted them my custody. Thereafter, I was tossed between police stations, abused and beaten.

'A few months after my arrest, six chargesheets were slapped against me. I was named conspirator and shooter in cases I hadn't even heard of. They also threatened to book me in many, many other cases of extortion – every man whom Jaidev Reddy had threatened – from Lakshmiprasad Mittal, Cyrus Mistry and Mahesh Bhatt to Bhoomi Developers, Ronnie Screwvala and Pritish Nandy. The cops did not file charges against me in these cases because they got the real accused; they could not be bothered with more fake evidence to implicate me. You can check my records with Arthur Road Jail. Each of the investigating teams in these cases has taken my custody, tortured me to a point where the assault not only broke my bones, but also crushed my soul.

'I'm innocent, sir – and no innocent man can survive such humiliation. No family can survive such infamy. I often think of suicide. Why won't I? I have six false cases to fight, and no money.

'I come from a lower-middle-class family, and no lawyer has been willing to represent me for free. After hearing I was associated with Reddy, one advocate did show up, but kept asking me if money had arrived. I asked him where the cash would come from. He said Jaidev Reddy. I said I don't know any Jaidev Reddy, why will Jaidev Reddy send money for me? He never returned. What could I do to help the situation? Nothing. I had no money. How will I have money? I don't work for Reddy or the underworld.

'With all these arguments in view, it is my humble request that the honourable court grant me bail. There is no cognizable or non-cognizable complaint registered against me in any police station prior to my arrest and the entire story thereafter – the barrage of allegations – is purely false and malicious.'

'What's your qualification?' the judge asked Rahul after his speech, interrupting the silence that had gripped the courtroom.

'Twelfth standard, but I have studied computers. I'm a graphic designer,' said Rahul, sniffing to convey that he was crying. 'When will I get bail, sahib?'

'When's the case from?' the judge seemed to be convinced. Rahul's defence matched the evidence presented by the prosecution. The magistrate did not challenge his claims of torture either. It was a strong possibility. India had reported 55,991 complaints against police officers over the preceding year. The allegations included police excesses like illegal detentions, fake encounter killings, torture, indignity and extortion.

'From two years ago.'

'I'm granting you bail. However, looking at your situation, I don't think you can afford the bail amount of Rs 50,000. If you'd like, we can start the trial.'

The magistrate required the refundable amount since allegations against Rahul showed he wasn't a small-time criminal who could be let off on regular solvency certificates. He was a flight risk. There had to be a significant cash amount to guarantee he wouldn't go absconding.

Seeing Rahul confused, the judge turned to noted criminal defence lawyer Shahid Azmi, who was seated on the advocates' desk in front of the judge.

'Mr Azmi, this is a request. Would you be willing to represent these boys? They're poor, and cannot afford legal aid.'

'Of course, sir,' Azmi agreed.

The gangster was overjoyed, but he did not show it to the full courtroom. He pretended to wipe his tears, and walked to his co-accused. The men patted his back, aware of the magnitude of his feat. It was October 2009 and according to Rahul, only two other MCOCA accused had availed bail across Maharashtra that year. Those two had lawyers representing them, the gangster boasts, 'while I managed the impossible on my own.'

Over the next few weeks, advocate Gavaskar managed to secure bail for Rahul in his four Dombivli shootouts, arguing that he was framed. With those interim wins in each of his six cases, the hitman felt a mammoth sense of achievement. Just as he did when he won the cricket match for his team as a boy. Six wickets in six balls.

17

The Noble Terror-Accused

---◆---

Since his trial was to commence in the MCOCA case at the special Mumbai court, Rahul was transferred to the city's Arthur Road Jail in late 2009. Unlike his previous arrival, he entered the prison with aplomb. To ensure he was not treated like a petty criminal, he filed an assertive application as soon as he entered prison. A guard deftly fetched him his rights – a plate, two bowls, one spoon, a mug sans handle, a pillow, a bed sheet, a mattress and a blanket.

Anticipating trouble, the officials showed him to the murder barrack, and not the one with underworld gangsters as in his previous stay. Most murderers in India are first-time killers, who kill over personal grievances like love affairs and property disputes. Accommodating the hitman with murderers was safer as these criminals are typically regretful, and least likely to pick a fight with grouchy inmates like Rahul. The gangster did not mind the switch. He would learn something new, meet more prospective recruits.

As soon as he entered his barrack on the November evening, Rahul noticed a group of seven inmates seated on their mattresses under the television set. *They must be the terrorists*, Rahul thought to himself. He knew that such accused are usually housed in murder barracks, far from jingoistic gangsters, who tend to abuse and attack them. There were several other signs, too – their long beards and their attire of white lungis and shirts, the way they stayed confined to a corner of the barrack, how they did not mingle with inmates outside their group, and how others kept distance. At least four mattresses around them lay vacant: a foam-and-cotton line of control.

As he laid down his belongings in a corner of the barrack, Rahul's mind wandered to an instance from two years ago in the same prison. With terrorists from Lashkar-e-Taiba, Students Islamic Movement of India, Hizbul Mujahideen and other terror outfits confined at Arthur Road, their jail population had grown substantially at the time. Irked with ill-treatment from prison officials and other inmates, the terror-accuseds started chanting 'Pakistan Zindabad' one afternoon. As punishment, the men – around twenty of them – had to circle the prison compound on their knees for hours. Those who tried to get up were beaten back to the floor.

'Always keep away from them,' Gabbar had told Rahul. 'They hate India. They can never be true friends to an Indian.'

Over the next few days, Rahul learnt that the terror-accuseds in his barrack were held for perpetrating the 2006 Mumbai train bombings. The carnage, known as the 7/11 terror attacks, was a series of seven coordinated blasts in suburban trains over eleven minutes, which killed 189 and left over 800 injured. Rahul did not endorse the attack, but terror outfits had always piqued his curiosity. It was their flawless modus operandi that appealed to his criminal mind the most. It also got him interested in the workings of Al Qaeda, and made him build a bomb. A few days after his arrival in the barrack, Rahul walked to one of the men in the group and sat on a mattress next to him.

'I see that you keep reading law books,' the terror-accused told Rahul. He must be thirty-five years old, the gangster gauged. He had scanty hair on his head, and a beard that touched his belly. Fair and tall, with an athletic frame, he spoke slowly, as if filtering every word in his mind.

'I'm trying to defend myself in a false MCOCA case,' Rahul said, glad the man was willing to talk. Courtesy kept the gangster from asking him his name or making enquiries about the charges against him. Even if he did ask, Rahul knew the man would lie. In the past, the gangster had known a terrorist who, whenever probed, would say he had been wrongly picked up for possession of detonators. He was being tried for a series of five blasts over a period of eight months in 2002–03 in Mumbai.

'All cases are false unless proven otherwise,' the terror-accused replied. 'It's good that you're working on your own defence. Lawyers are crooks. If you know your case well, even the nuances, you have a better shot at freedom.'

'Yes, I've secured bail in my MCOCA and Arms Act cases solely on personal merit. My advocate managed bail for me in my other four cases. They've to do with shootouts in Dombivli,' Rahul informed, almost boastful.

'If you've secured bail in all your cases, why are you still here?'

'Because I can't afford the sureties. I have to pay Rs 30,000 for each of my four Dombivli cases, Rs 50,000 for my MCOCA case, and Rs 5,000 for the Arms Act case. That's a total of Rs 1.75 lakh. My family doesn't have that kind of money. Only option now is to come clean in my trial, get acquitted, and walk out.'

'I'll help you,' the man offered in his soft voice.

Over the next few days, Rahul got closer to the terror-accused. The alleged jihadi reminded him of Bhaijaan, the underworld verteran and his mentor, who was eventually sentenced to life imprisonment for killing Dawood's henchmen. Rahul never saw the sharpshooter after the verdict. The gangster tried visiting him in prison once, but returned disappointed. Bhaijaan had refused to see him. The reason, Rahul guessed, was probably the Reddy–Mahajan split. While Rahul had picked Reddy, Bhaijaan had remained loyal to Mahajan.

Still unaware of his name, Rahul started referring to the terror-accused as 'Bhaisahab'. He figured the man must come from an affluent household since he would have ample dry fruits and drank bottled water. *Or maybe the bomber's terror outfit really values him.*

Rahul noticed that Bhaisahab would offer namaaz five times a day, and would remain sombre, his body, mind and tongue always in control. He never complained about the stale chapattis or loud television set. While other inmates laughed and joked with each other, he did not mingle with any of them. While others hugged and exchanged high fives, he'd never touch another inmate or indulge in a display of emotions. He spoke, but he never revealed he was interested. He saw, but he never showed he was observing.

Soon, Rahul started occupying the mattress next to Bhaisahab, their discussions centred on the gangster's cases. Since the most elite Mumbai Police squad had investigated him, Rahul was particularly sceptical about his acquittal in the Khar MCOCA case. The terror-accused subscribed to no such pessimism.

'Indian cops are brilliant investigators. They'll get their men, no doubt. But when it comes to nailing those men, establishing their guilt in the court of law, that's where they fail. They're disturbingly bad with paperwork. It doesn't matter that Salaskar was your investigating officer. It's what he's written in your chargesheet that holds consequence. Forget investigations, focus on evidence,' Bhaisahab explained.

'Got it.'

'Did they put you through an identification parade in the Khar case?'

'Yes.'

'Did the security guards identify you?'

'No.'

'Fantastic,' Bhaisahab exclaimed.

After browsing through Rahul's chargesheet, he added, 'But here, it says that they have identified you as the shooter.'

'Fuckers are lying,' Rahul was enraged.

'That's okay,' said Bhaisahab. 'Start gathering information on other witnesses, especially police witnesses, who've recorded their testimonies, stating they were present when you were arrested or interrogated or when the cops made recoveries. Get background information on these men. If they have police cases against them or any form of bad repute, their testimonies will lose credibility. Also, cops are lazy. They tend to use the same police witnesses for multiple gangsters. Go around the prison, and see if any other inmate has the same witnesses as you. If they overlap, you're gold.'

An enthusiastic teacher, Bhaisahab introduced Rahul to special and local laws, prison encyclopaedias and historic criminal judgements. He explained trial procedures, the types of offences, their respective punishments, and arguments that worked in favour of past gangsters.

Following his conversations with the terror-accused, Rahul decided on a major overhaul in his behaviour. He decided that like Bhaisahab, he would not pick fights or get into brawls with other inmates. If he did, prison officials would keep close tabs on him and would go the extra mile to make his life difficult.

Bhaisahab had also told Rahul that judges are often influenced by their own personal observations of a criminal. Thereafter, Rahul decided he would not request his magistrates for any luxury in prison. Other gangsters, he told himself, were idiots. They would file applications after applications, asking the court to grant them access to milk, fruits, cottage cheese, expensive biscuits and other food items. Their inane victories not only irked prison officials, but also told the judge of the men's affluence, providing indirect tip-offs on their alliance with the underworld.

'Because they're able to get judicial sanction for escaping the dirty food here, people think these dons have it going for them,' the terror-accused told Rahul. 'But that's not the case. They're morons. Look your worst for your court hearings – no shoes, the flimsiest of slippers, old shirts instead of t-shirts, no handkerchiefs and no shaving. You will file no application, make no demand.'

The alleged jihadi's advice made sense to Rahul. The trick had already worked on his MCOCA judge, who sympathized with the gangster's limited means, and asked advocate Shahid Azmi to defend him. He would appear unkempt and broken, the hitman told himself. He would feign defeat to win.

About twelve years after he first got into the underworld, Rahul was finally willing to let go of his pride. He had found a decent reason for the charade: his freedom.

———————

'By showing me injustice, he taught me to love justice. By teaching me what pain and humiliation were, he awakened my heart to mercy. Through these hardships, I learned hard lessons. Fight against prejudice, battle the oppressors, support the underdog.'
                              – Words by Roy Black, a New York-based
                                       defence lawyer, often quoted
                                            by advocate Shahid Azmi

Azmi, who was representing Rahul in his MCOCA case, was no ordinary solicitor. A year younger than the gangster, he was known as 'the terrorist lawyer' in Mumbai's courtroom corridors. The reason lay in his own incarceration under the now-defunct Terrorist and Disruptive Activities Prevention Act.

Azmi was accused of being an active member of a militant organization in south Kashmir. In 1999, at the age of nineteen, he was arrested for conspiring to murder a political leader. He spent five years in New Delhi's maximum-security prison, Tihar Jail. After he was exonerated of the terrorism charges, he turned resolute to fight injustices like the ones he had endured. A separatist leader in Tihar had told him that a lawyer must be a people's lawyer. Following his release, Azmi moved to Mumbai, studied law, and soon grew to be one of the most prominent criminal lawyers in the fraternity.

Over a career spanning seven years until he took up Rahul's case, Azmi had secured acquittals for seventeen men charged with terrorism. At the time, he was representing over four dozen others, including an alleged accused in the 26/11 Mumbai terror attacks of 2008, which killed 164. Rahul, who knew of Azmi's credentials, was confident that his advocate would get him an acquittal.

'*Khuda pe bharosa rakho,*' the soft-spoken advocate would tell Rahul, 'and if you do walk out free, don't do anything that'll bring you back here.'

The gangster admired Azmi. Not only had he never asked Rahul for money, but he was also an intelligent lawyer. Rahul had heard him argue in the MCOCA court many a time. He was amazed at how the advocate could prove or disprove a man's guilt through the simplest, unlikeliest of questions. A passionate lawyer, he would delve into the minutest of details, securing improbable acquittals through the art of witness examination.

One such cross-examination also helped Rahul's case. The man in the witness box was Green Court's manager, Ramesh Jagtap. A police witness, Jagtap told the court that Rahul was his friend, and that the gangster would often boast about his connection with Reddy. The bar manager also stated that Rahul had informed him of his plans to fire at the Raja Builders construction site. Jagtap's statement made him a key prosecution witness – his claims established Rahul's association with Reddy, and also proved his involvement in the Khar shootout.

'Since when have you been working at Green Court?' Azmi initiated Jagtap's cross-examination before the full courtroom.

'Ten years.'

'How many floors does the bar have?'

'Ground plus one.'

'Where is your desk?'

'First floor.'

'What's on the ground floor?'

'Bar and restaurant.'

'What's on the first floor?'

'I just said my desk.'

'Is that all there is?'

'We host clients on the first floor, too.'

'How many tables does the bar have?'

'Nine on ground floor, twelve on first floor.'

'Where's the television set?'

'Both floors.'

'Where's the music system?'

'First floor only.'

'How many tube lights does your bar have?'

'Six on ground floor, two on first floor.'

'How many bulbs?'

'Two on ground floor, thirteen to fourteen on first floor.'

'Why such discrepancy?'

'We have music upstairs. Clients listen to music upstairs. Bulbs create ambience.'

'Ambience, right. How many waiters work in the bar?'

'Thirty-seven.'

'All men?'

'Twelve men, twenty-five women.'

'Where do the ladies work?'

'First floor.'

'You mean the floor with the bulbs?'

'Yes.'

'Ambience, yes. What work do women waiters do?'

'They serve food and drinks.'

'What work do male waiters do?'

'They serve food and drinks.'

'So men and women, both do the same job?'

'Yes.'

'If men and women do the same work, why does the women's floor need ambience?'

'...'

'Why the ambience for women waiters?'

'I don't know. You should ask the bar owner.'

'Right. When Rahul is alleged to have committed this crime, were these men and women in your employ?'

'Yes.'

'What about a year before? In 2005?'

'Yes, they've been with us for many years.'

'Noted. Have you ever been to a police station?'

'Yes, I keep visiting.'

'Why?'

'The cops come around 1 a.m. every night to shut the bar. So when I'm called to the police station, I present myself.'

'Is that the only reason why you've ever been to a police station?'

'No.'

'What else then?'

'I don't remember. I was booked for some petty offence.'

'Is sex-trafficking a petty offence?'

'No.'

'Then tell us more about the case.'

'The cops accused us of having underage girls as waiters in our bar. It was a false allegation.'

'So you have a police record, and you keep visiting police stations.'

'Yes.'

'Then if Rahul Jadhav had told you he was a gangster, that he was connected with Jaidev Reddy, and that he was planning the Raja Builders shootout, why didn't you alert the cops?'

'...'

'Why didn't you alert the cops?'

'Because I was afraid.'

'Of?'

'Rahul.'

'But you've said he's your friend, and that he'd share all of this with you boastfully. Was he your friend?'

'Yes.'

'Do people fear friends?'

'No.'

'Do people protect friends?'

'Yes.'

After the final question, the judge smiled. He was impressed with Azmi's cross-examination, which had discredited Jagtap's testimony as well as his credibility. The lawyer had established that the police witness had a criminal case of his own, and that despite dance bars being banned in 2005, he was running his establishment illegally. Worse, if his statement that Rahul was planning the Khar shootout was true, he was looking like a co-accused in the case, who had tried to shield the gangster from the police. With the immoralities in the manager's character and discrepancies in his testimony, the judge decided to drop his statement.

Over the next few hearings, more witnesses in the case collapsed. Like the bar manager, the cops had recorded testimonies of many persons who knew Rahul and his association with the underworld – his friends, the cybercafe owner, the mobile shop owner, the bar staff and bar dancers. Each of these witnesses either failed to depose or denied their statements or their testimonies, as in the case of the bar manager, and were dismissed by the court. There was one final hurdle though – the two security guards, who were posted at the construction site when the shootout took place.

Soon after Rahul's arrest, the duo were called to Arthur Road Jail for an identification parade. Rahul was asked to stand in a horizontal line with five other handcuffed men. The guards walked by each of them, trying to identify the shooter. Neither of them had pointed a finger at Rahul, but the police, in the chargesheet, alleged that both had identified him as the assailant. When the victim, Aniruddha Shukla was called to the witness box, the gangster was nervous.

'Shuklaji, is this the man who shot at you?' the prosecution lawyer pointed at Rahul, who stood in the opposite witness box.

'I don't recognize this man.'

'Are you sure?'

'Yes.'

'But the chargesheet says that Rahul is the man who tried to kill you. The police are absolutely sure of his role.'

'How many times do I have to say no?' the victim was angry. 'How many times am I going to be called here? I've been shot for no fault of my own. I've had to bear the pain and the expenses. Plus, I'm being called to the police station, jail, court, everywhere – again and again and again. How many times will you call me here?'

'You will be called,' the lawyer was irked, too.

'I won't come.'

'I'll have a warrant issued against you.'

With the men barking at each other, the judge intervened. 'You must cooperate, Shuklaji. We're trying to get justice for you here.'

'No, sahib. You're shoving justice down my throat. I'm looking for peace. I gave up on justice years ago,' the guard, who had to move back to his hometown following the firing, said. He was in no mood for courtesies.

'So I'll note that this isn't the man who shot at you,' the magistrate conceded.

'He isn't.'

'You may leave. Thank you.'

As the trial progressed, the second security guard also refused to identify Rahul as the shooter. The MCOCA judge, while announcing the gangster's acquittal on 21 January 2010, noted that since all key witnesses had denied his involvement in the shootout, the prosecution 'had miserably failed to establish Rahul's guilt'.

After his acquittal in the MCOCA case, Rahul was moved back to Kalyan's Adharwadi Jail. The extortionist was thrilled. He knew that the only roadblock between him and his freedom was the bail bond of Rs 1.25 lakh in his five remaining cases. He coaxed his kin to arrange the money. He made promises he knew he wouldn't deliver on, and he feigned sentiments he didn't care about. His parents approached friends and relatives, and managed the amount from Rahul's brother-in-law, Kishor.

'Do you think he'll mend his ways once he's out?' Kishor asked Rahul's parents before lending the money. 'If not, let him stay inside.'

'He will,' his father said, praying it were true.

18

A Much Darker Fantasy

━━◆━━

Rahul's heart had built a home in his past. When he learnt he could walk out of prison, having secured one acquittal and five bails, he was most excited about returning to his life as a gangster. He was dwelling in his past, unaware that his past, too, was looking to dwell in him – a much darker fantasy.

The cruel intentions of his old days became evident the moment Rahul pushed open the tall iron gate of Kalyan's Adharwadi Jail, and stepped out. His father, brother and two uniformed police officers stood waiting for him. The gangster walked to his father, smiled his widest smile, and shook the teary seventy-year-old's hand. A hug would be a tad too dramatic, he mused, despite all that had conspired. Mangesh bothered with no such restraint and locked his brother in a tight embrace.

'Okay, okay, enough,' the policemen intervened. 'Rahul Ramakant Jadhav aka Bhiku?'

'Yes,' Rahul was surprised.

'The ACP wants to see you.'

The officers told Rahul that he was being picked up as part of 'preventive and precautionary measures' under Section 110 of the CrPC, which classified the gangster as a man, 'who habitually commits the offence of extortion', and is 'so desperate and dangerous that him being at large cannot be without security hazards to the community'.

'But I've just walked out after three years in prison,' the gangster said. 'Let me go see my mother at least.'

'You can go. This won't take too long,' stated one of the officers. 'Pay Rs 10,000 as security for your good behaviour, and you're a free man.'

'Money for what?'

'You're a big Bhai, Bhiku sahib. The money is surety against your future deeds. It promises that now that you're back in the free world, you won't be a nuisance to us or our society,' said the officer, producing a magistrate's order.

The document was irrefutable. Rahul did as he was told. As the cops drove the trio to the assistant commissioner's office, the miffed gangster started arguing with the officers.

'Section 110, CrPC states that I have to be in your area of jurisdiction for you to pick me up,' Rahul quoted from his legal knowledge.

'So?'

'So I'm not in your area of jurisdiction. I barely stepped out of prison.'

'Prison falls under our area of jurisdiction. Next argument.'

'The law dictates that you're supposed to issue me a show cause notice. I have to reply to the notice, explaining why I shouldn't be asked to pay sureties for my good behaviour. If you do not find my response appropriate, only then can you ask me for a security bond.'

'So?'

'You cannot pick me up now.'

'So?'

'So you're breaching the fucking law.'

'Yes, I am. And I think you must do something about it. How about complaining to the ACP?'

When Rahul faced the ACP, he repeated his arguments, only to be snubbed.

'Four firings and Jaidev Reddy's right-hand man,' the ACP stated. 'You're an obvious threat, beta. You're lucky you're out. Now, we need to have some guarantee that you won't continue to be the cunt you've been.'

'But I can't afford the amount.'

'Bring me your father and your brother's original ID cards. You may take them back once you've paid the bond. Also, until then, you've to present yourself here every morning at ten, sign the register, and let us know that you haven't absconded,' the ACP instructed, and turned to Rahul's father, 'Will you make sure he obeys, sir?'

'I will, sahib,' said Ramakant, his eyes fixed to the floor.

It wasn't the cops, Rahul told himself. It was just another peril of his precious job. He decided that he would not let the episode bring him down. Albeit provisionally, he was a free man that day.

When Rahul entered his home, his mother opened the door. Shalini did not speak, walked to the kitchen, and got busy with her cooking. She returned after a minute, looked at Rahul for a few seconds, and went back to her gas stove. Two more trips later, as her puzzled family sat amused, she began talking.

'I've made your favourite gulab jamuns,' she said. 'Eat six of them. Remove those jail clothes. Put them to wash. I've bought a new pair for you. You'll look good in them. And take a bath. Look at that hair. It's touching your waist; it's longer than mine. And god, that beard. Looks like a beehive. I can't see your face behind it. I want to see your face.'

As Rahul got off his chair and hugged his mother, she broke down in his arms.

'It's been three years since I saw your face, Chotu,' she said.

'Why do mothers react to everything with tears and food?' Mangesh tried to lighten the mood. 'Come on now; get those gulab jamuns. It's time to celebrate.'

26/11 Defence Lawyer Shot Dead in Mumbai
12 February 2010, *PTI*

Shahid Azmi, the defence lawyer for 26/11-accused Faheem Ansari, was shot dead by three persons in his office at the Taximen's Colony in Kurla (West). According to the police, Azmi was in his office when, at around 7.45 p.m., three persons entered and shot five rounds at him from point-blank range.

Four bullets pierced the thirty-two-year-old criminal lawyer's chest and he was killed instantly. The police said that two imported weapons, a pistol and a revolver were used in the firing, indicating that it was not the handiwork of any local or small-time criminal.

Four years ago, on 18 October 2006, Azmi had said that he was being threatened by the underworld. His complaint noted he had received a phone call from a person claiming to be from the Jaidev Reddy gang. The anonymous caller had told Azmi that his movements were being monitored and that he would be killed at his residence or office in Kurla.

Rahul was at Green Court when news about Azmi's murder flashed across television channels. Only three weeks had passed since the advocate had argued for his release – Azmi's final win while he was alive. Upon watching the news, the gangster fell to pieces. It is difficult for incarcerated men like Rahul to forget those who've helped them when they're at their lowest, when the world, even their families, abandoned them. There is no reason for strangers like Azmi to help hitmen like Rahul. They do so only because they are good men. In an uncharitable world, they're balance.

Rahul imagined his lawyer's final moments – the bullets to his heart, and how they must have killed him the moment they tore his skin. He thought of his handsome face – those big, kind eyes, and how they may have opened wide when the guns were aimed at his chest, how they may have remained unblinking. The image made him guzzle drink after drink. A few hours later, with the television remote still in his hand, he passed out on the bar table. The following morning, he woke up to a call from Azmi's assistant lawyer.

'Rahul, did you do it?' the female advocate did not bother with courtesies.

Rahul was devastated at the suspicion. It was his past and its tireless chase again. 'How can you say that, madam? Of course, I didn't do it. I could never do it. He helped me when I had no one. I can kill for him, and he knew that. How could you accuse me of this?'

'I'm sorry,' the advocate softened. 'I asked because they're suspecting Reddy's involvement.'

'You know I haven't been in touch with Reddy for years.'

'I'm sorry.'

'How's his family keeping up?'

'Everyone is too shocked. He had been getting threats from the underworld for a while now. He had also asked for police protection. I don't know what's happening. This is all too sudden.'

Before Rahul could respond, she added: 'I'll speak to you later. Let me know if the gangsters in your network have any clues about the murderers.'

Over the next few days, Rahul would reach the bar at eleven every morning. He would read every newspaper, and watch every news report about the murder. Four days after the crime, the Mumbai Police announced the case solved with the arrest of three contract killers allegedly hired by the notorious gangster Bharat Nepali. The police stated that Nepali, an erstwhile Rajan associate, had ordered the hit to establish his supremacy in the underworld. The arrests brought some solace, but Rahul could not get over the loss. He also brought it up when he spoke to Reddy again.

———◦|◦———

Rahul was still in mourning when, in March 2010, his advocate in the Kalyan Sessions Court, Nikhil Gavaskar, called him to his office. As the two discussed the progress in his four firing cases, the advocate received a call on his cell phone, answered it, and handed the phone to Rahul.

'Reddy here,' the caller said.

Rahul could feel a lump growing rapidly in his throat.

'Anna,' he said, his voice breaking. 'Where were you? I tried so hard to get in touch. I told everyone to get my message to you, whoever I could tell.'

'I know, beta. I know. I'm sorry, very sorry,' the don said. 'I sent men for you in Kalyan as well as Arthur Road Jail, but they couldn't find you.'

'Possible,' said Rahul, certain his Bhai could never have abandoned him. 'I was constantly moving between prisons, police stations and cops.'

'Yes, Gavaskar recently told me all about it.'

'They beat me up, Anna. They beat me real bad,' said Rahul, swallowing the ball that had again found its way to his throat.

'I know, beta. I'm sorry you had to go through all that. How's your health?'

'It's good, Anna. Prison was all food, charas and some alcohol. I ate a lot during these three years. I've lost some weight because of the hashish, but I'm feeling much fitter than I did when I was arrested.'

'Good, good. Are you still drinking?'

'Yes.'

'Don't tell me you're still drinking like a madman.'

'I wasn't, but I got hooked again after Azmi's murder. He got me out of MCOCA, Anna, and he did not charge me a penny. The cops are saying that you'd been threatening him.'

The don didn't reply.

'Did you get him killed, Bhai?'

'No, I didn't,' said Reddy. 'But I'm glad someone did. One Pakistani pimp less.'

Rahul stayed silent. He did not agree with his boss, but he didn't want to irk him either.

'Are you still drinking that dirty whisky?' Reddy broke the silence.

'Yes.'

'Start with scotch, boy. Cheap liquor fucks you in the long run.'

'No money for scotch.'

'Don't worry, I'll fix that.'

'Thank you, Anna.'

'So what were they saying about me in prison? Many of our men are inside.'

'Everyone was cursing you, Anna. They're all waiting for you to send money.'

'Arre, I understand. But how many men should I send money for? All my boys were locked up at the time, from Thane and Mumbai. You were in with ten of your co-accused. Plus, who could I have sent the money with? There's no one left outside. I'm not in India. How could I find trustworthy men to bring you the cash? I couldn't give it to just anyone. Had they farted to the police, the cops would have screwed you harder.'

'You could have sent it with the lawyer, or you could have just sent a lawyer.'

'I did. It was soon after you were arrested, at your very first hearing.'

'He was no good. He kept asking for money. I did not have money. I wasn't even paid for my last firing. My family had to pay for my lawyers and the bail bonds. You should have got me out, Anna. Whatever I did, I did it for you. Not as an employee, not as a recruit, as a brother. What if I were convicted in that MCOCA case? The cops were out to fuck me up. They slapped false cases on me and were threatening me with more.'

'I'm sorry for all the trouble you've been through, beta. I promise, no more.'

'It's not all your fault, Bhai. You'd asked me to be careful, to not sit in the same bar. It's me who didn't listen.'

'That's okay, child. It's over now. I'm sure Gavaskar will get you acquittals in your remaining cases.'

'Let's start afresh, Anna,' said Rahul. 'If nothing else, prison has added to my profile. Many more people fear me now. Money is waiting to flow in. I'll make the calls, and our boys will pick up the cash. That way, I'll have time to focus on Mumbai; turn the storms there, as we had planned.'

'Yes, that would be great.'

'Please write down my number.'

'No, don't give me the number you're using. The cops might be tapping that one. Get a new one, and ask Gavaskar to pass it on to me.'

'I'll do that, Anna.'

'Gavaskar will give you Rs 50,000 in cash. It's for you, but don't drink too much. Spend it on your family. And take good care of your health. I'll get in touch soon.'

'I'll wait for your call.'

Although his family had sold or mortgaged every little possession they had to secure his release, Rahul spent the money on alcohol. He would pay them back later, he told himself. Now that Anna was back, there would be no dearth of cash. Soon after the conversation, Rahul returned to his gangster life – drinking three quarters of a bottle of whisky a day, frequenting dance bars, and looking for friendships in the free alcohol he offered his bar mates. Soon, his joy grew manifold. Gavaskar had managed to get him an acquittal in the Anish Shah firing case.

Rahul had claimed trial, pleading not guilty to the crime. His defence, as in all the cases against him, was that of total denial. In the judgement delivered on 24 May 2010, the Additional Sessions Judge stated his findings as follows:

ALLEGATIONS	FINDINGS	REASONS
Does the prosecution prove that on 6 July 2006 at 6.15 p.m. in the shop of the complainant, Anish Shah, the three accused [Rahul, Machmach and Kaalya] along with absconding accused Jaidev Reddy, in furtherance of their common intention...?		
...committed house-trespass by entering into the shop of Anish Shah, having made preparation for causing hurt to him?	Negative	When Anish Shah was asked to identify the accused present in Court, he stated that these were not the same persons who had come to his shop and fired a shot.

...fired a shot at Anish Shah with such intention that if their act had caused his death and that of Vicky Sachdev, they would have been guilty of murder?	Negative	Vicky Sachdev, an employee of Shah's neighbouring shop, had received an injury after the shot was fired. He says that he had not seen anybody when the shot was fired.
...in order to commit extortion, put Anish Shah in fear of death?	Negative	It is the case of prosecution that two pistols were seized from the possession of the accused [Machmach and Kaalya]. The pistols, according to the prosecution, were used in committing this crime. But the prosecution has failed to produce the said pistols.
...committed criminal intimidation by threatening Anish Shah with injury to his person with intent to cause harm to him?	Negative	The prosecution has examined Dr Surendra Wankhede, and has brought on record the injury certificate of Anish Shah. The doctor states that on 6 July 2006 at 10.40 p.m., he had examined Anish in Kalyan Dombivli Municipal Hospital. He found that Anish had sustained contusion over the upper part of the lateral side of left thigh, circular in shape, and diameter 5 centimetres. Since Anish does not say that he had received the injury at the hands of these accused, the evidence of this witness also does not assist the prosecution.

What order?	Accused are acquitted.	The above evidence clearly shows that eye witnesses failed to support the case of the prosecution. Absolutely no evidence is brought on record by the prosecution to prove its case. In view of these facts, the accused are entitled to be acquitted.

Even three months after his conversation with Reddy, the don hadn't called Rahul. The gangster decided that instead of waiting anxiously for his Anna, which made him jump every time his phone rang, he would start laying the groundwork for his return to the world of organized crime. Smarter after his arrest, he now knew better than leaving a trail of cybercafe owners and telephone booth operators behind. He decided he would first buy a laptop for his research, and multiple cell phones and SIM cards for his extortion calls. The purchases required money, and the cash his don had given had drained out.

'My parents have been through a lot of heartache. I need to start working,' Rahul approached a real-estate developer in Dombivli, who also knew his family. The gangster had decided on politeness since he knew the cops were watching him. It would be stupid to have eyebrows raised without the don by his side. 'To start work, I need to buy a laptop.'

'Will Rs 40,000 be enough?' the developer asked.

'Yes,' Rahul was surprised at his quick compliance. Prison had indeed added to his clout, he mused.

'Don't you dare think I'm paying you out of fear,' the builder interrupted his thoughts. 'I'm doing it for your parents. They are good people. Mend your life.'

'I will.'

Rahul took the money, and bought a laptop for Rs 37,000. Similarly, he told one of his bar friends that he needed cash for his daily expenses. The friend, whom Rahul had treated to alcohol and women several times over the years, obliged with Rs 25,000 in cash. Rahul purchased three mobile phones with the money, and as many SIM cards. When the basic paraphernalia for his extortion racket was ready, he started with his research. He returned to the internet, and once again began extracting numbers of prospective extortion victims. The future looked promising, but Rahul's past had other plans.

Two men shot dead at Andheri building site
15 March 2011, *Hindustan Times*

Two men at a construction site in Andheri (W) were shot dead by unidentified men, allegedly from the Jaidev Reddy gang. Yogesh Khule, 29, site supervisor, and Samrat Devarsia, 28, the site engineer, were shot at point-blank range. While in Khule's case the bullet pierced his right eye, in Devarsia's case, the bullet hit him in the head. He died during treatment. Khule, a resident of Navi Mumbai, had got married just a month ago.

Before fleeing, the two men left a letter with an international number and Jaidev Reddy's name on it. Crime Branch sleuths suspect that the shoot-out could well be a desperate attempt by Jaidev Reddy to regain his turf in Mumbai's extortion market which he had lost following the arrest of several of his gang members.

Three days after the shootout at Reddy's behest, while Rahul was asleep, two armed police officers barged into his home. Before the gangster could react, they shoved him into a police van with his father. Rahul sat between the two cops, his father in front of him. As the van raced towards Mumbai, the officers started beating Rahul – slaps across his face, kicks on his legs, blows to his head, and a shower of abuses.

'What have I done?' Rahul tried to speak between the assaults as his father begged for mercy.

'You'll know soon.'

At Andheri's DN Nagar Police Station in suburban Mumbai, Rahul was told that he had been picked up for investigations in the double murder case. The gangster had read about the killings in a newspaper. His thoughts had fleeted to Reddy, who was active on ground, yet hadn't called him.

'I haven't done it,' Rahul told the cops.

'That is for us to decide,' the investigators moved him to an interrogation room. Three policemen surrounded Rahul as he sat on a wooden chair in the middle of the room. Ramakant stood in a corner.

'I was in Dombivli when the murders happened. You can check with the bar where I was sitting. You can also check my cell phone tower location,' Rahul offered.

'I will check, yes,' said the only plain-clothed officer among the three. 'Now, tell me, how did you get in touch with Jaidev Reddy?'

'I've explained everything to the Mumbai Anti-Extortion Cell as well as the Thane Police. I have nothing new to say.'

'I know. You're here on their reference,' replied the officer. 'Now, answer my questions, or you know the consequences.'

Thereafter, Rahul was put through a barrage of enquiries: Since when had Reddy been planning the double murder? Did you source the Andheri developer's number for him? If not you, who could have murdered the two men? Could they be contract killers or history sheeters? Who are Reddy's gangsters in Mumbai? Look at these pictures – could any of these be the murderers? What threats did you leave unfinished? What must Reddy be thinking now? Did he tell you of his plans? What else is going to happen in Mumbai?

If Rahul answered, the cops would move on to the next question. If he did not, they'd put him through rigorous rounds of whipping and beating. As the gangster shrieked in pain, his father stared emptily. His son's responses told him that he was indeed a gangster, close to one of the most dreaded dons in the underworld. The denial, which he had been dearly clutching on to, was shattered.

'I need you to call Jaidev Reddy right now, and get me the murderers' names,' the plain-clothed officer told Rahul.

'But I don't have his number. I haven't spoken to him in years.'

'I'll give you the numbers.'

A cop then took Rahul to an STD booth, and handed him five A4 sheets with at least 190 international numbers printed on them – numbers that Reddy had doled out to his extortion victims over the years.

'Dial each and every number until you have your boss on the line,' the escorting cop instructed.

While some numbers were off and others were not reachable, many were invalid. After calling over two dozen numbers, the gangster was exhausted.

'I told you I'm not involved in this. Why are you harassing me?' Rahul barked at the escort.

'Because your Bhai is harassing us, you son of a bitch,' the cop slapped him. 'Tell him not to trouble us, and we won't trouble you.'

Rahul sat in the booth for over two hours, dialling and redialling in vain. When he returned to the police station, he saw the plain-clothed officer shouting at Ramakant.

'If he doesn't give us the information we need, we will have each of your family members locked up,' the cop threatened. 'I won't spare your women either.'

The gangster felt sorry for his father. That kind, tiny man, his downcast gaze, his trembling chin, and his hunched shoulders. Rahul wanted to charge at the officer, beat him with fists and blows until he lay soaked in his own blood. The gangster could feel his muscles tighten, and his body turn hot. Aware that assault would be unwise, he spat the fury, walked to his father, and put an arm around his old man.

'Oye, Bhiku, I will call you again,' the officer warned as the two began to leave. 'This isn't over.'

19
The Burden of Guns

———◆———

To Rahul, crime had been easy. Being a criminal wasn't. What started with the double murder at Andheri quickly escalated to an average of two police summonses each month for the next two years. Cops from various police stations, the Crime Branch and anti-extortion units in Mumbai and Thane would call Rahul. Some suspected his role in Reddy's latest crimes, some hoped for intelligence on the don and his foot soldiers, and still others issued unofficial notices to monitor him. They would call him late at night, and as early as four in the morning. They would abuse him and thrash him. And they'd threaten to kill him in encounters. With fifty-three such instances, investigators managed to turn his life into hell, trapping the demon where he belonged.

Rahul would get paranoid every time his phone rang. He could not throw the handset away, confident the cops would come home. They had often arrived unannounced. While most had been courteous with his family, many hadn't. They would question his kin, or grab his father by the collar. To put an end to it all, Rahul thought of skipping bail and running away. He did not. He

222

couldn't have his family inherit his past, or the burden of his guns. The frustration remained with him, and quickly turned him into a chronic alcoholic. In his family's words, he became 'a monster'.

Once, in mid 2011, Rahul asked his father for money to pay his lawyer, who was representing him in the Arms Act case in a Mumbai court. The family – Rahul's parents and his brother – was watching television in their living room when the inebriated gangster, who had just returned from his bar, made the request.

'Why don't you ask your Anna for the money?' Mangesh replied for their father. 'You worked for him, you went to jail for him. He should be the one paying your lawyer's fee. Why us?'

'Aye, shut the fuck up,' said Rahul, barely able to stand straight. 'Speak when you're spoken to.'

'Look at you, Chotu,' said Mangesh as their parents watched in distress. 'Look what you've become. Despite all that we've done for you, look how you're speaking to me.'

'Ma and Baba have done everything. You haven't done shit,' he said, the alcohol throwing up words he probably did not mean.

Mangesh lost his cool. He leapt off his chair, and slapped his younger brother. As Rahul collapsed to the floor, he barked, 'Maderchod, what do you know? Do you think I was jerking off when you were inside those fucking prisons? I searched police stations, courts and jails to find you. I went begging around the world to get money for your bail. I went to our cousins, our brother-in-law, to every fucking one I knew. I've been meeting with your lawyers, paying them. Do you think they're working for you for free? Do you think you're some big Bhai? No. They're doing it because we, all of us, have given up everything we had only so that you could stand here. Why does Baba at seventy have to go to the police station? Why is Ma popping those pills? It's all because of you. No girl is willing to marry me because of you.'

Rahul jumped to his feet, 'No one's marrying you because you're an ugly buffalo, you stupid fuck. Don't you dare touch me again, or I'll kill you. One bullet. That's all it'll take to shut that trap of yours.'

'Kill me,' said Mangesh, now inches away from the hitman's face. 'Come on, do it now.'

Rahul rushed to the kitchen to fetch a knife. When he returned, his mother stood before Mangesh.

'Get out at once,' she said, her eyes bloodshot and voice shaking. 'Now!'

Rahul left, but not before pulling the television set off its stand, and bashing it against a wall. Mangesh had bought that TV for their family with his first pay cheque. Taken aback by the violence his brother now seemed capable of, Mangesh stood mum. The gangster laughed at the broken shards, and walked away.

—◆—

Considering all the facts, and if testimonies of witnesses are taken into consideration, there is suspicion created in the mind about happening of the alleged incident, and seizure of firearms from the possession of accused. Therefore, considering the evidence placed on record, the prosecution has miserably failed to prove its case. Accused Rahul Ramakant Jadhav @ Bhiku Mhatre is hereby acquitted under offences punishable under the Indian Arms Act.
— Judgement passed by the Additional Chief Metropolitan Magistrate, Esplanade Court, Mumbai
25 August 2011

After borrowing more money from relatives, Rahul's family had paid his lawyer, who was representing him in the Arms Act case in a Mumbai court. Salaskar's squad could not prove the story of his arrest, or that they had recovered a country-made pistol from him. Rahul was confident he would come clean in this case. Once he did, he had acquittals in three of his six cases. As the police's chargesheet again failed to prove its allegations against the extortionist, Rahul thought of Bhaisahab. The terrorist was right: The brilliant investigtors were poor penmen. The gangster felt optimistic about his freedom, albeit conditionally.

'We'll pay for your lawyer in the remaining cases only if you take up a job,' Rahul's mother told him, hoping that work would keep him busy and far from brawls and alcohol. 'Find a job or go back to prison.'

Rahul had little choice. Reddy hadn't called, and the Andheri cops, who were investigating the double murder, had taken away his laptop. They had sent the computer to a forensic science laboratory to determine if it had incriminating content, if Rahul was still in touch with his don. The gangster had also run out of acquaintances to borrow money from. His accomplices – friends he was closest to – weren't around either. Some were still in prison, while others had decided to keep away from him. Lonely, Rahul would spend his days and nights in the bar with other naaka regulars – men he had known but never trusted.

With no cash, friends or his Anna, Rahul figured a job would be useful, especially with the relentless cop summons. Every time a police officer questioned him, the first thing he would ask was, 'What are you doing these days?' Rahul's response of 'nothing' only made suspicions stronger: An idle gangster is a devil in his workshop.

'I'm not giving up on my underworld dream,' the extortionist reasoned, 'I'm only making a temporary diversion – until Anna calls.'

To find a job, Rahul had to first ready his curriculum vitae. He went to a cybercafe, and studied a few samples online. He realized it was impossible for him to make one. What would he write? What was he doing for fifteen years after his class twelve? It wasn't that he hadn't worked hard. It wasn't that he hadn't been exceptional. He was a Bhai – Reddy's top lieutenant, who had brought the highest and the mightiest to their knees. He had offered a lot of blood, brain and sweat to get there. Yet somehow, none of his accomplishments seemed good enough for the CV.

'Fuck this shit,' the gangster told himself. 'I can't waste the reputation I've built. I've given this work twelve years of my life, three more in prison. I've worked hard. And now, when it's time to encash the dividends, I can't do a nine to five and waste this.'

For the next few months, Rahul returned to extortion. He would threaten local shopkeepers and small-business owners, earning Rs 5,000 each time. Some paid out of pity, some out of fear. The gangster realized that he had sprung back to the petty extortion gigs of his initial underworld days but kept up with the crimes. He needed cash to afford his cigarettes, whisky and bar dancers. Trouble arrived only when one of his victims approached the police against the extortionist. As his threats were only verbal, the cops let Rahul off with an admonition: 'You've been an MCOCA accused. It's highly justifiable for us to kill you. Mend your ways, or kiss your life goodbye.'

The warnings soon grew violent. In September 2011, three renowned Bollywood personalities – actor Vivek Oberoi, actor-producer Sohail Khan and producer Ritesh Sidhwani – received extortion threats from Reddy, and were quickly provided police protection. A *Times of India* report revealed that the ganglord had targeted more Bollywood eminents. It said, 'This year, six film personalities, including the patriarch of one of Bollywood's biggest banners, got ransom demands of Rs 5 crore from Reddy. However, none of them lodged a police complaint.'

With a fresh campaign against Bollywood, Reddy was trying to make up for the losses, which accompanied the arrests of his many lieutenants over the past few years. To contain his reign of extortion, the Mumbai Police started hunting down his known associates, including Rahul. The summons and interrogations rocketed. The beatings and torture turned bloodier. The random police visits at his residence increased and the tension with his kin rose. *Maybe there is something wrong with me*, the hitman, who seemed to have hit his lowest, questioned himself for the first time. *Not everyone who has opposed or abandoned me – Dina, Aarti, my family, my friends, cops and my Anna – could have been wrong.*

Through a bar friend's reference, Rahul secured an interview with a Mumbai-based call centre. He did not get the job: he wasn't fluent in English. He considered working as a deliverer with a local courier service, but decided against it. A Bhai for a parcel boy would be too embarrassing. He then thought of approaching local businessmen for help, but his bar mates advised against it.

'You've terrorized these men, Bhai,' they said. 'You've made them shit their pants. And now you'll ask them for help. No, no. How would that look? What will people say? No, no, no. We cannot let you do that. It's beneath you.'

The men would put Rahul on a pedestal, and he would enjoy the puffery. He was still to realize that his precious, bullet-studded underworld crown no more existed. The don, his blessings were gone. The company, its clout, gone. The bundles of cash, his pistols, gone. What remained was a gangster's arrogance. And in his line of work, vanity sans guns meant barking dogs.

––•––

Two months after Reddy's threats to Bollywood bigwigs, Rahul joined a Thane-based razor manufacturing plant as a quality inspector – the work Ramakant did at the same firm. Rahul could not believe the job was his only option. All his years, he had wanted to be farthest from his father's tacks. Yet, here he was, in the midst of life and its annoying full circles.

When a hung-over Rahul reached the two-storey factory on the day of his induction, he was told he was being employed as a trainee. His monthly salary would be Rs 6,100, and his job was to ensure that razors produced in the factory lived up to prescribed standards. The unit employed over four dozen people, including a manager, two supervisors, forty-eight labourers who worked on twenty-four machines, and two quality inspectors other than Rahul.

To understand the technicalities, the gangster was handed a book on plastic engineering, which introduced him to ideal tower temperatures, melting point of plastic, how razor handles and blade cartridges are created and the types of probable defects. His supervisor also showed him around the blade-manufacturing machines to explain the process: steel is heated in furnaces, then cooled in freeze chambers and heated again. After rounds of coating to minimize friction and grinding to ensure sharp edges, the blade is ready to be attached to its plastic parts.

The job was of no interest to Rahul, the compensation humiliating. The gangster still decided to stick around – to shut the cops up, and to afford his daily half bottle of Bagpiper whisky, which cost Rs 286. Once he started with the job, Rahul couldn't drink the full bottle he used to, working his alcohol sessions around his shifts – if he was on the day shift, he'd drink at night; if he was working night, he'd drink in the afternoon; and for evening shifts, he'd get drunk in the morning. With his strong will, it was easy to find a way to the bar.

Over the next few weeks, Rahul made peace with his new life – an eight-hour job, five-hour alcohol sessions, six-hour sleep, and the remaining time on many days at police stations. His supervisors had no complaints about his work, but as the days passed he got closer to factory employees, which started creating trouble. Once, a labourer borrowed his cell phone to make a call and noticed that Rahul had only three numbers in his phonebook – his home landline, his sister's cell, and a friend's whom he would drink with.

'You're thirty-five years old, Rahul sir, and you only have three numbers. Meaning, you never made friends with anyone in thirty-five years?' the man asked Rahul.

'I have memorized all the numbers,' the gangster replied. Since most cops would ask questions about numbers in his phone book during summons, he had deleted all his contacts.

'And you haven't memorized your family's numbers?'

Unsure of the reply, Rahul walked away. However, he did not enjoy the luxury each time. Once, a quality-inspector colleague ventured into his professional history.

'What's your salary?' he asked.

'Rs 6,100.'

'That's it?' he was surprised. 'Where were you working before this?'

'Another manufacturing company.'

'Don't you think you're paid too little?' the man asked, confused. 'I'm eight years younger than you, but I draw Rs 15,000. I have one lakh rupees in my provident fund. You're thirty-five. You must have worked for at least twelve years. Why are you getting paid so little? Our supervisor is a class eight dropout, much younger than you. He's paid Rs 25,000. They're exploiting you. You must protest.'

'You're right,' said Rahul. 'I'll talk to the supervisor.'

'I'll come with you if you want,' he offered. 'I'll tell everyone to come.'

'No, no,' said Rahul. 'Let me have the first conversation. I'll tell you if he doesn't listen.'

When it wasn't questions about his professional life, it would be discussions around his marital status. Rahul's colleagues would pester him to get married.

'Look at your age. How will you go through life all alone?' his colleagues would worry aloud. 'What about sex? Sex is very important for a man's well-being. Are you having any? You must get it up and running once in a while. It keeps you potent. I'm telling you, you must get married. Are you dating anybody? No? Why don't you tell your parents to find you a wife? It'll be difficult because you're so old. But you can always find a divorcee. I know one, I can introduce you.'

To deter the persistent marriage proposals and sex-for-potency campaigns, Rahul, in mid 2012, distributed three boxes of sweets among his factory's employees. The celebration, he said, was because he had tied the knot with a woman named Shabana Qureshi, whom he had met on a train.

When congratulatory messages reached Rahul's father, the old man was stumped. It took substantial convincing before his parents believed that he had cooked up the lie to dodge his colleagues. At work, meanwhile, his fictitious wife led to many more confrontations, many more lies.

'Today, when you go home, refer to your wife as "Begum sahiba". She'll really like it,' a Muslim labourer once suggested to Rahul.

'Sure.'

'You must also read the Quran Sharif to understand her culture and beliefs.'

'Yes, of course.'

'I could read it to you after work if you like.'

'No, no. I'll tell her to take me through it. She'll be happy to.'

Rahul's job had begun to soften him, slowly leading to an overhaul in his self-image: from a dreaded, prodigious gangster to a meagre, easily replaceable, trainee. Eight months into the job and many instances of police assaults later, he was also beginning to resent his don and the whole universe of crime. They had left him as a man of no worth, he realized. Fifteen years, and he had nothing to show for them. All his criminal past did was pester his present, cast a shadow on his future.

Although Rahul was settling in at his workplace, there was one major hurdle: asking his supervisor for leaves to attend police summonses. Since his employers did not know about his murky past, he would ask for holidays, citing reasons like a relative had passed away, another was getting married, and yet another was having a baby. With repeated calls from the police, the gangster was running out of excuses. To worsen the leave crisis, court hearings in his remaining three cases got more frequent around mid 2012, demanding his presence.

In October that year, Rahul decided to quit the job. He was at the factory when three police officers came looking for him at his workplace. One of Reddy's gangsters, who had murdered three men in suburban Mumbai, was shot dead in an encounter. The cops wanted intelligence on the slain gangster's accomplices.

The supervisor summoned Rahul. As soon as the cops spotted him, they grabbed him by the nape of his neck and shoved him into their van.

'What's happening?' the supervisor was stunned.

'Nothing at all, sir. They're my friends,' Rahul hoped his boss would believe him since the Crime Branch officers were dressed in plain clothes. 'They're just messing around.'

'What friends pay visits with pistols and rifles?'

Rahul did not respond. Lying further would be futile, even silly. The following day, he put in his papers. He had the perfect excuse for his parents: He could not disfigure the reputation his father had built over decades of work at the firm.

—‖—

When Rahul returned to his alcoholism after quitting the job, drinking five quarters of whisky each day, he realized the ethanol was not working on him any longer. Despite the exorbitant consumption, he would remain worried over cop summons, jumping out of his skin every time his phone or the doorbell rang. To suppress the nagging fear, he would drink more and started indulging in cheap, local variants of drugs. The intake, as in his underworld days, led to instant diarrhoea if he ate, and he again started going without food for days. He'd stay lost in his inebriated stupor, waking up in gutters, abandoned buildings and footpaths.

As days melted into weeks, the extreme consumption started perpetuating paranoia. Rahul would feel he was being trailed, that some people were conspiring against him, and that just at the turn of the road, armed men were waiting to shoot him dead. He would keep switching bars, and he would brawl with strangers if they spoke over the phone, suspecting they were calling the cops on him. By the end of 2012, the hitman would also have frequent flashes from his past – shooting at innocent men and being chased. The conclusions to the images were always far from reality. Each time, in the end, he lay on a street, bleeding.

The gangster realized he needed something stronger to freeze out his mind. He found the answer in his mother's antipsychotics. Shalini would take half a pill every night to suppress the imaginary voices that had started calling out to her after her son's arrest. Hoping to kill his own voices, Rahul began to abuse the psychiatric medicine, consuming three pills daily. The dose would make his tongue heavy, and deaden his hyperactive mind. It would push him into a state of conscious drowsiness, where, although awake, he would forget all he had been, and all he had been through. Sitting in a corner of his home, he'd keep staring at a wall – calm, quiet, lost.

Since the pills were working, Rahul doubled the dose, using his mother's prescription to buy the medicine. Within two months, he became a madman. One afternoon, he did not emerge from the bathroom for four hours. His worried family broke the door down. The gangster was standing under the running shower, his clothes drenched, his eyes staring at the floor, looking at nothing. Another time, he returned from his bar, wearing only a vest and underwear. He realized his clothes were missing only when his mother questioned him.

'I know I had my clothes on – pants, one shirt,' he said, his eyes unblinking, his body shivering. 'Do you know where they are, Ma?'

'Where all did you go like this?' his mother asked, worried and furious.

'Where did I go?' he asked blankly. 'See, my vest and underwear, they're here. Let me go look for the rest.'

As he reached for the doorknob in his undergarments, his mother stopped him.

'I'm begging you, don't leave the house,' she said. 'Drink here, smoke here. Every time you go out, there's a problem. The other day, you were condoling with our neighbour for her husband's death. The man is alive and healthy. I'm very worried, Chotu. What has happened to you? What have you done to yourself?'

'Did you take my pants and shirt, Ma?' the semi-naked gangster asked in a monotone.

Rahul's health had deteriorated to the extent where he could not tell morning from evening. He could not cross the road without help, and had difficulty aiming his cigarettes on flames to light them. Every few hours, he would check newspapers to ascertain the date. When he couldn't read the time on clocks, he would crouch in a corner of his home, yelling in frustration. A rhythmic flow would govern the switch between his moments of sanity and insanity. Lights would become shadows, and colours would glow and fade. His acquittal in his remaining three cases is still a haze to him.

In each of the cases – the firings at politician-businessman Rajabhau Patkar's mall, Durian Furniture shop owner, Mohan Mavani, and head of Kalyan Dombivli Builders Association, Rajesh Mejari – the cops failed to prove their allegations. More than half a decade had lapsed between the crimes and their final hearings. The intervening years had blurred memories, and most victims and witnesses failed to identify Rahul as the shooter.

In the Mavani trial, the victim did recognize Rahul, but the judge dismissed the testimony, noting, 'Vague identification after more than six years after the incident, which the witness (Mavani) himself is doubtful about, leads to the inevitable conclusion that the identification of the accused is not free of doubt. Needless to say that benefit of the doubt is required to be given to the accused.'

The cops, too, committed many blunders, which failed their allegations against the gangster:

- Failure at witness deposition – many police witnesses did not show up or turned hostile.
- Revolvers, allegedly recovered from the accused, were never produced before the court.
- Chits with Reddy's numbers, allegedly recovered from the crime scene, were never placed on record.
- Although they claimed to have obtained handwriting specimens from Rahul to prove he had written those chits, investigators didn't place the handwriting experts' reports on record.
- Reports from ballistic experts were never shared with the court.
- A total of ten men were accused of being Rahul's accomplices. But the police didn't attribute specific roles to them in the crimes, nor did they produce convincing incriminating evidence against them.

While acquitting Rahul and his accomplices, the judge noted: 'It must be kept in mind that only the fact that the victim had sustained injuries and that the alleged offense occurred is not sufficient to discharge the burden of the prosecution. It is also necessary for the prosecution to establish that the accused and none else are the perpetrators of the crime beyond all reasonable doubt. All in all, evidence on record is severely short of sufficiency to make out the prosecution case.'

Rahul still doesn't remember how and why the courts set him free. He just knows he'd had enough to drink that night.

20
Chains

———•———

His arms, legs and stomach strapped tightly on a hospital bed, Rahul bellowed in pain. Three days had passed since his last drink, and alcohol withdrawals had commenced torture. His pupils enlarged, his body was riddled with frantic shivers, and his heart thumped furiously. He sweated and vomited. His head throbbed in pain, and his shaky voice begged for alcohol: 'One peg of whisky, just one, please.'

Exhausted, he passed out, only to tremor frenziedly. It was Thatrak again – the beast from his childhood nightmares, inching close, threatening to eat him up.

'No, Thatrak, no,' the thirty-eight-year-old gangster murmured in his sleep. 'I won't drink, I promise. Just go away, please. Please.'

When he woke up, Rahul asked to be allowed to the bathroom, and locked the door. Frustrated with his unabated craving, he balled his fingers to a fist and drove them through a glass mirror. He returned to the hospital bed bleeding, and told the doctors to tie him up again.

It was Rahul who had asked his family to refer him to a doctor. Although the courts had declared him innocent, his addictions continued. His frame of mind had changed – from tense to happy, but the bottles and pills remained as many.

Once, in March 2013, Rahul woke up in a gutter outside his building. His clothes were torn. He had scratches all over his face and limbs and his body ached. He was barely able to pull himself out of the nullah. His parents took him to a doctor, who informed them that Rahul had suffered two hairline fractures. As hard as he tried, he could not tell how he landed those bruises. The alcohol overdose had led to a complete blackout the previous night.

'I'm losing control, Ma,' the gangster told his mother the following morning, 'I think I'm going mad.'

His mother, already teary, knew he was right. She had seen him struggle to read simple sentences in newspapers. He would keep asking if the cops had come looking for him, if he really had been acquitted in all his cases. He could not retain answers, and kept asking the same questions over and over again.

'I feel scared all the time, Ma. There's nothing else I feel, only fear,' he confided in his mother, 'I feel like my head is a tiny, dark room, and I'm sitting in a corner all alone. There are loud noises, like gunshots, and the smell of blood. The unmissable stench of blood. I've shut my eyes tight, my palms have covered my ears, and my nose is pressed against my arm. But I can still see, hear and smell everything. It's scary, this dungeon in my head. I want to get out of it, Ma. Please bring me out of it.'

Rahul's family referred him to a psychiatrist. To make a diagnosis, the doctor showed him pictures with various patterns like a barbed wire maze and a mesh of colours. He asked Rahul what he saw in those images. 'Mountains,' he said. Also: 'A lake, ghosts, a few pregnant women and a naked one'. The doctor started his treatment for schizophrenia.

After visiting the therapist, Rahul stopped abusing his mother's pills. He had realized they were flirting with his sanity. Yet, the psychiatist's medicaments did no good since the gangster, after borrowing money from just about anyone, continued with his alcohol consumption. He was still being summoned to police stations. After every interrogation, he would return to his bar, and drink until he passed out. Rahul's family realized that the root of all his problems lay in alcohol; the solution, in medical detoxification.

In April 2013, Rahul was admitted at the Thane Institute for Psychological Health, where, along with treatment for his mental health, he went through cold turkey to quit the addictions. Withdrawal symptoms kicked in within eight hours of his last drink. Once they climaxed in three days, doctors had to tie him down. Two more days later, when the symptoms started subsiding, his medical treatment commenced. After ten more days in the hospital, Rahul could eat solid food again.

'This is only his detoxification,' the doctor told Rahul's siblings. 'He still needs treatment for de-addiction.'

'I don't understand,' said Mangala, Rahul's sister, 'He hasn't had a sip of alcohol in two weeks; he's healthy now.'

'Addiction has various layers – physical, emotional and psychological. We have fixed his body with detoxification; a de-addiction programme will fix his mind,' the doctor explained. 'Detox is temporary; de-addiction will make sure he never takes to the bottle again.'

Rahul's brother laughed. The idea seemed impossible to him.

'Does he have to do it in your hospital?' Mangala asked.

'Not necessary. Why?'

'I don't want him to stay in Mumbai or Thane,' she said. 'Any other city, where the cops won't hound him.'

'I'll have it arranged.'

Petrified of police interrogations and his own mind, Rahul allowed his family to take a call on his fate. His intoxicated brain would weave alternative realities, cast aspersions on every actuality, except for one: his family loved him. They had paid for his lawyers, secured his release, and did not leave him for dead despite his drunken debaucheries. So when they told him he was being taken to a de-addiction centre 150 kilometres away from his home, Rahul did not protest. No one would know him there, he figured. He could be anyone.

———

Muktangan Rehabilitation Centre, Pune, Maharashtra
May 2013
Admission I

When Rahul walked into the rehabilitation centre on the sweltering May afternoon, he did not know what a de-addiction centre was. Considering his hallucinations, he assumed it was a hospital, one for the mentally ill. If that was the case, he was happy to be there.

Rahul liked the unstable, having observed the special ward, 'Mental Separate' at Kalyan's Adharwadi jail. He would go near the isolated barrack to smoke charas, and had often glanced into the ward through its open door. He would feel at ease near those mentally challenged men – the only strangers in prison who did not reek of threat.

Rahul had noticed that the men in the jail's psychiatric ward had no restraint. They would shit anywhere or urinate in the middle of the barrack if they wished. They would walk around their circle, laughing, singing, dancing, and talking to themselves. If attendants brought them food, they would stare at it. After a few minutes, suddenly, they would pounce on it with both their hands, gobbling their rice and chapattis down in a frenzy. They were innocent, those men – no ego, no pride. And as long as they were kept from anything that could be used for a weapon, they were harmless. He'll have a good time at Muktangan, the gangster told himself.

Located in a quiet lane off a busy highway in the city of Pune, Muktangan provides medical treatment and rehabilitation programmes for addicts, with a focus on the psychological aspects of addiction. When Rahul learnt of the centre's function the day he walked in, he felt it was 'as laughable as voodoo'. Still consumed with conceit, he decided to stay on guard against counsellors, who would try to steal a peek into him.

'We've had many dons here – from Mumbai, Delhi, Pune and Bangalore,' a volunteer in the rehab told Rahul as he showed the gangster to his bed. The 300-square-foot room had twenty other single beds, hosting addicts from various cities, ages and income groups. All dressed in white, they were ready to go to bed after dinner. 'Addiction is not just a bad habit; it's a disease. You must first accept that.'

The man was about sixty years old. Although tempted, Rahul decided to avoid a war of words. 'I know,' he said instead.

'You don't know, beta,' the volunteer replied, checking Rahul's person for intoxicants, handing him a pair of white shirt and pyjamas. 'You just think you do. I, too, used to be an addict. I, too, assumed I knew. It steals your life away, this addiction – one cigarette, one drink, one chillum at a time. Plus, you were addicted to crime. You must work hard now, rebuild your life.'

'Don't bore me, chacha,' Rahul said. 'Leave, please.'

The silver-haired sexagenarian, who had been working at the centre for over three years, knew better than to argue. He left the gangster alone, checked on other patients in the room, and walked out.

Since doctors at Muktangan had given him a sleeping pill for his withdrawal-resultant insomnia, Rahul quickly passed out. The next morning, he had a problem: he was being asked to wake up at six.

'Why should I wake up so early? I've paid full money – 8,500 fucking rupees for thirty days. I'll wake up whenever I want to,' he told the old volunteer.

'The fee is to fix you,' the man replied sternly, 'You can wake up, or you can leave.'

'Okay, chacha. Don't get so worked up. Bring me a cigarette, and I'll go get fresh.'

'This is a de-addiction centre, there's no tobacco here.'

'I don't feel pressure until I smoke a cigarette. How will I shit without tobacco?'

'That's exactly what they'll teach you here.'

Rahul went to a doctor at the facility with his complaint. The doctor gave him a nicotine gum. It brought his craving to rest, but did not help him defecate. He was able to relieve himself only five days later, after a rigorous round of laxatives.

Although his bowel movements were resolved, Rahul had another problem: he could not sleep. Doctors had allowed sleeping tablets only for the first four days. Thereafter, he was expected to manage on his own. The gangster could not get undisturbed sleep without alcohol. He tried to argue, saying that even at the Thane hospital the pills had brought him sleep. But doctors refused to relent, and the addict started staying up at nights, showering and doing laundry to while away time. He would leave soon, he told himself – only three more weeks.

Although the rehab wasn't the most comfortable space for the gangster, he did take some interest in the daily group therapy sessions initially. Counsellors would gather twenty to twenty-five patients in a room, and use various interactive techniques to help them get rid of their addictions. A session called 'Lifeline', for instance, required addicts to pen down the most important events of their lives, and read them out before the full room.

'Do you really want me to read this out aloud?' Rahul asked the counsellor. None of the other addicts had a criminal past. Most were educated – doctors, lawyers or other professionals, with wives and children, who had fallen prey to vices mainly because of bad company.

'Yes.'

'Okay then, as you wish,' said Rahul. 'My name is Rahul Jadhav. I am famous as Bhiku. I was born in 1976, have one brother, one sister. I went to a Marathi school, failed class ten, passed the next year. After class ten, I went to college. Then class thirteen fail, class fourteen fail, class 14 fail again, then left college. One girlfriend, break up in some years. Started working, went to jail, came out of jail, then came here.'

The patients stared at Rahul; some shocked, all curious. Although he had barely shared significant details, the information was enough to interest and alarm them. After the session, a few addicts cornered Rahul to enquire about his past. 'Ask the counsellor. She knows everything,' he said curtly, irritated following the recollection. The 'Lifeline' exercise was meant to build peace between addicts and their past lives, but Rahul was convinced it was only to humiliate him.

Too proud to participate, the erstwhile gangster would hold on to his arrogance in most group therapy sessions. In a music workshop, for instance, he retorted with a flippant comment when the psychologist explained how lyrics and melody could break barriers to recovery.

'They help relieve stress,' she said, encouraging her patients to write and sing songs. 'Music helps you tap into hidden emotions.'

'It helps you more if you have a voluptuous bar dancer around,' Rahul commented.

Rahul's antics would often get him thrown out of the group therapy assemblies. He would throw paper balls and make bird sounds during sessions, as if he were back in school. Although his actions would bring laughter to the otherwise sombre patients, they would not go down well with psychologists. Worse, he wouldn't cooperate with personal counsellors in his one-on-one sessions. He would offer monosyllabic answers when probed, a rude remark if probed further.

The only thing Rahul did not despise at Muktangan was the time he spent drawing. To build the habit of self-introspection, one of the psychologists instructed the addicts to maintain journals. The men were asked to read the previous day's entry every morning, and figure what they could have done differently to make the day more productive. When Rahul asked the counsellor if he could draw instead, she agreed. Therafter, he would go to the library every night, and draw images imitating book and magazine covers – from Mahatma Gandhi and Rabindranath Tagore to Shah Rukh Khan and Mickey Mouse.

The day he was to return home, the gangster was happy to leave. 'Enough of this charade,' he bid goodbye to his roommates. 'I'm going to go out and get drunk.'

As soon as he walked out of Muktangan, Rahul pleaded with his father for money, saying he hadn't had a puff of cigarette or a drop of alcohol in forty-five days. Ramakant handed him Rs 200. Rahul walked to a wine shop and bought a quarter of Bagpiper whisky. He mixed the spirit in a bottle of water and gulped it down. Satisfied, he then walked to a roadside stall and smoked two cigarettes – as his father, who had travelled four hours to pick him up, waited. The old man stayed true to his patient nature, and the son to his.

Once home, Rahul, who was feeling much healthier after a month at the rehab, returned to his routine consumption of one whisky bottle a day. About four weeks later, the hallucinations and tremors returned. The palpitations and paranoia came home. The addict decided to return to Muktangan. He could not become the lunatic he was. The rehab was challenging, but it would keep him alive. Also, in a strange, unprecedented way, the mischief and the drawing had taken him back to his childhood – the only untainted time of his life.

—◦—

Muktangan Rehabilitation Centre, Pune, Maharashtra
July 2013
Admission II

When Rahul returned to Muktangan, he was moved to the Anubhav ward for relapse patients. His twenty-one-day stay, he was told, would be under the purview of Counsellor Habiba Jetha. Rahul liked Jetha's sessions. Through engaging activities for metaphors, she would compel her patients to dive deep within themselves, and raise pertinent questions. Rahul remembers a session, where she gave her group of twenty-five patients a metres-long thread each, and asked them to walk around in random circles. Once the threads had tangled up, trapping the patients in coils, she asked the addicts to untangle them.

'How's that possible?' Rahul asked. 'Are you stupid?' he did not add.

'This is exactly what you've done with your lives. You've messed it up. And now that we're asking you to disentangle it, you think we're crazy,' she responded, reading the gangster's mind in his ridicule-heavy tone.

In another session, she blindfolded the group, and asked the addicts to walk out of the rehab's main entrance. When they protested, saying they would be run over by a car on the street, she said, 'You've walked this way all your life. The blindfold has been of your arrogance, your ignorance. If you're drinking, you must know its consequences. Whatever action you take, you must know its fallouts. Get rid of the blindfold; take ownership of your deeds. Do not be a casualty of your own life.'

Jetha's words made Rahul ponder: 'Have I really been blind? Am I really responsible for this mess?' He knew he had tarnished the lives of his family, his victims, his co-accused and their kin, but he still wasn't sure of his own. 'I'm not responsible for the knotted up threads in my life,' he discarded the musing. 'It's the cops who've beaten my body and my soul, turned me into an addict, even a madman. But wait, didn't I give them reasons to do what they did?'

To find his answers, Rahul decided he would attend his personal counselling sessions with Jetha. He had avoided the interaction initially, but when her sessions raised questions about his own accountability, he was compelled to know more. At 12.30 p.m. on a Tuesday, he went to the counsellor's office. Still a gangster at heart, he leaned back on his chair, his legs wide apart, his head held high.

'Ask what you want to ask,' he stated.

Jetha knew of Rahul's past. She had guarded herself against being judgemental, and spent time observing him instead. She noticed that the former hitman hardly spoke to other addicts, barely smiled. She decided that the first thing she had to do was shatter his shields, and make him express himself.

'Put your Bhaigiri aside, only then will I talk to you,' she reacted to his body language. 'I'm a bigger don than you'll ever be.'

Apunko yeh sab bolneka nahi.' Rahul sat up, his defences springing up in his revised posture. 'If I lose my mind, it won't be good for you.'

'What will happen if you lose your mind, Mr Bhai?' she asked, her eyes tearing into his. 'Will you kill me? Come on, there's no one in the room. Now is the time. Do it.'

Rahul did not know what to say.

She continued: 'Sit here only if you genuinely want to talk to me. If not, get up and leave.'

'Ask what you want to ask.'

'Aye, listen.' Jetha was irked. 'No one's going to ask you if you answered my questions. There's no pistol to your head. Stay if you want to talk, or don't waste my time.'

'I'll talk,' the gangster relented. He realized that somehow, Jetha had authority over him. Without words, she had made it clear that she was the one doing him a favour, and not the other way around. Although hesitant, Rahul felt he could trust her.

'You're a good person, Rahul,' she softened, 'You're just wearing many masks. Talk to me without them, and I promise you'll never have a thing to worry about.'

Rahul agreed to open up. Over the next few sessions, the conversations got smoother. The addict narrated his story, revisiting and evaluating each of the significant moments of his life – when Dina jumped into the well, when schoolboys bullied him, when his girlfriend left him, when he shot at his victims, when the police arrested him, when they beat him up, when his don didn't show up, when the courts acquitted him, and when he woke up on streets after his drunken escapades.

Slowly and steadily, Rahul started expressing his deepest feelings to Jetha. On an occasion or two, his eyes welled up. He still didn't cry, but he felt a strong suggestion of tears. It wasn't vicious, the rivers in his eyes threatening to overflow. It was expression that cleared the haze and helped him experience the life he had lived.

Jetha would respond to Rahul's confessions with love and attention. She realized that his greatest grudge was that he was no more a criminal, but the cops still treated him like one – questioning him, beating him, and rubbing his past deeper into his skin. Another problem, one he was too proud to admit, was that he felt lonely. His girlfriend had left him, his don had abandoned him, and his friends had walked away. His family was around, but they were heartbroken, too. Although they took care of him, he could feel a distance. Rahul had started believing that whoever loves him, leaves him. His first abandoner – Dina.

'The people in your life were not bad, Rahul – nor had you trusted the wrong people. You just trusted them the wrong way,' Jetha would try to explain, hoping to calm the emotional turmoil inside him.

'When will we meet again, taai?' he would ask the counsellor after their sessions, now referring to her as an older sister.

Although Rahul had made progress with Jetha, all of it was insignificant once he returned home, and went back to his daily bottle of whisky. Within ten to twelve days, as his health rapidly deteriorated, he told his parents he wanted to return to Muktangan.

'We cannot afford it, Chotu,' Shalini told her son. 'Your second admission's fee was Rs 6,000, and a third will be as much. Plus, your travel expenses. Please fix yourself in this third admission. We don't have the money to pay for a fourth one.'

––—⊢—––

Although addicts typically take a maximum of two admissions at Muktangan, Rahul went on to admit himself thrice after his second stint. Each time, he would return home to his addictions. He couldn't believe how difficult it was to kick those lethal habits, how he'd become a slave to them. They were chains he did not know existed, not until they became too heavy to be broken.

'The problem isn't your drinking, it's your mind,' his counsellor, Mansi Satyekar, told him after his third admission in August 2013, 'You need to get rid of the baggage of your past. Once your mind is clean, you'll quickly drop every addiction, everything that's holding you back. Just listen to your counsellors. Put all your heart in the tasks they assign.'

Rahul took the advice. In the 'Lifeline' lecture with Counsellor Wrushali Gore, he again wrote down the key events of his life. This time, in much detail, enlisting his crimes and their punishments. He did not read the intricacies out before the full room, but he wrote each one down and repeated the murky details in his mind.

Gore then asked the group to write about their future: 'Five years from today, what would your health be like? How will your home look? Where will you be working? How much money will you have?'

Although the questions titillated Rahul's mind, he left the paper blank. He did not have the imagination for it. His past still obstructed the view of his future.

When he returned to his bottle after his third admission, Rahul called Satyekar.

'Why are you calling me now? You should have phoned before you took the first sip,' she admonished him.

'I can't understand what to do. I really don't want to drink, but I cannot keep myself from it,' he said.

'Come back here,' she said, 'and don't drink until then.'

Rahul drank before his fourth admission. His septuagenarian father, who was fatigued from travelling the distance, had asked him to go on his own. Certain that the fourth admission was his final, Rahul drank half a bottle of whisky in a Pune bar. Counsellors asked him to leave when he reached Muktangan drunk in September 2013. They let him in only when he returned sober with his father the following day.

'I think I need to get a job,' he told Satyekar upon his return. 'But I cannot find one. They want character certificates. They want to know what I was doing during the years I was with the underworld. When I return home, I try to smile at neighbours and acquaintances. No one returns my smiles. They still think I'm a gangster. Why can't they take me back? Even the courts have declared me innocent. My blood boils, madam. I feel like taking a gun and shooting them, exactly in those judgemental eyes.'

'People's thoughts about you echo your own, Rahul,' said Satyekar. 'You know you were not innocent. Now, you need to make peace with it. You need to develop a strong will power – against your addictions, your anger, your arrogance, and even the temptation of residing in the past. Believe you're a kind person, and let your actions show it's true. Others will come around.'

To trust he could change, Rahul started paying attention to the documentaries played at Muktangan every week. He particularly liked the story of Datta Shrikhande, who was then working as a coordinator at Muktangan. Shrikhande took to smoking when he was eight, and graduated to substance abuse in class four. The intoxicants – alcohol, ganja, brown sugar and 'almost everything that gave me a kick' – helped him forgo the memory of his parents, who died when he was little.

When he grew up, he started driving a rickshaw. His earnings could not afford his drugs, so he took to stealing. His criminal record spiralled, and he was externed from his city for two years. He was admitted at Muktangan in 1992, and soon kicked his addictions. He went on to obtain a bachelor's degree in psychology while working as a peon at Muktangan, and later became a counsellor at the centre. An ace cook, he was also one of the top thirty contestants in MasterChef India, a renowned television cookery show.

As a child, heroes had always inspired Rahul. He found the same motivation in Shrikhande. He, too, could change, the erstwhile extortionist started believing. His life, too, would offer him a second chance.

Although motivated during his fourth stint, Rahul again returned to alcoholism once he was home. He called Satyekar, but she refused to help.

'I'd told you to call me before you started drinking. I'd told you to come for follow-ups after you left Muktangan. You did not listen to any of that. I can't help you if you don't respect my word,' she chided.

A dejected Rahul spent weeks away from Muktangan even as his thoughts kept taking him back to the rehab, which had made him believe in the possibility of an alternative life. In October 2013, he returned to the centre for a fifth time, and again tried active participation in his sessions. A counsellor, Tehreen Sayyed, had asked the addicts to prepare solo skits for Dussehra. The theme, in keeping with the significance of the Hindu festival, was the victory of good over evil.

Sayyed noted her observations about Rahul's performance: 'In the first scene, he pretends to be in prison, and just informed that no lawyer was willing to represent him. He looks sad and decides to argue his case on his own. On the day of his judgement, he appears nervous, battling his thoughts on whether or not he should drink to keep up with the tension. He avoids the urge, argues his case and gets himself an acquittal. The win, he says at the end of the skit, was because he fought his internal demons, let sense (good) prevail over temptation (evil). With his performance, he was successfully able to vent out suppressed emotions.'

Over five admissions in Muktangan, Rahul got close to other patients. He would spend all his free time with the addicts, playing indoor games, singing and laughing. Once, he pushed the limit.

During Diwali, the centre's administration had arranged for a party, with music and dinner. The addicts jumped onto beds and danced. Rahul, who got overenthusiastic, stripped his clothes off and started dancing naked. He felt liberated that night, as if he need not feel shame, as if he had nothing to be ashamed of. The shocked patients, meanwhile, complained to the authorities. Since he was to leave in three days, no action was initiated.

In early November 2013, Rahul left Muktangan after his fifth stint, and again returned to his bottle. Only this time, accompanied with thoughts of suicide.

21

That Dare to Dream

———•❧•———

11 February 2014. 11.30 p.m. With a lit cigarette in one hand and a bottle of whisky in another, an inebriated Rahul walked along the railway tracks in Dombivli, looking for a spot where he could die in peace. A few metres ahead of the busy platform, he sat down on the tracks and uncorked his bottle. He went for a large sip, and pulled a long drag to dissolve the bitter taste. Hoping to find more courage in the spirit, he gulped another round. It was his third attempt at suicide in the past few weeks, and he wanted to be sure that this time, he did not disappoint death.

Until half an hour ago, Rahul had been sitting in his bar, Green Court. It was his birthday, and no one – his family, co-accused, bar mates, counsellors or rehab friends – had wished him. They probably did not remember. To Rahul, it meant alienation. Everyone's life journey had separated from his own. Worse, all his dear ones seemed to have chosen the diversion. The former hitman burned with a cold fire, his many unrequited loves springing from his hate.

Lonely, Rahul's thoughts took him to Aarti, his first and only real girlfriend. He hadn't spoken to her in a decade. Hoping to find her presence online, he pulled out his phone, and typed her name in the search engine of a social networking site. Her profile popped up. She had added her husband's last name, had a son, lived in Europe, and appeared happy. Looking at her smiling face, the gangster's heart ached. It was the same honest smile, one that ventured deep into her big, brown eyes.

'That kid could have been mine,' Rahul thought to himself. 'Only if I'd been man enough to do the right thing.'

Irked, he threw the handset to the floor, and smashed it under his feet. As bar patrons watched, he barked at the waiter: 'Did you see what I just did? Why don't you throw me out?'

The server did not respond. The gangster's histrionics were a regular feature at the bar.

Rahul then picked up his whisky glass, and dropped it to the floor. As the sound of glass pieces echoed in the tiny space, he picked up two more glasses, and hurled them at the wall. 'Here, now will you throw me out?'

The waiter stayed committed to his silence. His quietude told Rahul that his mother was right: No one wanted to indulge him. He was among the dregs of society.

'Do you think people like it when you visit their homes? No. They're disgusted by you. No one wants to be near you,' she had said one morning when Rahul woke up after blacking out the previous night. His bar acquaintances had carried him home.

'But when did I visit anyone?'

'You do not know what you do after you get drunk.' She was furious. 'They come after you, pleading with us to send you somewhere far. Neighbours have told their kids to keep away from you. You're a bad influence. Please, fix your life or leave us.'

His mother's words ringing in his ears and Aarti's happy face mocking his heart, Rahul picked up his bottle, and left for the railway tracks. It was the worst way to die: out in the cold, with no one looking for him. But he had made up his mind.

After a few minutes on the tracks, Rahul saw a train stop at Dombivli railway station. 'Two minutes, and it'll all be over,' the erstwhile gangster thought and stood up. As the train left the platform, he gulped another sip. Nervous, he started jogging on the spot. The train slowly picked up pace, and in moments Rahul could hear the wheels in motion, feel the tracks tremble under his feet. The engine's lights started blinding his vision, and he shut his eyes. With the train only a few feet away, his heart thumped furiously. Almost involuntarily, he opened his eyes and leapt off.

'Fuck,' he yelled in disappointment, lying on an adjoining track, his voice inaudible under the train's ear-splitting horn. 'Fuck!'

Certain that he'd have to let the next train crush him, Rahul sat up, and started recounting reasons that had brought him to the railway tracks that night. 'There's nothing to live for, you chutiya,' he tried convincing his mind, which, without instruction, had decided to rescue him. 'No one would care if you died.'

Thoughts of suicide had built up in Rahul's mind soon after he started drinking again upon his return from Muktangan after his fifth stint. His brain turned into the most dangerous place in the world for him. It started mocking and tormenting him. 'Five admissions and you still haven't managed to kick your addictions. Five admissions, and you're still a failure. You're no Bhai-vhai, Bhiku. You're just a big, ugly failure.'

Rahul had begun to realize that his life had been nothing but a relentless attack on his family's sanity. His friends did not want to be with him, and relatives and neighbours still saw him as the long-haired hooligan who'd have two pistols tucked into his trousers at all times. He'd turned thirty-nine that day, but he hadn't found love.

'What girl would want to be with me?' Rahul found himself thinking. 'I'm not stable. I do not have a job. All I have is a terrifying past, one whose shadow just wouldn't stop trailing my present.'

'All these years of Bhaidom, I've been no better than a fraudulent street urchin,' Rahul continued with the self-admonition after breaking for a sip of whisky, 'When such men beg for money, they touch you, get uncomfortably close to your face. People pay out of irritation, not fear. The same is true with me. People don't fear me. They hate me. And why wouldn't they? What have I done to gain respect? Fuck being a Bhai, I'm not man enough to earn five rupees without a pistol in my hand. '

Motivated once again, Rahul sprung to his feet. A train was approaching in his direction two tracks away. He rushed to the track, and turned around. Maybe it would be easier if he didn't look death in the eye. Once again, the tracks trembled, and once again, Rahul leapt off. Killing another man, he realized, was much easier than killing himself.

As Rahul sat on the railway tracks, counting more reasons to end his life, two railway guards rushed towards him. The driver of the previous train had probably informed the railway control, and the drunkard was asked to leave.

'But I'm here to die,' he tried to explain. 'I won't harm anyone, I promise.'

'Not today,' one of the guards snatched his bottle.

—————||—————

Muktangan Rehabilitation Centre, Pune, Maharashtra
March 2014
Admission VI

As his father waited on a platform at Pune railway station, Rahul ordered his quarter of whisky at a nearby bar. Ramakant, who had never had a sip of alcohol, had refused to accompany him. He hadn't even spoken to his son during the three-hour train ride. He was still upset. The railway guards had taken Rahul home, told his family about his suicide attempt. Ramakant had slapped his son, and as his family stood shocked at the unlikeliest source of violence, the seventy-five-year-old broke down. It wasn't just about what his son had become; it was also what he'd made of him.

'Leave us, Chotu,' he told Rahul amidst his tears. 'For everything we've done, I only have one favour to ask of you. Don't ever come back.'

Weary of neighbours' complaints, his mother had already asked him to leave. Now his father, too, had demanded the same. Rahul decided he would not stay in a house where he was no more welcome. With nowhere else to go, he called one of his Muktangan counsellors, Madhav Kolatkar. The psychologist was hesitant about admitting him for a sixth time. He agreed only when Rahul offered to stay at the rehab until his counsellors decided he was ready to leave, even if it meant years.

'Are you absolutely sure you won't run away?' Kolatkar asked Rahul when he reached the rehab with his father.

'I have nowhere to run to. I have no one to run to.'

Rahul was again admitted in the 'Anubhav' ward for relapse patients. He was told that after three weeks in 'Anubhav', he would be moved to the 'After Care' section for three months. His monthly fee would be Rs 9,000.

'I know your family can't afford the fee,' said Kolatkar. 'If you want a reduction, you'd have to accept three conditions: quit tobacco, do any job you're assigned while working as a volunteer, and commit to stay at Muktangan for at least three years.'

The addict nodded in agreement.

Rahul took three days to cross off the first condition. During his previous stays at Muktangan, he would borrow chewing tobacco from visitors. After consuming the nicotine, he would remove the wet blob, and wrap it in a piece of paper. He would chew the blob many times later, until the juice wore out. Often, addicts would share tobacco whenever they had access. To abstain from it, Rahul first started with regular doses of nicotine gum. He also avoided common areas, where addicts usually savoured the forbidden stimulant. Ten days after he quit, he was put through a urine test, and came out clean. His monthly fee was reduced to Rs 6,000.

For the next three months, Rahul, as part of his second condition, did four jobs at Muktangan. He would manage accounts at a shop inside the rehab that sold soaps, toothpaste, toothbrushes and other daily essentials to patients. He worked with nurses twice a day, distributing medicines among addicts. He would tend to patients in withdrawals, cleaning their vomit, bathing them, and tying them up during their cold turkey. Fourthly, he would help addicts' wives who cooked in a kitchen inside Muktangan, preparing lunch boxes to be delivered in offices across Pune. The women's husbands would not work, and the income helped them keep the pot boiling at home.

The chores kept Rahul busy. Over weeks, he stopped mingling with other addicts and kept away from most of his counsellors. He had consciously decided on the distance. The addict was filled with fury at the time, like an inferno blazing inside of him, wanting to burn him and everyone around him.

'Get up, and get it on your own,' Rahul barked at a counsellor when the latter requested him for a cup of tea one afternoon. 'Volunteers are not your servants. Stop ordering them around.'

'I'm not ordering you, Rahul. I'm requesting you,' the psychologist replied.

'I'm not your servant,' the former outlaw stood by his response.

'Getting tea doesn't make you my servant. It's just a nice gesture.'

'I don't think so.'

'It's your ego that keeps you from agreeing.'

'It's not my ego, it's the system. Nowhere have they written that volunteers are personal stewards to counsellors.'

'It's your ego, and it'll be a barrier in your recovery.'

'I'll deal with it.'

———◁I▷———

Four months after his sixth admission, Rahul's monthly fee was reduced to Rs 3,000. A further reduction meant further labour, and Rahul was moved to the housekeeping department. His counsellors knew he had spent a considerable time without alcohol and tobacco. All that needed to be fixed now was his rage. The erstwhile gangster was pissed at the world – for abandoning him, for not rescuing him from his lows, for not taking him back and, simply, for not fearing him.

For the first six months in the housekeeping department, Rahul cleaned common areas and toilets in the three-storey building. He washed dishes, gathered the leftover waste following meals, and put it in dumpsters in the rehab's backyard. After half a year of diligent work, his fee was waived off, but counsellors still weren't convinced that he could leave the facility. During these six months, he was caught for lending his urine to an addict who used it to cheat in his tobacco test. When confronted, Rahul stayed arrogant.

For a monthly salary of Rs 1,000, which started ten months after his sixth admission, Rahul continued to work at Muktangan as a volunteer. He would wake up at four in the morning and assemble his cleaning apparatus – broom, toilet cleaner, phenyl, disinfectants and a piece of cloth. He would begin his day by scrubbing the guest and staff toilets. He would then sweep the reception area, the clinic, the library, the auditorium and the group therapy rooms. After having breakfast with other addicts at 8 a.m., he would start cleaning the compound area. After lunch, if he was in the mood, he'd attend counselling sessions for the next four hours. He would have tea at

6 p.m., and then work at the fertilizer plant in the rehab's backyard. He would gather heaps of garbage – cooking waste, leftover food, medical waste – and put it in the plant to produce manure. He would distribute medicines with the nurse at 8 p.m., and then have his dinner. After an hour of drawing or reading in the library, he would retire to his bed at 10 p.m.

'He was only asked to clean toilets, and sweep the common spaces. Everything else, he did on his own,' says Kolatkar. 'He cleaned dozens of ventilators, which had gathered layers of dust over the years. He would climb onto ladders and parapets to clean the ones on the upper floors. He'd fixate. He would keep rubbing and scrubbing until the glass was spotless. On an average day, he'd do the work of five volunteers alone.'

Rahul's counsellors believes that the rigorous cleaning was a way to channel his anger against the world, and his disappointment in his own self. Perhaps, in all that washing and mopping, he was looking to vacuum his past, tidy his soul.

As days passed, Rahul started taking up more tasks that belittled him, unaware that he was trying to punish himself. Once, two workers in the fertilizer department told him that they required cow dung for composting. The former gangster said he would not stoop to picking up shit but, in moments, agreed on his own. He could have refused, and no one would have objected. Instead, he went to a nearby shed, scooped heaps of fresh dung with a bucket, and loaded it on a hand cart. He pushed the cart back to Muktangan as strangers watched. He was melting with humiliation, but he kept pushing the cart. He was shaking with anger, but he kept pushing.

Another time, he went down a manhole in Muktangan to unclog the sewage line. Using his bare hands, he threw out kilos of filth that had blocked the flow. When he emerged, he was covered in human faeces. As he started collecting the grime in a bucket, he heard a man call out his name. When he turned, he saw it was an acquaintance from Green Court – a man who had known of Rahul's reign of terror in Thane and the dread he once commanded.

'Is that really you, Bhiku?' the visitor asked, his eyes glued to the faeces on Rahul's body.

The recovering addict froze. The embarrassment had numbed his mind. After a few seconds, as the vistor still stood shocked, Rahul quietly returned to transferring the sludge to the bucket.

Looking at him absorbed in his chores, fellow addicts started worrying about Rahul. He wouldn't talk to anyone. He would just keep working as if he would die if he stopped.

'Rahul, we think you should speak to one of the counsellors,' a group of three addicts once accosted him. 'They've been telling us all along: Express how you feel. You're expressing yourself through all this mindless work. That isn't healthy.'

'I don't need to run to counsellors,' Rahul replied. 'They can't fetch their own tea, how will they help me? Apparently, they're trying to fix my ego by asking for tea. Have you ever heard anything more stupid? I don't want their therapy. I'm working because Muktangan has pardoned my fee. I won't bother anyone, that's all the recovery I need.'

Of all his counsellors, Rahul would only attend sessions with Habiba Jetha, Tehreen Sayyed and Mukta Puntambekar, deputy director of the rehabilitation centre. The women would nurse him with affection – they would get cake for his birthday, treat him to homemade biryani and would buy him coffee mugs and sketch pencils. Soon, Rahul started referring to the women as his sisters. Every time they hosted a session, he would gladly take part. He could not recognize the gradual emotional healing. He was only happy to feel appreciated again, even loved.

Although he was opposed to most of his counsellors, they had his well-being in mind. In mid 2015, a senior officer of the Thane Anti-Extortion Cell went looking for Rahul at Muktangan. Instead of summoning the former hitman, counsellors showed live CCTV footage to the cop where Rahul was busy cleaning the auditorium.

'I cannot believe my eyes,' the officer was stunned. 'This man is Jaidev Reddy's topmost gangster. He's an ace shooter, a star extortionist. And he's cleaning your floor.'

'How did you know he was here?' counsellor Madhav Kolatkar asked him.

'His co-accused told us. They're just cronies. Rahul is the real Bhai.'

'He was,' the counsellor corrected.

The psychologists told the officer that police enquiries would beat Rahul down, and the progress he was making. The officer left without questioning the former gangster. He noted Kolatkar's number, and would follow up with the counsellor every few days to ensure Rahul was still in Muktangan, still redeeming his past.

———◆———

Seated on a bench in a session with Puntambekar in December 2015, Rahul struggled to put pen to paper. The deputy director of Muktangan had asked the group of ten 'Aftercare' volunteers to list their future goals. Rahul did not know what his aspirations were. He did not have any. A life beyond rehab was unfathomable to him. His family wouldn't take him back, and the world wouldn't take him back. At Muktangan, he felt safe. No one judged him here. No one reminded him that he was a parasite to society. But even as he was at peace with his present, Rahul hadn't thought of his future. It was still too wild, that dare to dream.

'All of you have stayed at Muktangan for months, even years,' said Puntambekar. 'You've successfully kicked your addictions. But I'm worried you're getting comfortable here. True rehabilitation means reintegrating with society. You have to affirm your ground in the outside world, make sure they see this changed side of you, and applaud it. Now, tell me your goals.'

While some addicts said they wanted to get married and start a family, others spoke of getting jobs. Still others, including Rahul, stayed quiet.

'You have to be more to get more,' Puntambekar continued, 'I need you to leave Muktangan within the next year. Pick a skill, make a plan and execute it. If you'd like to learn driving, we'll pay for your training. If you'd like to learn cooking, we'll train you, and issue certificates. Just tell me what you'd like to do, and we'll figure a way.'

Rahul kept mum.

'In addition to skill building, I need you to get fitter. You're eating right, yes. But you need to get some exercise. Do yoga, join the gym at Muktangan, go for runs in the morning. In fact, there's a ten-kilometre marathon coming up next month. Would any of you be interested?'

Rahul raised his hand.

'Good. Do you have any experience running?'

The former shooter stared at the floor. After a few seconds, he shrugged the hesitance and said, 'I have experience running from cops, from the men I shot at, and from the crowds that chased after me. The longest I've run is four kilometres – after I shot a furniture store owner in the heart.'

'That'll work.' said the counsellor. 'I'll have a gate pass issued for you. You must run outside the facility to train for the marathon.'

'Okay,' Rahul was hesitant. Addicts and volunteers required the pass to leave Muktangan, and Rahul hadn't had the courage to get one issued. He did not trust himself. He knew he would never return.

On 30 December 2015, Rahul stepped out of Muktangan at 6 a.m., his first faceoff with the outside world in almost two years. It was quite congenial, he noticed – nothing like the dystopia he had painted in his mind. The winter sun was amiable, the air fresh with morning dew, and naked trees swayed in the cold winds, dancing to the joy of green leaves to come. Standing at his imaginary starting line outside the rehab's gate, Rahul mulled over the futility of his decision, but decided to run because he had given his word. Then, as he took his first step, running uncaged him from his first fear: the fear of new beginnings.

Rahul stopped after running for a kilometre. Sweat-purged and panting, he could hardly breathe, and walked to a nearby garden. As he settled on a bench, he saw a group of people standing in a circle, laughing hysterically. He wondered if he was the reason, but soon realized it was a laughter therapy assembly.

Men and women jogged about the garden's peripheral running track, while some stretched and performed yoga on the grass in the centre. A few others sat with their eyes shut, meditating. Rahul was happy to be in the park. Here, he was no more the gangster he was in Mumbai. He was no more the addict he was in Muktangan. In that garden, he had a new, unblemished, even respectable identity – of a fitness enthusiast. The realization slowly started crushing his second fear: the fear of rewriting his story, of dreaming.

Elated, he left the garden and started running again. After two kilometres, he walked back to Muktangan. As the day progressed, his muscles ached. The pain worsened over the next three days, but he did not stop with his morning runs. He wasn't acquainted with the science of the sport, but he'd liked the essence of it. There was something deeply liberating about running without being chased. To comfort his sore muscles, he approached Puntambekar for painkillers.

'No, no. You're doing it wrong,' the counsellor, an avid marathoner, told him. 'First, you need to develop a proper pre-run routine. For at least ten minutes, you must do a few dynamic stretches like butt kicks, leg swings and high knees. Blood must reach your muscles before you hit the road.'

After demonstrating a few stretches, she added: 'Start your run with jogging for a few metres. Then, slowly, pick up pace. Your speed will increase gradually, not immediately. And for marathons, you must build your endurance so you can run faster and farther.'

'What's endurance?'

'In a word, stamina. You should be able to cover long distances without your body giving up.'

'That won't be a problem.' Rahul smiled. 'As a child, I'd walked fifty kilometres from Dombivli to Mumbai twice. No water, no food, only endurance.'

The following morning, Rahul performed the stretches before his run. He covered five kilometres that day, and over the next two weeks, he was running eight kilometres daily. He was happy with his progress. The increased endorphin levels had elevated his mood, made him feel rewarded.

Rahul started liking the sport. There was another perk: the gate-pass had allowed him access to the city of Pune, which he hadn't explored beyond the bar outside its railway station. He would run in the old city, where Muktangan was located, and then explore the city centre flanked by new, luxurious hotels and ageing, dilapidated buildings. The modern infrastructure boasted of the city's development as sculptures of his favorite hero, Shivaji Maharaj smiled at the progress. It was like him, the city of Pune: crazed to get to the future, still clutching tightly to its past.

About three weeks after he first started running, Rahul collapsed on a sidewalk one morning, eighteen kilometres away from Muktangan. When strangers nudged him back to consciousness, he didn't know where he was, or that he had come that far. Somewhere, in the middle of the run, Rahul had begun thinking about his life. His mother's tearful voice had started ringing in his ears: 'People are on their deathbeds because of you. We've lost all respect because of you. We don't want to live anymore because of you.'

The words rushed like adrenaline through Rahul's veins. To punish himself, he started running as fast as he could. He ran until he dropped, until the words faded with the closing of his. When strangers woke him up, he had a smile on his face. He knew that the run had first transcended his body, then his mind, and then laid bare his soul.

At the Pune marathon, around the end of January 2016, Rahul covered the ten-kilometre distance in fifty-five minutes. As the crowd cheered him on, the erstwhile gangster exuberantly crossed the finish line. He had begun to heal.

Epilogue

———◆|◆———

Looking at the high perimeter walls of Yerwada Central Jail in Pune, Rahul smiled, a gleam of irony on his face. He knew that stone walls and iron bars did not make prisons. If they did, the former underworld hitman would belong on the other side of the wall – with the inmates inside, many of them locked up for felonies lesser than his. He wasn't one of them. He was 'free', sentenced to live with his unforgiveable past and his unforgiving future.

Earlier that morning, when Rahul left for a run from Muktangan, the former outlaw was feeling particularly powerless. To the man, who had once terrorized his city, a lack of power was menacing. He knew he could make the barrel of his pistol sing again, that he could just take what he wanted at gunpoint. Although tempted, those could not be his choices anymore. He couldn't bear the tiresome circle of sin and repentance again, so he decided to do what his father advised – 'Stay put, don't fuck our lives.'

A day ago, on 11 February 2016, Ramakant had travelled 150 kilmoetres to wish his son on his fortieth birthday. The underworld prodigy was happy to see his old man.

'Where's Ma?' he asked his father.

'She can barely walk. Her osteoarthritis has taken a toll on her feet.'

'Since when?' Rahul was concerned. After his sixth Muktangan admission, he had spoken to his family over the phone a few times, but they had never mentioned their troubles. They would disconnect after confirming he hadn't been drinking, that he hadn't harmed another man.

'It's been a while,' said the seventy-six-year-old. 'Here, she's sent gulab jamun for your birthday.'

'Baba, I think I'm ready to return home. I participated in a marathon here, haven't touched alcohol or cigarettes in two years. I don't feel the urge to drink anymore.'

'No, no, there's no way you're coming back,' Ramakant was unusually curt. 'You won't come alone, cops will follow. We're done with the interrogations. I'm done being shoved into the police van. Stay here, that's ideal for everyone.'

'What if I get a job?'

'Who's going to give you a job? You've tried to kill people. Staying idle will take you back to the bottle, and us to our graves. No, no. You're not coming back.'

Rahul knew his father was right. In his mother's words, he was 'godless' – a man who did not fear the devil because he *was* the devil. He agreed he was best confined, and let his father go. *Karma*, he told himself, *I'm paying for the blood I've spilled.* But even as he tried to accept the cards fate had dealt him, his head felt heavy, as if being poked with a thousand needles, as if on the verge of exploding.

The following morning at 6 a.m., Rahul put on his running shoes, and left the facility. A barrage of emotions plagued his mind: anger, remorse, helplessness and self-pity. He knew that the last few years had killed the criminal and addict in him, but his own family wouldn't acknowledge that. The rehab had faded his past, but his family still stood guard against it, unwilling to allow him a second chance. As he left the centre, Rahul decided he would run as far as his feet would take him. Like his life, not all journeys required destinations.

———

At Yerwada Central Jail, Rahul turned right towards the Mula-Mutha River. Although he had fallen in love with Pune, he wished to leave the songs of the city behind – the honking horns, the prancing eyes, and the constant rush to get to the end of the day. Rahul wanted no confrontation with time that morning, so he ran onto the 150-year-old Yerwada Bridge to get away from the city. A few metres later, he saw young couples seated along the side-rails of the overpass. Holding hands, they were gazing at the still river underneath, its bed flanked with cannabis plants.

The hazy figures in the morning twilight took Rahul back to his own great love. He, too, would take Aarti to a lake, he reminisced. They, too, would hold hands, watch days melt into nights. He wondered if his life would be any different if she were still with him, if he had fought for her, and hadn't settled for her resemblances in sparsely clad bar dancers. *These musings are pointless*, he quickly reminded himself. He had to accept his reality – he had loved and won, and he'd loved and lost.

From the Yerwada Bridge, Rahul started running towards the old Mumbai–Pune highway. One and a half hours later, when he reached the city of Chinchwad, he was sixteen kilometres away from the rehab. He knew his body would not support him for long – the farthest he had run was eighteen kilometres. Yet, he did not stop. As he ran amidst the white noise of winds in trees, he felt lighter. It was the running: A mental sport, it kicked in when his senses got out of the way, when he let his mind wander, and forgot his body.

It was after a decade that Rahul seemed to like the road ahead of him. The worldly trades of the city had given way to patiently ageing trees, the quaint poetry of birds, and the illustrious Western Ghats. The peaks made him feel dwarfed, but this time, he did not think of pulling the trigger to maim the mighty. He decided to surrender.

As he ran along the highway, Rahul spotted a police SUV racing in his direction. He quickly ducked to the road, and hid his face behind his right forearm. His eyes throbbed, his fingers curled into a fist, and his nails dug into his palms. The cops paid no heed, and drove past him. As Rahul rose, he felt uncomfortable again: it was fear. Fear of what had been, fear of what was to be.

After he unfroze, Rahul started walking towards Mumbai. He picked up pace only when he thought about his time in a police lock-up, his investigators' words ringing in his ears. 'Men like you belong in the coffin,' renowned encounter specialist Inspector Vijay Salaskar had told Rahul, 'You don't love anyone – not your family, not your friends, not your don. You're just a flesh-devouring carnivore – an animal living inside the body of a human.'

As he thought of Salaskar's words, Rahul could feel his breathing accelerate, but he did not try to stop his feet. Almost masochistically, he thought of another custodial encounter. The cops had been beating him at Turbhe Police Station to get intelligence on Reddy's whereabouts.

'Find out where his girlfriend lives,' Shailesh Kumbhare, the investigating officer from Thane Anti-Extortion Cell, ordered his subordinates.

'That's my personal life, don't you dare go there.'

'Really? Is it not personal when you barge into people's offices to fire at them? Aren't you destroying their personal lives? And those of their families?'

Rahul did not argue. A few kicks and blows later, when he still hadn't revealed the details, the cops bundled him up in a police van, and drove him to Aarti's housing society. They had gauged his reaction when they mentioned her. Although he hadn't said much, the cops knew this was a soft spot. If they pounded this spot, the gangster would spit out vital information.

The cops made Rahul stand in the central compound, visible to residents in most apartments of the society's five buildings. They stripped him, and pushed him to the floor. For the next half an hour, as residents watched, the six cops took turns to beat him. Whenever Rahul could catch a breath, he would look up at Aarti's second floor apartment, glancing to see if she was party to the audience. She wasn't. The door to her balcony was shut.

'Looks like she isn't home,' a cop observed. 'Must be out fucking.'

As his colleagues laughed encouragingly, the officer continued, 'Haan, Bhiku Bhai? Are her legs public or do they open exclusively for you?'

Rahul did not respond. He was aware that the cops were using a classic interrogation technique: the pride-and-ego down method. He knew they were attacking his perceived weaknesses, hoping to make him lose control over his silence. They wanted him to vindicate himself, and blurt out the information they were seeking. He stayed quiet.

'*Haan, maderchod.* Has the don been fucking your mother?' another cop kicked his cheek. 'No? Then why the fuck don't you tell us where he is?'

Although Rahul continued to hold his own, his body was on fire with rage. He could see his skin turn red, feel his hands attempt to wreck the handcuffs. He knew on any other day, in any other setting, it would take him moments to knock those cops out. But that had to be left for another day. This instant did not belong to him.

As he ran across the Mumbai–Pune highway, Rahul remembered how he did not allow himself a single screech when the cops broke his bones, and his spirit. He had seen the fear in his victims' eyes when he would point his 9 mm pistol at them. He drew his power from that fear, from their dilated pupils. He did not want his investigators to derive the same pleasure out of him. He kept mum when the cops assaulted him, even as the screams inside his head made him dizzy.

As Rahul remembered the torture, he could hear his silent shrieks all over again. This time, after a decade, he allowed his throat to voice those subdued wails. The pain busted through his lungs, the only weapon he had. He ran like a madman, his long, loud, piercing cries reverberating through the mountains. He shrieked as if he was being beaten in that instant, as if the cops would have mercy, listening to his wails. There was no one. It was the first time Rahul had allowed himself that vulnerability – he could; his secret was safe with nature.

The pace at which he was running, Rahul could not feel his legs. As he darted past hills and trees, he couldn't tell if his heart was still beating. He kept running, his mind faster than his feet, begging him to accept that his precious pride could not be redeemed, that he had to take the fall for his transgressions.

When he stopped thinking of the police torture, Rahul's mind wandered to his parents, who lost all to save him. He thought of Mallik, his friend, who died a month after the Mumbai Crime Branch took Rahul to his residence. He thought of Machmach's father, who succumbed after he learnt of his son's arrest. He thought of Tochan, whose wife abandoned him a week after their marriage. He thought of each of his ten co-accused, and how he had destroyed their lives. And then, for the first time, he thought of his victims, the men who lay bloodied on the floor, as the gangster walked away, proud.

The faces, once again, accelerated Rahul's feet. He could feel an enormous lump gaining strength in his throat, attempting to choke him. He tried to swallow the ball, but his eyes had already started welling up. His body had begun to feel heavy, as if he was being weighed down, wading through a deep, muddy river. His throat parched, his jersey and shorts drenched, and every inch of his body was covered in sweat. He hadn't realized that he'd been running for four hours, had almost reached the hill station of Lonavla, sixty kilometres away.

As he ran, Rahul kept thinking about his crimes, the wreckage of men and blood. When he neared a green patch off the highway, he rushed into its overgrown grass and collapsed. His heart thumped furiously, and cold air bit into his lungs, but the erstwhile hitman could not care for his body or its protests. Then, he just lay under the open skies, and as the winter sun soothed his open wounds, he closed his eyes and wept.

———⊣⊢———

Six months after the Pune–Lonavla run, Rahul returned home. His counsellors convinced his parents to take him back. The former gangster had made genuine progress. During that run, he had recognized the emotion that perpetuated his anger, fuelled the inferno inside him. It was remorse. Guilt was robbing him of his chance at at a new life, as his past laughed heartily at his depleting soul.

The sixty-kilometre run built courage in Rahul to own up to his crimes, and to feel ashamed, even sorry. Slowly, he began to make peace with his history. It was evident in his speeches in the 'Alcoholics Anonymous' sessions at Muktangan. Unlike earlier, the hitman started delving into the darker details of his life, narrating instance after instance, as the grime of resentment left his skin.

Rahul had realized that he could not let his past overpower his present, or annihilate his future. He could not change bygones, and if he spoke about them, no harm would come to him. The cops weren't out looking for him, nor did his family or the society hate him. His only enemy, he had realized, was him.

'I, Rahul Jadhav, was a gangster and addict,' he said in his first such admission before a group of ten to twelve Swedish students, who visited Muktangan in February 2016 for a study tour. Rahul knew that since his English was poor, the students wouldn't completely understand him. The communication barrier was the perfect solution to his hesitance, and he willingly told the group about his life and everything in it.

'I want to go out in the world. But not like this. I want to go out like, how do you say, gentleman. I want to go out as gentleman,' Rahul concluded his speech.

As the Swedes applauded, the former gangster felt lighter. It was a burden off his chest. Although he had attempted to kill men, he had defended himself in courts, and fought his way out of the allegations. While his well-dressed lies had kept him bound, the naked truth was setting him free.

Impressed with his progress, the Muktangan administration asked Rahul to deliver lectures to other recovering addicts. He was happy to oblige. By the time he left the facility, he had counselled 175 addicts over five months. His counsellors say that he inspired many others with his story of alcohol and de-addiction, crime and redemption.

When he went home in June 2016, Rahul's family was certain that he would return to his addictions and debaucharies, but he surprised them. He did not get in touch with any of his friends or gang-mates, and continued to abstain from alcohol and tobacco. He would spend his days at home, tending to his bedridden mother, and taking care of household chores. He would cook and clean for his family, and returned to many of his childhood hobbies: sketching, reading, and sharing his feelings with a diary. If he left home, he would walk out late – when dark nights and deserted streets lent him a cloak of anonymity.

Rahul also kept up with his morning runs. After leaving home at five, he would quickly cover the few kilometres to the highway, where no one recognized him. He would run for twenty kilomentres, and take a train back home, his face covered with a muffler and hooded jacket. Although he aspired to be a professional runner, he didn't want to approach trainers, who would inadvertently get friendly and venture into his past. Instead, he downloaded a few applications on his phone, and would sincerely follow the training tips. For heel training, for instance, he would climb and descend stairs of a railway station far from Dombivli.

Rahul knew that running was healing him. The sport had forced a structure into his day-to-day schedule, and increased his sense of being in control. Running was ridding him of the feeling of helplessness that mars most addicts. It was building self-esteem in the former gangster, offering greater hope for the future.

After he returned to Dombivli, Rahul would purposely leave home at 4 a.m. at times, running about places from his past: Dina's home, the creek, his street corner, the bar, Bhaijaan's building, the four spots where he fired, the police stations he was beaten at, and the Adharwadi jail. He'd also run to Mumbai at times, deliberately taking the route along Mumbai Sessions Court, Qilla Court and the Arthur Road Jail. He wouldn't stop at those places, he'd just run by them in nostalgic silence, recounting his past days, feeling grateful for better ones.

One afternoon, during a follow-up session at Muktangan, Rahul ran into Ankush Morde, a fellow recovering addict at the rehab. As the two spoke, Rahul told his friend that he was looking for a job. Ankush had seen the former gangster slave at Muktangan, how he'd throw his body and heart into his work. Ankush set up a job interview for Rahul with his brother, Harshal Morde. He assured Harshal that the former hitman would be an asset to their company.

When Rahul went for the interview in Mumbai, he did not know that the Mordes were one of the biggest chocolate manufacturers in the country. He showed up with no expectation, as he had with Bhaijaan, and once again his life was left altered. Since Ankush had recommended Rahul, his brother immediately offered him a job in the delivery department. His monthly salary would be Rs 12,000, he was told – and he could have the weekends off to train for his running.

In late October 2016, Rahul started with the job. He moved into a tiny room in an industrial building in south Mumbai, which Morde Foods had arranged for him. The former outlaw was relieved that his boss could distinguish between his past and his present. Harshal did not look down upon him for who he was; he respected Rahul for who he had become.

During one of his trips to North America, Harshal bought Rahul a GPS-enabled sports watch. The gadget, which could monitor heart rate, speed and performance, was to help him with his training. The expensive gift left Rahul overwhelmed. In a way, like his don's generosity with bundles of cash, it also validated his work.

Rahul was just settling into his new life when the Mumbai Crime Branch landed a tip-off about his shift to the city. Soon, he was being summoned at police stations and anti-extortion units across Mumbai. They'd ask him to show up every fortnight, and each time, he would carry medals and certificates from the many marathons he had participated in. Although the cops wouldn't assault him, they'd make him wait at police stations. In those long hours, Rahul would return to his past, again tense and angry, again begging for clemency.

In May 2017, Rahul was home when he received a call from inspector Vinayak Vats, a highly decorated officer in Mumbai's Anti-Extortion Cell. Vats, at the time, was heading Salaskar's squad, one that had first arrested him. A jittery Rahul visited Vats the following morning, his medals and certificates in tow. The moment he displayed his achievements, offering he had changed, police officers broke into guffaws.

'This is Bhiku Bhai, sir,' one of Rahul's investigators told Vats. 'He's Reddy's top lieutenant. He only runs from the law, no marathon-varathon.'

Vats asked his subordinate to shut up, and patted Rahul's back. He then turned to his colleagues, 'No one will bother this man again. He's no more a criminal. He has a job, and is training to become a runner. Tell other anti-extortion cells as well. Let him rebuild his life in peace.'

Rahul's eyes welled up. The tears flooded out when Vats felicitated the former hitman with a juice box and a rose as the cops, who'd once assaulted him, cheered and applauded.

———◦———

Rahul worked as a delivery person with the Mordes for almost three years. He continued to live in Mumbai, visiting his family over weekends. He would run along the Mumbai sea-face every morning, an average of twenty-one kilometres a day. Apart from Muktangan, he would also lecture at schools, colleges and de-addiction programmes. Of the ten-member gang he had created, he helped a few get jobs, and convinced a few others to get married. He thinks many of his friends and neighbours have now accepted him: 'I'm part of their Whatsapp groups, and they've also befriended me on Facebook. Some even invite me to their weddings and birthdays.'

As of early 2020, Rahul has had no summons from underworld investigators. He works as a de-addiction counsellor at Muktangan, and lives in Pune with his wife, Shashi Khandagale, a nurse he met at the rehab. The couple tied the knot in September 2019. The only hurdle in their union was the enquiries from Rahul's brother-in-law, who, as irony conspired, is a police officer! Shashi adores her husband for the man he is, even for the man he was. 'He couldn't have found himself if he hadn't been lost,' she says.

As for running, the sport has turned Rahul into a dreamer. Four years after the Pune–Lonavala run, the former gangster no longer hears his mother's indictments when he runs. He hears applause. The ambition of his childhood has returned; only this time, he isn't looking for magic bullets. Despite his job, the forty-three-year-old trains for four hours every day, and follows a strict diet. He is part of professional running groups, where fellow runners know of his past and applaud his present. He aims to shatter the national stadium run record one day. He also hopes to travel abroad, not to ride the double zero rail, but to participate in international marathons.

An endurance runner, Rahul has participated in over two dozen marathons, where he has covered more than 3,000 kilometers over hundreds of hours. His total run so far is nearly 10,000 kilometers. When he runs long distances, he does not heed the blisters on his feet, the fire in his calves, or the nausea in his gut. His mind flees with his body and, unaware of the destination, he savours the journey. Running, to him, is now bigger than a sport – he runs in joy, and he runs in melancholy. His runs are heartaches and celebrations, breakdowns and prayers. He exerts himself to his fullest each time he runs, hoping to make the effort a metaphor for his life.

As an ultra-marathoner, Rahul has run across the country. His greatest achievement, he says, is his marathon from Mumbai's Gateway of India to Delhi's India Gate – a distance of 1,431 kilometers, which he covered in a fortnight in January 2019. Sponsored by the Mordes to spread the message of de-addiction, Rahul delivered lectures in many villages and cities on his way. When he reached India Gate, journalists had gathered to marvel at his feat, celebrate his triumph. Rahul stood beaming. The last time he had such press attention, he was inside a black veil.

The day he started the Mumbai–Delhi run, the former hitman learnt that his Anna, don Jaidev Reddy, was arrested in Senegal. News reports told him that Reddy, who was being extradited to India, had resisted the arrest, stating that his detention was a case of mistaken identity. As he stood at the starting line, Rahul wished his don had given in. He knew it was wilder: surrender.

Acknowledgements

———•‖•———

I first met Rahul to interview him for a long-form news feature. Those six hours told me that the man was walking around with a book in his belly. Thanks, Rahul, for sharing your story with me, even the uncomfortable parts.

Thank you, Debu da (Debasish Panigrahi), for introducing me to Rahul. This book would have been impossible without you.

I'm immensely grateful to Rahul's family, friends, co-accused, other former gang-mates, lawyer, counsellors and employer – and those whom I've promised not to name – for their time and their invaluable recollections. My sincerest gratitude to his investigators in Maharashtra's anti-extortion units, who helped me dig out decades-old documents, and strained their memories to help me bring balance to the manuscript.

Many thanks to the officers of Mumbai Crime Branch, who offered unparalleled insights into the world of organised crime.

I count myself fortunate to be working with editors like Prerna Gill and a publisher like Diya Kar, whose passion for this book is so encouraging and so contagious. Thanks also to Kanishka Gupta for being the friend and critic that he is.

Finally, my love and gratitude to my family and friends. I'd be lost without you.

About the Author

———◆—◆———

Puja Changoiwala is an award-winning journalist, and author of the critically acclaimed true-crime book, *The Front Page Murders: Inside the Serial Killings That Shocked India*.

As a journalist, Puja writes about the intersections of gender, crime, social justice, human rights and technology. Her work has featured in *The Guardian*, *The Hindu*, BBC, MIT's *Undark*, Al Jazeera, *Stanford Social Innovation Review* and *South China Morning Post*, among other esteemed publications in Asia, the UK, and North America.

Previously a human rights correspondent with a London-based magazine, Puja has also worked as a senior crime reporter with *Hindustan Times*. A 2019 fellow with the Global Investigative Journalism Network, she is a recipient of the prestigious Laadli Media Award for Gender Sensitivity, Red Ink Award for Excellence in Indian Journalism and Iceland Writers Award, among other acclaims.